D0464831

THE EXPLORER IN ENGLISH FICTION

THE EXPLORER IN ENGLISH FICTION

Peter Knox-Shaw

St. Martin's Press   New York

First published in the United States of America in 1986

Printed in Hong Kong

ISBN 0–312–27763–6

Library of Congress Cataloging-in-Publication Data
Knox-Shaw, Peter, 1944–
The explorer in English fiction.
Bibliography: p.
Includes index.
1. English fiction—History and criticism.
2. Explorers in literature. 3. Travel in literature.
4. Voyages and travels. 5. Melville, Herman, 1819–1891
—Criticism and interpretation. 6. White, Patrick,
1912–   —Criticism and interpretation. I. Title.
PR830.E985K6   1986   823′.009′35291   86–13857
ISBN 0–312–27763–6

For Barbara

Contents

Acknowledgements

The passages from *Voss* by Patrick White (copyright © 1957 by Patrick White, renewed © 1985 by Patrick White) are reprinted by permission of the publishers, Viking Penguin, Inc. and Jonathan Cape Ltd.

Chapter 1 is based on my article, 'The Explorer, and Views of Creation', *English Studies in Africa*, 27 (1) 1984, © Witwatersrand University Press, 1984.

Preface

Although there have been a number of critical works on the novel given over to topics such as adventure, colonization or the politics of the frontier, a comparative study of novels in which an encounter with unknown territory holds central importance has till now been lacking. My aim in this book is to analyze and relate a variety of texts which show representatives of a home culture in confrontation with *terra incognita* or with unfamiliar peoples. There is, as it turns out, a strong family resemblance between the novels that fall into this category whether they belong, like *Robinson Crusoe*, *Coral Island* or *Lord of the Flies*, to the 'desert island' tradition where castaways have exploration thrust upon them or whether they present, as in the case of *Moby Dick*, *The Lost World* or *Voss*, ventures deliberately undertaken. There are frequent indications, too, that many of the novelists in question are aware of working within a particular, subsidiary genre. This means, in sum, even when it comes to texts as culturally remote as, say, *Captain Singleton* and *Heart of Darkness* that there is firm ground for comparison. The emphasis of this study is, in consequence, historical as well as critical.

In order to show that many conventions which are basic to the fiction inhere in the actual business of coming to grips with the unknown, I begin with a theoretical introduction illustrated chiefly from the writings of explorers. Travelogues reveal how large a part projection plays in every rendering of unvisited places. So much is imported that one might hypothesize, for the sake of a model, a single locality returning a stream of widely divergent images over the lapse of years. In effect it *is* possible to demonstrate a shift of cultural assumptions by juxtaposing, for example, a passage that tricks out a primeval forest in all the iconography of Eden with one written three centuries later in which – from essentially the same scene – the author paints a picture of Malthusian struggle and survival of the fittest. And since the explorer is not only inclined to embody his image of the natural man in the people he meets beyond the frontiers of his own culture, but is likely also to read his own emancipation from the constraints of polity in terms of a return to an underlying nature, the concern with genesis is one that recurs with particular persistence in texts dealing with exploration. With varying degrees of awareness novelists have responded, ever since Defoe, to the idea that the encounter with the unfamiliar mirrors the identity of the explorer. Their presentations of *terra incognita* register the crucial phases of social history – the institution of mercantilism, the rise and fall of empire – but generally in relation to psychological and metaphysical questions of a perennial kind. In his poem 'Le Voyage', Baudelaire remarks that travel leads to bitter knowledge: what the world shows us, in the end, is ourselves. Novelists have capitalized on this parallel between the discovered object and disclosed subject by raising a variety of structures on a recurring triad of interconnected ideas – projection, human nature, genesis – each of which supplies a means of relation. Though forms and emphases alter, the nature of man is a theme that proves remarkably tenacious in works of this kind, ultimately for the reason that Lawrence sums up in *Kangaroo*: 'There is always something outside our universe. And it is always at the doors of the innermost, sentient soul'.

After the introductory chapter I proceed chronologically with the four novelists who have contributed most, in my view, to the genre – Defoe, Melville, Conrad, Patrick White. In each case I deal principally with two texts: *Robinson Crusoe* and *Captain Singleton*; *Typee* and *Moby Dick*; *An Outcast of the Islands* and *Heart of Darkness*; *Voss* and *A Fringe of Leaves*. *Moby Dick* and *An Outcast* appear to touch on exploration only tangentially, but I have included them because they play a crucial part in the development of the genre – to which they are, in any case, consciously approximated: Melville enlarging repeatedly on the idea of the sea as an 'everlasting terra incognita'; Conrad strategically invoking the desert island idyll as an ironic backdrop to his dark tale. Wealth of reference is often a mark of literary stature, and in following these books any attentive reader is led from Genesis to Aboriginal myths of creation, from Hobbes to Rousseau and Darwin. Major works have a way, too, of declaring their genetic traits. Allusions to *Rasselas* and *The Ancient Mariner*, for instance, spell out Melville's glorious debts to diverse traditions, while his hybrid forms record the impact of a scientific spirit that did much to transform travel writing. I draw on accounts by explorers throughout, not only where immediate sources are concerned (Woodes Rogers, Stanley, Leichhardt among others), but so as to trace the correspondence between the non-fictional and novelistic realms. And although my comments on them tend to be brief, novels about exploration by writers other than the principal four come in for discussion when pertinent to the issues at hand: so Verne and Haggard, for example, provide a perspective to Conrad's treatment of recidivism in *Heart of Darkness*, while Coetzee and Brink supply comparisons with Patrick White's handling of the return to polity in *A Fringe of Leaves* (1976), a text even more fully receptive than *Voss* to the culture it penetrates.

My work on this book was eased by two three-month periods of relief kindly granted by the English Department at Cape Town University where I teach. To the librarians and staff at the British Museum, the Public Record Office, the South African Library, and the University of Cambridge my thanks are due for much patience and frequent help. I am grateful also to the editors of *English Studies in Africa* and *The Commonwealth Novel in English* for allowing me to repeat material that first appeared in their journals, though in a different form. I owe much to my editor, Margaret Leach, for her generous attention to my manuscript. And while my chief intellectual debts are acknowledged in the pages that follow, I should mention the stimulus given by my lively colleague Dr John Coulton. To my wife, who encouraged and assisted me at every stage in the gradual realization of this book, I owe as ever the most.

1 The Explorer, and Views of Creation

Not far from what he took to be the site of Eden, Columbus turned back. A fierce tide at the Orinoco mouth decided him against sailing up-river to look for Paradise, and to judge from his account of the scene the dangers he faced were real enough:

> And behind this current, there was another and another which all made a great roaring like that of the sea when it breaks and dashes against rocks . . . This was continuous, night and day, so that I believed that it would not be possible to go against the current, or to go forward owing to the shallows.
> And in the night, when it was already very late, being on the deck of the ship, I heard a very terrible roaring which came from the direction of the south towards the ship. And I stayed to watch, and I saw the sea from west to east rising, like a hill as high as the ship, and still it came towards me little by little.[1]

Columbus's reading of the situation was, however, far from simply a practical matter. What he saw from the deck of his ship proves to have been shaped by a mental image; and the instance is one among many in a venture which points, as a whole, to the force of the preconceived. The continent that rose out of the sea not only answered his dream of finding land far to the west but continued to be seen through it. So it was that America remained the eastern seaboard of Asia, and in consequence the region of Paradise also. Although a densely tangled skein of reference, ranging from the Apocrypha to *Imago Mundi*, coloured Columbus's view of the New World, the influences informing his particular impression of the Orinoco can be pin-pointed by going no further afield than to two books which he had with him on his voyages, the Bible and *Mandeville's Travels*.[2] The Book of Genesis spoke of four rivers flowing out of Eden, the third of which moved

1

eastward through Asia (2:14); and Mandeville who situated his
paradys terrestre 'towards the est at the begynnynge of the erthe',
indeed so far east as to occupy the opposite side of the globe, drew
his tall story to a close with a description of the torrents that
barred its approach:

> No man that is mortelle ne may not approchen to that Paradys
> . . . be the ryueres may no man go, for the water renneth so
> rudely and so scharply because that it cometh doun so
> outrageously from the high places abouen that it renneth in so
> grete wawes that no schipp may not rowe ne seyle agenes it.
> And the water roreth so and maketh so huge noyse and so gret
> tempest that no man may here other in the schipp, though he
> cryede with alle the craft that he cowde in the hieste voys that he
> myghte. Many grete lordes han assayed with gret wille many
> tymes for to passen be tho ryueres toward Paradys with fulle
> grete companyes, but thei myght not speden in hire viage . . . So
> that no mortelle man may approche to that place withouten
> specyalle grace of God.[3]

That it was in the thrall of this passage that Columbus watched
the racing waters at the river mouth is clear not only from the way
he echoes Mandeville's conclusions, but lingeringly returns to the
saving clause, 'withouten specyalle grace of God':

> Not that I believe that to the summit of the extreme point is
> navigable, or water, or that it is possible to ascend there, for I
> believe that the earthly paradise is there and to it, save by the
> will of God, no man can come.[4]

Columbus who had in earlier days regarded himself as the great
voyager prophesied by Isaiah,[5] conveys an impression of self-
doubt when, in a further passage on the confluence, he presents
the currents as responding to the pattern of a familiar moral
conflict, the besiegement of innocence by vice:

> Then I surmised, concerning the streaks of current and the
> rolling waves, which went out of and entered into these straits,
> with that great and violent roaring, that there was a battle
> between the fresh water and the salt. The fresh struggled with

the other to prevent its entrance, and the salt with the other that it might not come out ... the fresh water was always victorious.[6]

Whatever the strength of the tides Columbus's assessment of his chances on the estuary evidently depended also on other less physical considerations – partly on an item of topographical lore, partly on a reckoning of his state of grace. Various aspects of his cultural life were focused in the immediate scene, and so brought to bear upon his judgement.

For the critic who studies novels about exploration, travelogues have a value quite apart from any importance they might have as sources, in that they show how themes which are basic to the fiction (and subject to the usual trafficking of literary influence) belong in the first place to the actual business of coming to grips with the unknown. In this respect Columbus's account of the Orinoco mouth is particularly instructive for it points to two features – more specifically to a process and a concern – which recur in travel writing and hold a central place, moreover, in novels about exploration. The process is projection: a mental image is transferred to an object outside the self – for our purposes most commonly to a physical setting. The concern is with genesis: the unfamiliar setting returns the image of an original state, or is seen as charged in some way with the evidences of creation. It is with this last issue, which obviously presents a special case of the first, that I shall chiefly be dealing. Just how decisive a part it plays in the fiction I hope to show, but my aim in this chapter is to look at the ways in which explorers have written about the immanence of the primeval; and while I shall do my best to trace the main developments in the history of this concern I can hardly fail to indicate its remarkable persistence.

To generations of voyagers in the wake of Columbus the New World gave substance to a vanished, legendary past, but long after faith in Genesis had faded, explorers continued to view distant places in the light of some belief as to how life began. Specific economic or political motives play their part in these views as we shall see, but no single reading of this kind seems adequate to explain the variety of primordial states in question; and here I shall try to account for the prevalence of this concern by considering whether there may not be an intrinsic as well as functional relationship between it and projection, a process at work in every rendering of the unknown. In any case it is this last topic that we need first to approach.

To *project*, in the sense we shall be using it, is to locate a mental image in the external world. An obvious feature of this process is that an inward tendency presents itself as – and sometimes gets mistaken for – an objective reality. Although the idea goes back a long way the term came into currency only in the nineteenth century, and it is appropriate that Coleridge who so insistently questioned the limits of subjective vision should have been the first to use it. The figurative sense he introduced seems to have owed its force less to the original Latin root (meaning to throw forward) than to an already standard usage in optics. When Emerson, for example, speaks of the hero-worshipper as one who

> intoxicated with his admiration of a hero, fails to see that it is only a *projection* of his own soul which he admires

he carries over the sense of the special scientific term:

> with a Prism you strike the Rainbow-colours upon a wall, and observe where red is *projected*.[7]

Even where the word itself has not been at issue, the idea of projected light has frequently served to illustrate the influence of a mental disposition. So Proust finds an emblem for the shaping work of the imagination when he describes how a magic lantern flooded the familiar outlines of his childhood bedroom with scenes from a romantic tale.[8] But although the optical metaphor provides a striking model of the mind's power to impose, it proves in other respects inadequate, or even misleading. When it comes, for instance, to accounting for the ways in which images attach themselves to objects, the metaphor selects from a wide range of possible transformations only that extreme typified by the hallucinatory. For the external world, in so far as it enters the optical analogy at all, does so as a blank screen or incidental backdrop, devoid of the capacity either to suggest or control. Yet if we turn to a representative case of projection, the famous passage in which Columbus portrays the island he had named La Espanola as an earthly paradise, we find among a few details that he may have conjured out of the air others that suggest the recalcitrant identity of the setting, and much else that falls into a middle realm to which a forgotten sense of projection, denoting alchemical change, would do more justice than the optical term. The paragraph is from his opening description of the New World:

> This island and all the others are very fertile to a limitless degree, and this island is extremely so. In it there are many harbours on the coast of the sea, beyond comparison with others which I know in Christendom, and many rivers, good and large, which is marvellous. Its lands are high, and there are in it very many sierras and very lofty mountains, beyond comparison with the island of Teneriffe. All are most beautiful, of a thousand shapes, and all are accessible and filled with trees of a thousand kinds and tall, and they seem to touch the sky. And I am told that they never lose their foliage, as I can understand, for I saw them as green and as lovely as they are in Spain in May, and some of them were flowering, some bearing fruit, and some in another stage, according to their nature. And the nightingale was singing, and other birds of a thousand kinds in the month of November there where I went. There are six or eight kinds of palm, which are a wonder to behold on account of their beautiful variety, but so are the other trees and fruits and plants. In it are marvellous pine groves, and there are very large tracts of cultivable lands, and there is honey, and there are birds of many kinds and fruits in great diversity. In the interiors are mines of metals, and the population is without number.[9]

Columbus already looks with the appraising eye of the colonist as his bracketing of mines and people in the last sentence shows, but this does not prevent him from relying on traditions of a more sacred character. The landscape he presents, while remaining particular and distinct, is always at the point of coalescing into a Renaissance image of Paradise. Just as tall trees 'seem to touch the sky' so the scene as a whole is referred to the imaginative properties of Eden, chief of which here are invariance and plenitude. Rather than describe a perpetual spring Columbus relates what he sees to the notional image of a climate unspoilt by the Fall. So he finds the leaves of early winter as fresh as those of Europe in May, points at trees in varying stages of their season, and yet allows that it is only through hearsay that he supposes the woods never bare. So long as his eyes are on the scene the things he describes enjoy a fair measure of independence. The climate and evergreen forests of the Caribbean were of a kind, of course, to feed his expectations. Only when he brings in the *November* song of the nightingale, a bird absent from Europe over the winter, does he make the principle of invariance fully explicit; and at the cost, then, of some infidelity to the setting, for there never have been nightingales in America. It is not uncommon for explorers to lump unknown creatures into familiar categories; and were it not for the resonance of this detail and its dramatic placing (almost comparable to Milton's telling use of the bird in his account of twilight in Eden) Columbus might be assumed to have grown tired of ostensive definition – the process responsible for his odd phrase, 'there where I went' – and fallen back on an approximate label.[10] It seems more likely, however, that the nightingale was the result of a metamorphosis contrived by his ears.

Certainly the other organizing principle of the passage, the ideal of plenitude, gives away its a priori character much sooner, indeed from the very first sentence. For here Columbus introduces the word 'limitless' into a context that fails to support its meaning – he speaks of all the islands being 'fertile to a limitless degree and this island extremely so'. The idea continues, all the same, to inspire his syntax. Trains of co-ordinated clauses underline his impression of immeasurable abundance ('there are . . . and there are . . . and there are . . .' etc.), and the effect is heightened still further by his marking off of 'some' against 'all', and by his related noting of single or easily counted items against a blurred backdrop of 'a thousand' or 'very many'. Whether it was the Book of Genesis with its insistence on the variety of creation ('every tree', 'every beast', 'every fowl'), or the radiant pictorial detail of some Quattrocento treatment of the subject that lay at the back of Columbus's mind it is impossible to tell, but the presence of Eden makes itself deeply felt, and seems, moreover, to have sharpened rather than dulled attention to the setting. It is entirely consistent that Columbus should wish to distinguish eight species of palm, or elsewhere supply the first European account of the yellow-wood, which he describes as a pine with berries like the olive. Yet the blend of observation and received ideas that characterizes his writing is not, after all, far from that found in the updated medieval maps which survived into his period.[11] The world is shaped on these as a perfect trefoil or, since it seemed reasonable that the *Orbis Terrarum* should emblazon its own initials, in the form of a T within an O. Jerusalem – in view of the text, 'I have set her in the midst of nations' – invariably stood at the centre. It was against this ground that details from the portolan charts and early voyagers were, as far as possible, fitted. A similar uniformity of design underlines Columbus's report of *terra nuova*.

Travelogues show how basic projection is to any reading of the unknown. However evocative the features of a newly observed setting prove, they are likely, at most, to play only a limited part in the development of an overall impression. For while they may challenge, as well as confirm, they cannot significantly *contribute to* those habits and beliefs that make up the disposition of the observer. It is easy to suppose that Columbus would have failed to find a paradise had he been confronted with a less amenable coast outside the tropics; but, in fact, throughout the following century, in landfalls made along the entire seaboard of the continent, the same pattern of response recurs. Writing of the place that would be named Virginia, Arthur Barlowe comments on how the natives live 'after the maner of the golden age', and goes on to spell out the notion that sustains his rapturous and often minute descriptions: 'the earth bringeth foorth all things in aboundance, as in the first creation'.[12] Despite the northerly latitudes a similar understanding runs through the account of Newfoundland by Edward Haie who breaks off a long list of animals with the remark – 'we could not observe the hundreth part of creatures in those unhabited lands: but these mentioned may induce us to glorifie the magnificent God, who hath superabundantly replenished the earth'.[13] Writing in the next century of country between these two regions (the Plymouth district, on which earlier explorers spent many a superlative)[14] the Pilgrim Fathers, on the other hand, present an altogether different picture. Ironically enough it is often the observation of abundance that supports their sense of the land as a menacing waste. In this as well as in other respects, the following passage from the retrospect of a Puritan spokesman is typical:

what could they see but a hideous and desolate wilderness, full of wild beasts and wild men – and what multitudes there might be of them they knew not . . . For summer being done, all things stand upon them with a weatherbeaten face, and the whole country, full of woods and thickets, represented a wild and savage hue. If they looked behind them, there was the mighty ocean which they had passed and was now as a main bar and gulf to separate them from all the civil parts of the world.[15]

Of course the Pilgrim Fathers came not as discoverers but as exiles, without the hope – as the last sentence makes clear – of any return. Equally to the purpose, however, they came equipped with the identity of Israelites who had exchanged captivity for the pains and trials of the Wilderness. Exodus rather than Genesis presided over their encounter with the interior. Their outlook was sustained, moreover, by a Calvinist repugnance towards the natural state. Whereas to the more orthodox it seemed that the seeds of Eden (Gen. 1:11–12) had carried the vestiges of perfection into a fallen world, the American Puritans inclined to the view that original sin had obliterated all trace of the divine image in man. Differences of a profound theological cast underlay the changing faces of the New World.

From the standpoint of Richard Hakluyt, the great Elizabethan anthologist of voyagers, it is the *individual* difference between his explorers that calls for comment. He hits on a vivid metaphor to describe the way 'the desires of divers men' mould impressions of the New World. 'If an oxe bee put into a medowe', he writes, 'hee will seeke to fill his bellie with grasse, if a Storke bee cast in shee will seeke for Snakes, if you turne in a Hound he will seeke to start an Hare: So sundry men entring into these discoveries propose unto themselves severall endes'.[16] The work of projection is thrown into relief by comparison, but Hakluyt's meadow – the paradigmatic case of a single object drawing a whole spectrum of response – belongs less to the historian than to the creative writer. Shakespeare offers just such an exposition in *The Tempest* where each character creates, in effect, an island in his own image – a circumstance made conspicuous by the rather special treatment of the setting. It is, of course, common practice in Renaissance drama for characters to report repeatedly on what they see but they do not, as a rule, disagree about what there is to be seen. In *The Tempest*, however, the island takes on as broad a range of aspects as there are characters, and it goes through all the fluctuations of a chameleon when the characters clash their differing points of view. In the following extract, for example, while the level-headed Adrian asserts a nature unpolished but not intemperate, and the well-meaning Gonzalo transmits a golden age, Antonio and Sebastian, about to plot the death of Alonso, chip in jointly with their jaundiced asides, producing between them an image that strongly suggests the predatory:

ADR. The air breathes upon us here most sweetly.
SEB. As if it had lungs, and rotten ones.
ANT. Or as 'twere perfum'd by a fen.
GON. Here is everything advantageous to life.
ANT. True; save means to live.
SEB. Of that there's none, or little.
GON. How lush and lusty the grass looks! how green!
ANT. The ground, indeed, is tawny.
SEB. With an eye of green in't.[17]

The tawny beast with the green eye is planted in the landscape by the conspirators who, when they are later caught with their swords drawn, summon further wild creatures of their making. For while Gonzalo and Alonso wake, respectively, to music and to silence, Antonio and Sebastian explain their aggressive stance by peopling the island with a 'herd' of roaring lions.

What the characters in *The Tempest* project onto their setting they also project on each other, but the setting which keeps its mystery intact (owing partly to the effaced omniscience of the dramatic presentation) returns the clearer if less complicated image. The desert island serves Shakespeare as a mirror which he holds up to the nature of his characters, and the play reminds us of the way distant places reflect the traits and beliefs of those who observe them. It alerts us to the fact that while projection colours every facet of experience it declares itself most forcibly where the unfamiliar is concerned. The less familiar the setting the more highly burnished the surface presented to the observer. There are a number of reasons why this should be so. Conrad pointed to one when he likened Europeans in a tropical environment to 'blind men in a large room'.[18] The unknown resists assimilation, and accordingly leaves a wide margin for the imaginary. Without invoking Whorf one can recognize that the absence of an appropriate nomenclature blunts perception, and there are, besides, a variety of psychological influences that curb attention to experience that is out of the way. The well-attested case of the Eskimo tribe who decided, after their encounter with some Russian explorers, that they had been visited by a party of squid,[19] points to a further corollary. When the unknown cannot be ignored there is a tendency to approximate it, at any cost, to the familiar.

Analysis along these lines confirms the idea that *terra incognita* acts as a mirror to the habitual. But allowance must also be made for the imaginative stimulus imparted to explorers by unvisited places, a stimulus often sufficiently strong, it proves, to arouse deep-seated feeling, and to stir public assumptions that ordinarily go unstated. For all these reasons the travelogue can be put to work as an instrument exceptionally sensitive to historical change. In place of the model supplied by *The Tempest* we have only to think of a single place giving rise to a succession of widely divergent images over the lapse of years. In the comparison that follows more than three centuries separate the accounts of what we can treat as the same setting. For although the scene viewed in 1562 by the French explorer Ribault was situated on the coast of Florida, and that viewed by Stanley in 1887 at the heart of the Congo, the particular landscape described by either explorer could as well have supported the conclusions drawn by the other. A setting, effectively constant, indexes in this case a crucial shift in the understanding of creation.

Translated from the French by Hakluyt and included in his first volume, *Divers Voyages Touching the Discovery of America* (1582), Ribault's narrative includes one of the many passages,[20] broadcast through the literature of travel in the late sixteenth century, which show the New World in the image of the golden age:

We entred and viewed the countrie thereaboutes, which is the fairest, fruitfullest, and pleasantest of al the world, abounding in hony, venison, wilde foule, forests, woods of all sortes, Palme trees, Cypresse and Cedars, Bayes ye highest and greatest, with also the fayrest vines in all the world, with grapes according, which without natural art and without mans helpe or trimming will grow to toppes of Okes and other trees that be of a wonderfull greatnesse and height. And the sight of the faire medowes is a pleasure not able to be expressed with tongue: full of Hernes, Curlues, Bitters, Mallards, Egrepths, woodcocks and all other kinde of small birds: with Harts, Hindes, Buckes, wilde Swine, and all other kindes of wilde beastes, as we perceiued well, both by their footing there, and also afterwardes in other places, by their crie and roaring in the night.

Also, there be Conies and Hares: Silke wormes in merueilous number, a great deale fairer and better then be our silk wormes. To bee short, it is a thing vnspeakable to consider the thinges that bee seene there, and shalbe founde more and more in this incomperable lande, which neuer yet broken with plough yrons, bringeth forth al things according to his first nature, wherewith the eternall God indued it.[21]

Where Columbus set out to quantify the illimitable, Ribault attempts to utter the inexpressible. Twice he insists that the scene cannot be encompassed by words, and in view of the superiority he ascribes to nature's products over those of art (wild vines supply the fairest grapes), his claim seems to relate to a belief that the original state of nature – which it is his privilege to view – offers a perfection beyond that of the arts, the redemptive institutions available to fallen man. This is the idea which informs Montaigne's famous essay 'Of the Cariballes', published two decades later, in which it is argued that the natural state exceeds 'all the pictures wherewith licentious Poesie hath proudly imbellished the golden age'; and that language itself is tainted by human corruption – 'The very words that import lying, falshood, treason, dissimulations, covetousnes, envie, detraction, and pardon, were never heard of amongst [the savages]'.[22] Of course, when Montaigne pronounces that the original state was without *nomos*, or what he calls 'human combination' – 'no intelligence of numbers, no name of magistrate, nor of politike superiority . . . no contracts, no successions, no partitions' and so on – he departs from Christian orthodoxy. Eden was tilled by Adam.[23] Ovid, however, in his account of the golden age had supplied the model of an existence, free of codes and laws, over which a benevolent, self-cultivating nature presided. Whereas Columbus points to land that can be cultivated, Ribault follows the *Metamorphoses* ('the earth itself, without compulsion, untouched by the hoe, unfurrowed by any share, produced all things spontaneously')[24] in celebrating nature's sufficiency – 'this incomperable lande, which neuer yet broken with plough yrons, bringeth forth al things according to his first nature'; and the same emphasis pervades his description of the vigorous creepers: 'the fayrest vines in all the world, with grapes according, which without natural art and without mans helpe or trimming will grow to toppes of Okes and other trees that be of a wonderfull greatnesse and height'. On this last detail the poet Drayton clearly drew for his lines addressed to Hakluyt, entitled 'To the Virginian Voyage', and it is amusing to observe that he restores the full Ovidian context that underlay Ribault's impression, introducing the 'golden age' itself, zephyrs and *otium*:

> Where nature hath in store
> Fowle, venison, and fish,
> And the fruitfull'st soyle
> Without your toyle,
> Three harvests more,
> All greater then you wish.
>
> And the ambitious vine
> Crownes with his purple masse
> The Cedar reaching hie
> To kisse the sky,
> The Cypresse, pine
> And use-full Sassafras.
>
> To whose, the golden age
> Still natures lawes doth give . . .[25]

Writing with further information at his disposal Drayton was able to identify Ribault's bay tree as the sassefras – a name for the American laurel of probable Spanish–Indian derivation. Ribault's taxonomy is by contrast unrelievedly European; and Hakluyt takes the French explorer's process of approximating the unknown to the familiar a step further when he glosses the egrets – a species indigenous to France but not to England – as 'beautiful birds, like herons, but white'. Unlike Adam who himself gave the names to the beasts and birds of Eden, Ribault is equipped only with an imperfect index to the myriad forms of creation; and language, even if not exactly in the ways he expected, *does* betray his perceptions. The clause that leads into the passage quoted supplies an instance. Here Ribault in describing his encounter with the inhabitants of the region evokes an aura of natural fellowship, but his vocabulary imposes a structure of feudal relations on the tribesmen, further reinforced by the nature of his gifts:

After we had a good while louingly entertained and presented them with like gifts of habersher wares, cutting hookes and hatchets, and clothed the king and his brethren with like robes, as we had given to them on the other side: we entred and viewed the country.

The easy parataxis of the ensuing list of creatures – which seems to assume Isaiah's prophecy of the lion lying down with the lamb, and certainly dispels any notion of subjugation and mastery – is hardly in keeping with his conversion of the Indian headsmen into a robed aristocracy. But as is the case with Shakespeare's Gonzalo, steeped in Montaigne –

> GON.   contract, succession,
>   Bourn, bound of land, tilth, vineyard, none;
>   No use of metal, corn, or wine, or oil;
>   No occupation; all men idle, all;
>   And women too, but innocent and pure:
>   No sovereignty; –
> SEB.   Yet he would be King on't[26] –

the latter end of Ribault's commonwealth forgets its beginning.

Midway through *In Darkest Africa* (1890) Stanley devotes a chapter to 'The Great Central African Forest' in which he repeatedly impresses on his readers that he is dealing with a primeval setting, with 'that old growth untouched by man, and left since the earliest time to thrive and die'.[27] Self-sufficient and self-generated, the scene expresses the absence of man rather than the presence of God. The sole creator here is the perceiver – a sense conveyed by Stanley's adoption of a descriptive mode which proceeds by fiat:

> Then from tree to tree run cables from two inches to fifteen inches in diameter . . . fold them round the trees in great tight coils . . . let slender cords hang down also in tassles . . . Work others through and through . . . Now cover . . . with a thick moss.[28]

The recipe format is kept up for paragraphs at a time but in context the effect is far from quaint. Stanley is among the most articulate of explorers and his descriptive passages, which never fail to be graphic, are interspersed with commentaries that are apt as well as lavish. Towards his pivotal statement that 'the forest is typical of the life of humanity' he moves with poise, fully aware of the animation which he has already imported into his account of the setting. His prose pullulates. In the course of a single sentence he introduces 'a mushroom staring out of a fern', 'fungi clinging like barnacles to a deeply-wrinkled log', 'the grey green face of an elephant-eared plant', 'tumorous lumps' and 'tears of gum'. The sentence finally winds to its close in vivid mimicry of the creepers (an endless source of fascination), instinct as ever with rapacious life:

> [the eye caught] length after length of whiplike calamus –
> squirming and twisting lianes, and great serpent-like
> convolvuli, winding in and out by mazy galleries of dark
> shadows, and emerging triumphant far above to lean their
> weight on branches, running coils at one place, forming loops at
> another place, and then stretching loosely their interminable
> lengths out of sight.[29]

In contrast to Ribault, Stanley pictures his scene in movement, typically in movement that recapitulates growth; and while he presents natural forms in terms of their function, his unsteady zoological metaphors – his objects are always at the point of turning into something else – challenge the fixity of their labels. There is, of course, no trick about the way he projects a full biological spectrum onto the vegetable world in order to establish an equivalence for human life. He is concerned with an evolutionary conception of man as a being continuous with lower forms of creation, and comparably engaged in a struggle for survival. From the lianes whose triumph is manifest in the firm support they have found at the top, Stanley now switches to a scene from the civilized world and pursues his analogy further:

> [The forest] has suggested a morning when I went to see the
> human tide flowing into the City over London Bridge between
> half-past seven and half-past eight, where I saw the pale,
> overworked, dwarfed, stoop-shouldered, on their way to their
> dismal struggle for existence. They were represented here
> faithfully, in all their youth, vigour, and decrepitude; one is
> prematurely aged and blanched, another is goitrous, another is

organically weak, another is a hunchback, another suffers from poor nutrition, many are pallid from want of air and sunshine, many are supported by their neighbours because of constitutional infirmity, many of them are toppling one over another, as though they were the incurables of a hospital, and you wonder how they exist at all. Some are already dead, and lie buried under heaps of leaves, or are nurseries of bush families and parasites, or are colonised by hordes of destructive insects; some are bleached white by the palsying thunderbolt, or shivered by the levin brand, or quite decapitated; or some old veteran, centuries old, which was born before ever a Christian sailed south of the Equator, is decaying in core and vitals; but the majority have the assurance of insolent youth, with all its grace and elegance of form, the mighty strength of prime life, and the tranquil and silent pride of hoary old aristocrats; and you gather from a view of the whole one indisputable fact – that they are resolved to struggle for existence as long as they may. We see all characters of humanity here, except the martyr and suicide. For sacrifice is not within tree nature, and it may be that they only heard two precepts, 'Obedience is better than sacrifice,' and 'Live and multiply.'[30]

Onto the forest Stanley projects a version of the social Darwinism popular in his day, a notional system to which economic individualism contributed perhaps as much as Darwin's biological theory. The *co-operative* aspects of survival, whether symbiotic or intra-organic – though certainly underdeveloped in the evolutionary sciences themselves at this period – hardly enter into Stanley's ruthless portrayal of competitive strife. In so far as he finds anything in the forest to correspond to ameliorative institution, it is in the least dignified features of the scene – a hospital translates into a huddle of stunted trees. Indeed the primeval setting supplies Stanley with the means of separating 'ought' from 'is' for through it he spells out the codes of a particularly abrasive natural law, before which the martyr stands condemned with the suicide. Through his process of projection Stanley calls the status of ethics into doubt; and perhaps he ventured into deeper water than he knew, for while he pretends to be divided in his loyalties he seems to have little more than lip service to offer the official god. Just as the older parts of the forest survive from an era before Christians ventured South, so the

precepts which govern forest lore, he notes, antedate the coming of
Christ. In conjunction with the command from Genesis – 'Be
fruitful, and multiply',[31] the words of Samuel – 'To obey is better
than sacrifice', through which Jehovah admonished his people for
sparing the Amalekites,[32] not only conjure up a nature red in tooth
and claw, but fairly exactly frame the Malthusian concept of
expansion controlled by constraint. Again, in the paragraph that
immediately follows, the old proverb 'the devil takes the
hindmost', prefixed by a version of 'self do, self have', takes on the
force of an evolutionary credo:

> And as there is nothing so ugly and distasteful to me as the mob
> of a Derby day, so there is nothing so ugly in forest nature as
> when I am reminded of it by the visible selfish rush towards the
> sky in a clearing, after it has been abandoned a few years. Hark!
> the bell strikes, the race is about to begin. I seem to hear the
> uproar of the rush, the fierce, heartless jostling and trampling,
> the cry, 'Self for self, the devil take the weakest!' To see the
> white-hot excitement, the noisy fume and flutter, the curious
> inequalities of vigour, and the shameless disregard for order
> and decency![33]

Stanley begins by upholding the pieties, but his show of dismay –
even here – is uneasily balanced between moral deprecation and
distaste for the mob. He is given away by the note of irrepressible
jubilance on which his commentary ends, and the same
exhilaration at energies released, and recoil from the weak,
underlies his earlier inventory of types.[34] From Stanley the
primeval forest elicited a primitivism that was to become
widespread, and more openly avowed, as the century moved to its
close.

The accounts of Ribault and Stanley illustrate a pattern that
proves general to the travelogues of explorers. A setting which is
taken as primeval reflects a set of conceptions which derive from
the explorer's understanding of genesis. The ramifications of the
myth in question are not only far-reaching philosophically but
often palpable in their consequences: they invade human relations
and their immediate effects can sometimes be traced. Such is the
case with the sequel to Ribault's voyage to Florida. Recalled to
France, Ribault left behind him, under the care of his friend
Captain Albert, a small band of men who pledged themselves to a

utopian constitution outlawing all forms of servitude; but, falling on hard times, these colonists soon reneged on their principles, and when Captain Albert tried to oppose their enslavement of a local Indian tribe, he was hounded through the countryside and put to death.[35] It seems that the image of the golden age seldom survived the experience of settlement. When it came to the point, intimations of paradise failed to restrain even Columbus from capturing hundreds of Indians for the slave markets of Seville.[36] Over the centuries the image of virgin territory was itself increasingly prostituted, the golden age cynically transposed into terms of hard cash. Urging hasty exploitation, Sir Walter Raleigh, for example, writes:

> Guiana is a countrey that hath yet her maydenhead, never sackt, turned, nor wrought . . . the graves have not bene opened for golde, the mines not broken with sledges, nor their Images puld downe out of their temples.[37]

Although the Ovidian emblem of an earth unbroken by ploughshares still persists, its ironic presence passes without acknowledgement. It was not only greed, however, that corroded the image of Eden. The very concept of colonial settlement implied a nature wanting redemption and control.

For Stanley as much as for Raleigh there was, at any rate, little risk of hypocrisy. The drama that Stanley observed among the leaves required no aesthetic frame. In his diary at least, first published in 1961, he was ready to apply the same scheme directly to experience, as in this description of his escape from a fired village:

> There were at least 600,000 human beings struggling in a solid body in the same direction, trampling down the weak, aged and sick in their devouring haste to be away from the sea of fire below. It was a grand scene but a cruel one – for hundreds of sick, little ones and witless men and women perished in it. The flames almost took my breath away, they seemed to lick the air before it entered my lungs, but with heads bent low we charged on blindly, knowing no guide save self interest and self preservation.[38]

Stanley's sense of the sublime is aroused on this occasion by the unmasking of blatant natural impulse. He finds the cruel scene grand because it shows up what he takes to be an underlying truth about human behaviour.

The advent of evolutionary theory was to sharpen, if only fitfully, the distinction between 'ought' and 'is', and over the course of years to encourage the view that moral codes were created rather than discovered. To the modern reader familiar with Nietzsche's distinction between the Apollonic and Dionysian, or with George Moore's naturalistic fallacy, the obvious contrast between Ribault's and Stanley's accounts might seem to boil down to the difference between a prescriptive and descriptive undertaking. Yet, while it is true that Stanley is partly prompted by a scientific theory and that his view does justice to the force of instinct and the ferocity of strife, it is equally clear that his description is selective – so much so that even a feature as conspicuous as the flowering of the forest trees would represent (since energy is spent without individual gain) 'sacrifice' rather than 'selfishness' in the terms of his own metaphor. On the other hand, while it is true that Ribault sustains his vision of a preordained order by drawing a veil across many aspects of the setting, and true moreover that legend and dogma rather than observation inform his sense of it, he clearly believes that it is from the scene itself that he reads the precepts of his creator. In short, while Ribault writes an idyll and Stanley a tendentious report neither shows himself at all ready to recognize any element of prescription. But, of course, the tendency is general. The notion that ethics is a prescriptive undertaking invariably resists acceptance. The unseen solicits proof, and – where martyrs are lacking – to found a system of values in nature is to supply some kind of sanction. In this context a nature untouched by man or existing beyond the realms of polity – and whether seen thus as most wild or least unfallen – carries particular potency. For, as every variety of primitivism shows, the extraneous confers a special status, and accordingly provides a distinctive means of designating the essential. To jungles, to deserts, to the unvisited places of the world, men over the centuries have turned. One of their less official aims there has been to embody the image of their creation so as to *see* what they themselves are like under the coverings of civility. Some have regarded their home culture as a corrupt crust; some as a veneer of manners; the deeply redemptive role of social institution has been recognized by others. But every doctrinal system, whatever its drift, requires anchorage.

'The remotest parts of the world are the richest':[39] Herodotus meant his remark to be taken literally, but the staling effects of familiarity make its application universal. Explorers and for that matter their readers (for, as Mandeville with a canny eye on his public noted, 'newe thinges and new tydynges ben plesant to here')[40] have always been enticed by novelty. Is it perhaps because the desire for freshness finds a supreme satisfaction in the idea of a pristine world that explorers have so frequently preoccupied themselves with the evidences of genesis in distant lands? A simple process of transference is sufficient to account for the elision from things newly-observed to things as-if-newly-created: to see freshly is to confer freshness on what is seen. But this notion is perhaps more easily conceded in principle than in practice, and the concern with genesis requires, in any case, further illustration.

Explorers are as diverse in professional type as the regions they explore. But the concern with genesis although seldom, if ever, given a role as focal as that it consistently plays in the fictional genre nevertheless crops up repeatedly in travelogues, regardless of the outlook and circumstances of the explorer. Again and again in the face of settings altogether opposed in character, the same imaginative directions are taken. The image of an original state is as readily furnished by a polar landscape as by a tropical jungle. Moonlight in the Antarctic opens for Edward Wilson a vista into a remote, and pre-evolutionary past:

> The stillness was almost uncanny, one could imagine oneself on a dead planet, – that we were standing, not on the earth, but on the moon's surface; everything was so still and cold and dead and unearthly, with an absolute silence which one felt as broken by nothing but wild Nature's storms since the beginning of the world.[41]

For Burchell, writing a century earlier, the reward of travelling in southern Africa, through 'country still in a state of nature', is his access to 'the works of creation, ever delightful to all but those of a corrupt and depraved mind'.[42] Likewise for Le Vaillant, writing of the same region on the eve of the French Revolution, the hinterland represents the natural state, and accordingly holds all the allure of original innocence.

Although his understanding of the process of projection is far from complete Le Vaillant is among those explorers who are aware of an equivalence between the outer scene and inner life. Poised on the outskirts of settlement, Le Vaillant converts the physical frontier into a psychological one when he writes:

> From this place the last post belonging to the Company was not far distant, and we arrived at it after a quick march of three hours. I was now about to withdraw myself from the dominion of man, and to approach a little towards his original condition.[43]

What he means by this personal recovery of the 'original condition' becomes clear when he reflects on the sensations of freedom that attend his departure from the beaten track:

> Proud of his origin, man thinks it an indignity that people should beforehand dare to number his steps. I . . . never thought myself completely free, but when surrounded by the rocks, forests, and desarts of Africa . . . By the freedom of my will, which commanded them with sovereign sway, and by my complete independence, I really perceived in man the monarch of all animated beings, the absolute despot of nature . . . [these] are only the pure and natural sentiments of liberty, which rejects, without distinction, every thing that seems desirous of prescribing its bounds.[44]

Autonomy and freedom are equated here, and to further reflections in this vein (arising out of his relationship with a pet baboon) Le Vaillant adds that never before had he experienced the 'full value of existence'.[45] He is ready, however, to suspend an earlier resolve to refuse invitations and avoid all unnecessary contact when he meets the Gonaqua, since they exemplify for him 'the state of nature', a phrase often repeated in this connection. The comparison he proceeds to draw between these tribesmen and the Hottentots of the colony – 'who bear no marks of their ancient origin but an empty name; and who enjoy, only at the expense of their liberty, a little peace, purchased at a dear rate'[46] – is a revealing one for it re-echoes the terms in which he describes his own emancipation from the constraints of polity. What in essence he does is to project his own highly individualistic understanding of liberty onto the collective existence of the Gonaqua, whom he presents not only as a 'free and brave people, valuing nothing but independence', but as incapable of '*obeying any impulse foreign to nature*'.[47] Le Vaillant follows Rousseau when he affirms that 'in an uncivilized state man is naturally good';[48] but his notion of primitive society as a corporation of autocrats is informed by his own newfound sensations of absolute despotism. In common with many explorers before and since, Le Vaillant superimposes his own freedom from social restriction on the people he observes. Typically, again, he equates life beyond the realm of his own civilization with the natural, and consequently assumes that to be beyond polity is to be without it. In effectively turning a blind eye to the culture of the various tribes he encountered, to languages, laws and religions – the details rather than the implications of which he was sometimes ready to ponder – Le Vaillant contributed to a pernicious error that anthropological awareness would later only gradually dispel. His intentions were benevolent, his view of the original state sustained by a strong French tradition of radical deism; but that linkage of the exotic with the natural, to which he among many others subscribed, was to prove unfortunate when less beneficent views of nature prevailed.

Canoeing down the Orinoco River more than three centuries after Columbus had approached its mouth, Alexander von Humboldt – whom Darwin was to describe as the greatest of travellers, and whose comments on the earlier literature of exploration are invariably shrewd – pointedly noted the absence of Eden:[49]

We enjoyed the repetition of the same spectacle at several different points, and I may add, always with new delight. There came down together, to drink, to bathe, or to fish, groups consisting of the most different classes of animals, the larger mammalia, being associated with many coloured herons, palamedeas, and proudly-stepping curassow and cashew birds (Crax Alector and C. Pauxi). 'Es como en al Paraiso;' it is here as in Paradise, said, with a pious air, our steersman, an old Indian who had been brought up in the house of an ecclesiastic. The peace of the golden age was, however, far from prevailing among the animals of this American paradise, which carefully watched and avoided each other. The Capybara, a Cavy three or four feet long, (a magnified repetition of the Brazilian Cavy, Cavia aguti), is devoured in the river by the crocodiles, and on shore by the tiger.[50]

Humboldt never attempted a theory of evolution, but in common with many of Darwin's precursors he keeps a sharp eye both on biological variation and processes of change. In his idiosyncratic travel-book, *Aspects of Nature* (1808), he often speculates on prehistory, reconstructing lost landscapes, those 'storied cemeteries of perished organic forms', and reviving gigantic creatures long buried in earth's 'indurating crust'.[51] That he was aware of projection is clear from his story about the pious Indian from the passage above, and in his late encyclopaedic work, entitled *Cosmos*, he articulated the process by quoting from a German critic who had observed of Shakespeare, 'the descriptions of natural objects become as it were only mirrors in which the mental emotions of the actors in the scene are reflected'.[52] But the delight which Humboldt takes in the sight of the animals drinking on the Orinoco bank (despite his awareness of the unidyllic reality) is in keeping with a much earlier observation of his on an animistic correspondence between subject and object. 'The inward mirror of the sensitive mind', he writes, 'reflects the true and living image of the natural world.' From which it follows that a 'free and vigorous setting' stimulates a spirit of adventure, and that 'distant richly endowed lands' convey 'the earlier youthful age of mankind'.[53]

Long before the separate components of his theory dove-tailed together to inspire *The Origin of Species* (1859) Darwin, like Humboldt, had travelled into the past as an explorer. For while it is true that numerous scientific works, notably Lyell's *Principles of Geology* (1831–3), impart a specialized bias to the observations recorded in *The Voyage of the 'Beagle'* (1839), the concern with origins in this travelogue is typical of the explorer, and altogether endemic to the form. Like Wallis or Bougainville, Darwin sees in the Tahitian islanders 'a fine picture of man inhabiting some primeval land'.[54] Poised on a mountaintop he notes, like Cook,[55] the excitement of being the first observer; and though granite meets his gaze and he wryly confesses to not being the first, what he sees is nonetheless 'coeval with the beginning of the world'.[56]

The disclosure of prehistoric forms arouses his imagination, and his writing is at its most charged when he describes a silicified forest, or a fog-bank that fortuitously restores an earlier level of the ocean.[57] The volcanic landmasses of the Galapagos islands constitute a turning point in the imaginative trajectory of his voyage, as also – it was to prove – in the development of his theory (for from his study of variation among the finches there, he was later to infer the crucial concept of environmental modification). 'Both in space and time', he writes of the archipelago, 'we seem to be brought somewhat near to that great fact – that mystery of mysteries – the first appearance of new beings on this earth.'[58] In the 'retrospect' to his travelogue, Darwin accounts for his intense delight in the life of exploration in a way that develops Humboldt's equation of the exotic with the youthful:

> It has been said, that the love of the chase is an inherent delight in man – a relic of an instinctive passion. If so, I am sure the pleasure of living in the open air, with the sky for a roof and the ground for a table, is part of the same feeling; it is the savage returning to his wild and native habits. I always look back to our boat cruises, and my land journeys, when through unfrequented countries, with an extreme delight, which no scenes of civilization could have created. I do not doubt that every traveller must remember the glowing sense of happiness which he experienced, when he first breathed in a foreign clime, where the civilized man had seldom or never trod.[59]

But just as Le Vaillant's self-emancipation left its impression on his view of indigenous people, so Darwin's recovery of an instinctual life is reflected in his alignment of the primitive with the wild:

> I do not believe it is possible to describe or paint the difference between savage and civilized man. It is the difference between a wild and tame animal: and part of the interest in beholding a savage, is the same which would lead everyone to desire to see the lion in his desert, the tiger tearing his prey in the jungle, or the rhinoceros wandering over the wild plains of Africa.[60]

But while the projection of a liberated self supplies a common pattern, Le Vaillant and Darwin celebrate very different values through their spurious embodiment of the natural. For Le Vaillant the natural upholds, miraculously, a model of both personal and social harmony. For Darwin it denotes instinctual forces which threaten polity, but vitalize the individual. Yet for them both an urge to equate the unfamiliar with the original distorts perception of the exotic people they encounter.

Myths of creation are multifarious but, as far as Western culture is concerned, Genesis and physical evolution pretty well subsume the various kinds. The differences between these two are, of course, radical. Where the first provides for a universe created for once and all, its categories fixed and instinct with design, the second postulates the continuous development of new forms arranged in layers of ascending complexity. In the exchange of theory for doctrine, the old hierarchy is thrown into a temporal perspective and its order reversed. Descent from God gives place, on the new model, to an unfinished ascent from the lowest reaches of creation. The Ladder of Perfection – to make the point graphically – is chopped in half and turned upside down. To the layman seeking marks of origin in the external world, the most obvious difference between the two accounts lies, perhaps, in the contrast between their static and dynamic character. The Book of Genesis had ordained a single steady state; but the nascency posited by science declared itself in successive states, and implied a locus of endless vicissitude. Among many repercussions the scientific theory complicated the bearing of the present upon the past: on the one hand history was present in the fossil deposits which could be placed in temporal sequence by the palaeontologist; on the other hand the relationships between living forms themselves held the key to physiological change. Often under only the most tenuous of scientific cover, odd beliefs about the immanence of the past gained currency. According to a biogenetic theory, dating back to the late eighteenth century but first acquiring empirical pretensions in the third quarter of the nineteenth,[61] each stage of evolution was rehearsed by the human foetus in the course of its growth. While in this, as well as in many other ways, the development of each individual was seen to recapitulate that of the kind – 'ontogeny' seen to 'repeat phylogeny' to use the contemporary phrase – phylogeny in its turn was telescoped into the present through a variety of racial dogmas. These proceeded on the assumption that all evolutionary process was single and uniform, and lined up exotic cultures as so many fossil specimens of vanished stages in the development of Western man.[62]

Given the drastic implications of the shift in world view that occurred in the nineteenth century, it might seem that the respective mental operations entailed by the quest for genesis in the external world were so distinct as to belong to an entirely different order. But if we return to the figure of the explorer, and consider the matter existentially, we shall see that this is not so. The point is perhaps best made by insisting on the evolutionary tendencies that pervaded the moral and social – indeed all but the cosmological – aspects of Judaeo-Christian belief itself. Traditionally the categories of physical creation (if not its nature) were held to remain static, but man had decisively fallen, and had fallen only to be re-engaged in an unfolding drama of redemption. Accordingly, for the traditionalist as much as for the evolutionary thinker, the idea of genesis readily converted into a sense of buried potential in the self. And although from the turn of the eighteenth century (the period which constitutes a watershed in the rise of evolutionary thought) an emphasis on the self as many-layered became increasingly pronounced, this only extended an already assumed correspondence between the inner and outer worlds. Whereas to Le Vaillant an unspoilt landscape responded to a source of innate goodness in the corrupted self, for Emerson the 'concentrical . . . geological structure of the globe' provided the appropriate metaphor for the human mind, seen as impenetrably deep yet discontinuous.[63] In the case of Leichhardt, an Australian explorer enthralled by the evolutionary geology that preceded Darwin, an almost obsessive interest in stratification tallies with his claim that year after year of his past unfurled as he penetrated the Centre:

As I proceeded on my journey, events of earlier date returned into my mind, with all the fantastic associations of a dream; and scenes of England, France, and Italy passed successively. Then came the recollections of my University life, of my parents and the members of my family; and, at last, the days of boyhood and of school – at one time as a boy afraid of the look of the master, and now with the independent feelings of the man, communicating to, and discussing with him the progress of my journey, the courses of the rivers I had found, and the possible advantages of my discoveries. At the latter part of the journey, I had, as it were, retraced the whole course of my life.[64]

Later in the century this pattern of personal reclamation would be extended to incorporate exotic cultures, and to include animal, vegetable, and even inorganic creation.[65] Under the stimulus of evolutionary theory, the psyche as much as the external world was viewed as the accretion of previous states. No lapse in historical continuity is implied by this, however; for to the traditionalist the image of paradise corresponded to an unfallen state of the soul, obscured – but not irrecoverably so – by original sin.[66]

Given that genesis, on either model, implies a process of uncovering a hidden self, let me re-open the issue posed at the start, the relation of projection to genesis; and return to the question of what it is that leads explorers to search for the evidences of creation in the external world. To this question two answers have already proposed themselves – first, the need to found a prescriptive system in the natural world; second, the transference of a perceptual freshness to the object. Though both these answers touch on the occupational circumstances of the explorer (as a person who ventures beyond the realm of polity in search of new things) and involve projection (since in each case mental concerns are located in the external world), neither touches on the nature of projection itself. But in accordance with my original aim of showing an intrinsic connection between this process and the concern with genesis, I shall now turn to one that does, even though it implicates the explorer only in so far as projection is least impeded when it engrosses the unknown.

Virtually by definition, to project is to be unaware of importation. Ideas that are fully owned do not belong to external objects; those that appear to are likely to surprise their engenderer. In its special psychoanalytic usage introduced by Freud, the term is exclusively reserved for unconscious ascription, and associated with censorship. Hence Charles Rycroft in a dictionary entry supplies the gloss: 'projection of aspects of oneself is preceded by DENIAL, i.e. one denies that one feels such and such an emotion, has such and such a wish, but asserts that someone else does'.[67] Since, like a dream, it gives expression, however disguised, to what the conscious mind censors, projection in this special context comprises the first step in a

return of the repressed. But over a wider sphere it preserves its
function as a vehicle of self-divulgence. For, from the object which
has drawn a fully charged response, the conscious mind can
retrieve what time and habit, as well as censorship, have effaced.[68]
In view of its capacity for baring the hidden, projection constitutes
a dreamwork of the daylight self.

For a model of this operation it is once again to literature that
we need to turn. The famous passage from *The Prelude* in which
Wordsworth describes his childhood experience of rowing across
a lake by moonlight not only shows how projection serves as an
instrument of self-disclosure, but relates this process to the act of
exploration.[69] Led by a 'Nature' which consists as much in inner
impulse as external setting, the child begins his adventure by
unmooring a boat, and this small social transgression unleashes
a train of uncovenanted feelings which lead to a decisive
recognition. Wordsworth begins, characteristically, with the
experience:

> One summer evening (led by her) I found
> A little boat tied to a willow tree
> Within a rocky cave, its usual home.
> Straight I unloosed her chain, and stepping in
> Pushed from the shore. It was an act of stealth
> And troubled pleasure, nor without the voice
> Of mountain-echoes did my boat move on;
> Leaving behind her still, on either side,
> Small circles glittering idly in the moon,
> Until they melted all into one track
> Of sparkling light. But now, like one who rows,
> Proud of his skill, to reach a chosen point
> With an unswerving line, I fixed my view
> Upon the summit of a craggy ridge,
> The horizon's utmost boundary; far above
> Was nothing but the stars and the grey sky.
> She was an elfin pinnace; lustily
> I dipped my oars into the silent lake,
> And, as I rose upon the stroke, my boat
> Went heaving through the water like a swan;
> When, from behind that craggy steep till then
> The horizon's bound, a huge peak, black and huge,
> As if with voluntary power instinct

> Upreared its head. I struck and struck again,
> And growing still in stature the grim shape
> Towered up between me and the stars, and still,
> For so it seemed, with purpose of its own
> And measured motion like a living thing,
> Strode after me. With trembling oars I turned,
> And through the silent water stole my way
> Back to the covert of the willow tree.

The unmooring is defined as an act of stealth, but registered also as an act of release through the terms applied to the boat, which leaves home, freed of its chain. This poetic transference is the first of many through which Wordsworth dramatizes the sensations of the child, and it is a figure appropriate to his original experience, for from the point of view of the boy, locked in the grip of panic, terror is located in the external scene itself. For him it is the mountain that voices the sounds of his own making; the huge peak that rises and, as he flees, pursues; the oars that tremble. But the singleness of the child's experience is conveyed to the reader through the mature consciousness of the narrator who, even as he conjures up a scene which abets illusion, demonstrates the tricks of parallax and referred motion:

> When, from behind that craggy steep till then
> The horizon's bound, a huge peak, black and huge,
> As if with voluntary power instinct
> Upreared its head. I struck and struck again . . .

Even the serpent-like aspect of the peak receives its force from the rower's action ('upreared' : 'struck'). Yet Wordsworth leaves us in no doubt that in the throes of sensation he was blind to his own agency, unaware even of the way in which his flight created pursuit, or his fear an object of terror:

> and still,
> For so it seemed, with purpose of its own
> And measured motion like a living thing,
> Strode after me.

He seems, moreover, to relate this sheer externality to a dread of admitting feelings of fear and awe. For no sooner is the boat unchained than the poet shows how the boy keeps his responses in check. As so often in Wordsworth's poetry the double negative in 'nor without the voice' is pointed: by hinting at the relief of silence it suggests that the sounds are unwelcome, and that the attention of the boy is selective. The troublesome echoes cannot, like the water, be left behind but they are soon displaced by a reassuring impression – the moonlit wake receding into steadiness. Then, almost it would seem as a planned diversion from his latent unease, the boy (– 'like one who rows, / Proud of his skill, to reach a chosen point / With an unswerving line') imposes the form of a game on his venture. Even the summit of the craggy ridge is pressed into service as a beacon. And only once the space within the 'horizon's bound' has been conquered in this way, by reason and by will, can he freely revel in a scene to which stars, a grey sky, the image of a swan, and some ornate poetic diction ('elfin pinnace') lend the aura of an idyll. When, because of its greater height and the ever-increasing distance, a further peak begins to rise beyond the frame of the ridge, his composure is instantly shattered.

As Wordsworth turns to the reflective impact that the experience had on him as a boy, the expanding horizon that dominates the action in the first half of the paragraph converts into a metaphor for self-discovery, and the work of projection is carefully dismantled. Answering the '*huge* and mighty forms' of an interior landscape the once hidden peak (twice described as 'huge') now takes its place in a fresh map of the psyche:

> for many days, my brain
> Worked with a dim and undetermined sense
> Of unknown modes of being; o'er my thoughts
> There hung a darkness, call it solitude
> Or blank desertion. No familiar shapes
> Remained, no pleasant images of trees,
> Of sea or sky, no colours of green fields;
> But huge and mighty forms, that do not live
> Like living men, moved slowly through the mind
> By day, and were a trouble to my dreams.

The setting sparks off a psychological recognition. But the rendering of the inner world remains colourless, and comparatively vague, so that we are grateful for the further layer

of reflection supplied in the paragraph that follows. Here
Wordsworth celebrates his acceptance of 'the passions that build
up our human soul', adding that it was in the absence of 'the mean
and vulgar works of man' that he learnt to '[sanctify] both pain
and fear'. The notion of escape from a constricting social
consciousness proves central in a variety of ways. If the passage
displays two facets – the one adventurous, the other diagnostic –
each reflects an instance of truancy, as appears from the way the
exploring and projecting unfold in parallel. Led by nature into
conflict with taboo, the boy unchains the boat from its usual
home, and ventures out to discover a peak beyond his ken. The
emotions with which he invests this peak undergo a similar
enfranchisement: apparently extraneous to the daylight world of
men, they break through the defences of censorship with sufficient
force to be identified and fully owned.

Projection (when followed through, at least, to the point of
analysis) finds an apt metaphor in exploration, for both involve
the recovery of what exists but remains hidden beyond the realm
of the known. Yet although there is a real, though limited, sense in
which emotions and desires precede the objects which excite their
expression, they cannot be defined without these objects, any
more than a planet – as Feuerbach once observed – can be
understood without its sun. His remark prefaces a penetrating
comment on the heuristic potential of the external world:

> In the object which he contemplates, therefore, man becomes
> acquainted with himself; consciousness of the objective is the
> self-consciousness of man. We know the man by the object, by
> his conception of what is external to himself; in it his nature
> becomes evident . . . Even the objects which are the most
> remote from man, *because* they are objects to him, and to the
> extent to which they are so, are revelations of human nature.

Feuerbach goes on to align man's nature with his origin:

> The eye which looks into the starry heavens, which gazes at that
> light, alike useless and harmless, having nothing in common
> with the earth and its necessities – this eye sees in that light its
> own nature, its own origin.[70]

How we came to be determines what, beneath the skin, we are –

the idea dies hard, for the sense of an essential human identity, underlying the changing faces of polity, is something to which every version of genesis infallibly gives rise. It is for this reason that there is only a short step between searching unexplored places for vestiges of the primeval, and finding in them symbols of the unconscious mind. Because the process of projection provides a means to baring a hidden self, it has served as an analogue as well as a vehicle to the revelatory myths of creation.

2 Crusoe, Desert Isle Ventriloquist

If his first narrative is viewed as the start of a new kind, Defoe appears to have fathered both realist fiction and the novel of exploration at a single stroke. In fact his parenthood is more obvious in the case of the sub-genre. For while *Robinson Crusoe* (1719) centres in the lone hero and so hardly touches on those 'social and relative duties' which were to provide the stuff of the mainstream novel from Richardson onwards, there is scarcely a story dealing with the exploits of either adventurers or castaways which does not bear the mark of its influence.[1] Models for the restless spirit that keeps Crusoe on the move, even once he is stranded, have never been lacking; but when it came to the shaping of his tale Defoe left an imprint that was to prove indelible. Crusoe finds himself cut off from society, undergoes a period of growth in a fresh environment and finally returns home. This three-stage plot became conventional to the adventure story, and wherever we encounter it we are likely to come across some allusion to Crusoe. Defoe's other and more famous legacy, his contribution to the realist novel, needs no rehearsing.[2]

Because of its double lineage *Robinson Crusoe* demarcates common ground between concerns that are special to exploration and perennial to the novel as a whole, and it may well be an indication of the firmness of this ground that works such as *Moby Dick*, *Heart of Darkness*, or *Voss* rate as classics of the wider genre. There seem, in fact, to be three main points at which Defoe's adventure story abuts on the central tradition. Firstly, Crusoe poses a question typical of the explorer when, pondering the mysteries of genesis, he asks 'what am I, and all the other Creatures?' (p. 92).[3] The question reaches deeply into the text as we shall see, and it is certainly one kept alive by the work of major novelists. Then, eccentric though his treatment of the issue may be (he seems out to show at times that solitude is man's proper state), Defoe uses the solitary situation of his hero as a base from which to investigate the rival claims of independence and relation, a theme as important later to, say, *Women in Love* as to *Voss*. Lastly, it is certainly true that one of Defoe's most forceful contributions to the rise of the novel lay in his creation of what Pat Rogers has called the narrator's 'sustained intimacy' of address.[4] Here, again, it seems to have been in response to the challenge of his hero's isolation that Defoe pioneered new routes of access to inner states, and he was well served in this regard by the projective procedures that characterize travel writing. It is with the last of these three areas of interest that I shall more particularly be concerned, for my chief aim is to examine the way Defoe objectifies the inward tendencies of his hero through his use of setting.

After six years of uninterrupted solitude on the island, and a month or two of absence from his second dwelling Crusoe is woken from the rest he takes, on his return there, by a voice that insistently moans, '*Robin, Robin, Robin Crusoe*, poor *Robin Crusoe*, where are you *Robin Crusoe*? Where are you? Where have you been?' (p. 142). Although the words are really his own, since he himself has put them into the mouth of his parrot, Crusoe fails to recognize them and, slipping back into sleep, imagines that it is a man who calls out to him, and speaks. His attitude to this figure proves ambivalent. Reassurance rapidly gives way to fright in his dream until he wakes, for a second time, in a state of panic only to hear his repertoire of self-pity relayed by his pet. The peculiar quality of this parrot-talk becomes evident to Crusoe at the moment he places the voice:

> no sooner were my Eyes open, but I saw my *Poll* sitting on the Top of the Hedge; and immediately knew that it was he that spoke to me; for just in such bemoaning Language I had used to talk to him, and teach him.
>
> (p. 142)

For the first time Crusoe takes in, as if from an external source, the plaintive phrases which, only half-consciously it appears, he has confided in himself or in Poll over the years. Just as in the course of his circumnavigation of the island (the episode that immediately precedes his return to the bower) Crusoe adopts a fresh perspective towards his 'captivity', so now he learns to view his former condition from the outside. Like the dictaphone in *Krapp's Last Tape* the parrot begins as an instrument of self-expression and ends as a means of self-disclosure. As a mark of his eerie recognition Crusoe reports that he continues to be disturbed by the incident after his practical fears have been allayed.

The parrot-sequence is a *tour de force* as Defoe certainly knew for he advertises it in advance and keeps Poll conspicuously posted.[5] But although 'very diverting', the scene is also functional, gathering, as it does, several of the novel's chief themes into vivid relation. Both Crusoe's latent craving for human society and his recoil from it are embodied in the man he creates from the parrot in his sleep; and this figure looks forward to the later dream in which he pictures the companionship of a victim rescued from a cannibal horde (pp. 198–9). In Friday he finds – once this dream has come to pass – a being who can fully occupy the role in which a succession of pets have fallen short. The first of these, the dog he saves from the wreck and values as a 'trusty servant', has one shortcoming:

> I wanted nothing that he could fetch me, nor any Company that he could make up to me, I only wanted to have him talk to me, but that would not do.
>
> (p. 64)

The parrot has the advantage, here, in catering more completely to Crusoe's need:

> the sociable Creature came to me, and sat upon my Thumb, as he used to do, and continu'd talking to me . . . just as if he had been overjoy'd to see me again.
>
> (p. 143)

One favourite supplants another, and the moment Friday speaks Poll's accomplishments are forgotten. Before he finds his companion and has done with pets, however, Crusoe makes up for deficiency with number until he has surrounded himself with a 'family' of creatures – dogs, cats, sea-fowl, parrots and kids – each allotted a regular place at his household table (pp. 147–8). When Friday arrives on the scene he is taught to address Crusoe as 'master', and generally referred to as 'my man'. He *realizes* the metaphors of servitude applied to every pet in turn, but never quite transcends the portion of his predecessors. Seldom is he more acceptable than when approaching his rescuer with gestures of fawning submission (p. 206); and Crusoe is soon to take his surrender of will for granted: 'I took him out with me', he will write, or again, 'Having thus fed him with boil'd Meat and Broth, I was resolv'd to feast him the next Day' (pp. 210–11, 212). A continuity between Crusoe's education of Friday and his taming of creatures from the wild is apparent fairly often.

The relationship with Friday represents the fullest expression of Crusoe's desire for company; on the strength of his social passions he insists, nevertheless, time and time again. He describes, for instance, how, overwrought with disappointment, he falls into a trance after the disappearance of the Spanish ship, constantly chanting, '*O that it had been but One!*', until his hands and mouth fasten in a convulsive clench (p. 188). Crusoe's social desires are, of course, of a limited kind. Like most of Defoe's heroes he never betrays a flicker of sexual response, managing even to keep the report of his marriage to a single sentence so that Mrs Crusoe dies on a participial phrase embedded within a subordinate clause (p. 305). In any case we are left in no doubt that his relationship with Friday comprises the culmination of his social life:

> the Conversation which employ'd the Hours between *Friday* and I, was such, as made the three Years which we liv'd there together perfectly and compleatly happy, *if any such Thing as compleat Happiness can be form'd in a sublunary State.*
>
> (p. 220)

Nor is it by chance that this specially fulfilling bond should be of a master–servant kind, for throughout the text Crusoe's thirst for relation is countered by his delight in autonomy. Whenever he thanks God for making life on the island 'better than sociable' (p. 135) his independence is not far from view and it amounts, as he once explains, to nothing less than sovereignty:

> I had nothing to covet; for I had all that I was now capable of enjoying: I was Lord of the whole Mannor; or if I pleas'd, I might call my self King, or Emperor over the whole Country which I had Possession of. There were no Rivals. I had no Competitor.
>
> (p. 128)

The itch for self-determination is with Crusoe from the start: it is
no other than the happy 'original sin' which prompts him to 'act
the Rebel' to his father, and to shy away, twice over, from 'the
middle state' (pp. 4, 40, 194). He can understand his confinement
on the island as a punishment for transgression precisely because
it comes as the consequence of his resistance to 'confin'd Desires'
(p. 194). When he finds the footprint, the prospect of human
presence is wholly soured by the lack of any compensating
assurance of control. In context it is clear that Crusoe's
relationship with Friday answers to the shape carved out by a
confluence of warring needs. It represents a compromise between
what he calls his 'Desire after the Society of my Fellow-Creatures'
(p. 188), and his urge to be monarch of all he surveys.

One reason why Crusoe, on returning to his bower, is slow to
recognize Poll's sad refrain is that in the course of his voyage
round the island he undergoes a change of mood. No sooner has he
been swept into a dangerous current than daily existence appears
to him in a favourable light:

> Now I look'd back upon my desolate solitary Island, as the most
> pleasant Place in the World, and all the Happiness my Heart
> could wish for, was to be but there again.
>
> (p. 139)

It is while bathed in the afterglow of these sentiments that he hears
Poll relaying the litany of his gloom, '*Poor* Robin Crusoe, *Where are
you? Where have you been?*'. Ambivalence is a feature of Crusoe's
experience as much as it is the mental habit of his schizophrenic
creator, and it would certainly be extravagant to suppose that
every antithetical movement of the narrative adds to a design. All
the same, this particular antinomy in Crusoe's reading of his
situation is an important one, for it not only ramifies through the
novel so as to produce, as Carnochan has noted, the sense of two
distinct islands;[6] but also points back to the decisive change of
outlook that attends Crusoe's religious conversion. In short, the
'*Island of Despair*' – the phrase confided to his journal (p. 70), and
the 'pleasant Place' that he sees (yet again) from the ocean, are
used to denote the 'before' and 'after' of his repentance.

The impressions Crusoe forms of his island are mixed from the
outset, and so they continue to be, for they are founded in the
paradox of his solitary state. The volatile bouts of joy and terror he

experiences on landing (sensations so intense, he notices, as to be equally overwhelming, pp. 46–7) give way to feelings that are more stable and prolonged, so that he is soon able to analyse the causes of his fluctuating moods by drawing up a table in which he enters the good against the evil aspects of his plight. This table shows Crusoe simultaneously elated and depressed by the fact that he is sole survivor. If it is reason for joy that he alone of the crew should have been saved it is no less a cause for terror that, stripped of all companionship, he should face the undisclosed dangers of his new world without any aid. He is at once the miserable *solitaire* banished from society to fribble away a hopeless life, and the lucky man singled out to make the most of a pleasant setting. For Crusoe, solitude holds two faces, and both are reflected by the island when he sees it for the first time from the crest of a hill:

> after I had with great Labour and Difficulty got to the Top, I saw my Fate to my great Affliction, (*viz.*) that I was in an Island environ'd every Way with the Sea, no Land to be seen, except some Rocks which lay a great Way off, and two small Islands less than this, which lay about three Leagues to the West.
>
> I found also that the Island I was in was barren, and, as I saw good Reason to believe, un-inhabited, except by wild Beasts, of whom however I saw none, yet I saw Abundance of Fowls, but knew not their Kinds, neither when I kill'd them could I tell what was fit for Food, and what not; at my coming back, I shot at a great Bird which I saw sitting upon a Tree on the Side of a great Wood, I believe it was the first Gun that had been fir'd there since the Creation of the World; I had no sooner fir'd, but from all the Parts of the Wood there arose an innumerable Number of Fowls of many Sorts, making a confus'd Screaming, and crying every one according to his usual Note.
>
> (pp. 52–3)

When Crusoe confirms from his vantage point that he is indeed on an island, renewed despondency clouds his response to the scene. So he is the prisoner of his landscape, 'environ'd every Way with the Sea'; the place 'barren', and full of 'wild Beasts'. But even while recording this impression, Crusoe pauses to note some anomalous details. Although there is 'no Land to be seen' he makes a point of mentioning two islands which lie at no great distance to the west; or, again, admits that he has no reason to assume the presence of the beasts – 'however I saw none'. Despite himself Crusoe thrills to his surroundings and, as his attention is increasingly absorbed by the foreground, soon forgets that he is on an island at all. But while he is impressed by the abundance of wildfowl and rejoices in the great size of a bird, or of the wood, he makes no attempt to disguise the source of his feeling, the power he enjoys over everything in range. Indeed, as the paragraph reaches a climax with the firing of his gun, he quietly acknowledges that his inheritance is nothing less than a world still fresh from God's creation. He relishes the terror of the wheeling birds and remembers, at the same time, to notice the variety of their kinds. It is with disturbing rapacity that Crusoe acts out Marvell's dream of living in Paradise alone.[7]

In little more than a paragraph Crusoe shifts between his customary states of grief and contentment, states that relate directly to the interplay of his warring needs. On the one hand, the island frustrates his need of social intercourse; it gives free reign to his love of power on the other. Yet although it is plain to every reader that Crusoe is subject to wavering moods throughout, in his retrospect of his first two years on the island he presents his experience of despair as the distinctive trait of his unregenerate days:

> how much more happy this Life I now led was, with all its miserable Circumstances, than the wicked, cursed, abominable Life I led all the past Part of my Days; and now I chang'd both my Sorrows and my Joys; my very Desires alter'd, my Affections chang'd their Gusts, and my Delights were perfectly new, from what they were at my first Coming, or indeed for the two Years past.

He proceeds with an account of what he has called the *Island of Despair*, now identified as a symptom of his sin:

> Before, as I walk'd about, either on my Hunting, or for viewing the Country, the Anguish of my Soul at my Condition, would break out upon me on a sudden, and my very Heart would die within me, to think of the Woods, the mountains, the Desarts I was in; and how I was a Prisoner lock'd up with the Eternal Bars and Bolts of the Ocean, in an uninhabited

Wilderness, without Redemption: In the midst of the greatest Composures of my Mind, this would break out upon me like a Storm, and make me wring my Hands, and weep like a Child: Sometimes it would take me in the middle of my Work, and I would immediately sit down and sigh, and look upon the Ground for an Hour or two together; and this was still worse to me; for if I could burst out into Tears, or vent my self by Words, it would go off, and the Grief having exhausted it self would abate.

(pp. 112–13)

Here Defoe enlarges on his hero's isolation with a metaphoric force that is unusual in his writing, and once again it is the experience of a vast expanse ('the Woods, the Mountains, the Desarts') bearing in on the frail, exposed soul, that epitomizes Crusoe's sense of claustrophobic confinement, an irony driven home by the phrase, 'the Eternal Bars and Bolts of the Ocean'. It is not surprising to find a similar oxymoron used, in an address by a Puritan spokesman, to describe the sinking spirits of the Pilgrim Fathers on reaching America:

If they looked behind them, there was the mighty ocean which they had passed and was now as a *main bar and gulf* to separate them from all the civil parts of the world.[8]

Unsurprising in that Defoe continually relates his imagery of imprisonment to the Book of Exodus, an episode of Biblical history that has always held strong appeal for the Nonconformist mind. Shortly before he prays for the first time in 'the true sense', Crusoe alights on a text, 'Can God spread a Table in the Wilderness?', which, in common with most of the scriptural allusions in this part of the novel, refers to Moses' deliverance of the Israelites from Egyptian bondage.[9] Even his moment of conversion is couched in the same terms:

Now I began to construe the Words mentioned above, *Call on me, and I will deliver you*, in a different Sense from what I had ever done before; for then I had no Notion of any thing being call'd Deliverance, but my being deliver'd from the Captivity I was in; for tho' I was indeed at large in the Place, yet the Island was certainly a Prison to me, and that in the worst Sense in the

World; but now I learn'd to take it in another Sense: Now I look'd back upon my past Life with such Horrour, and my Sins appear'd so dreadful, that my Soul sought nothing of God, but Deliverance from the Load of Guilt that bore down all my Comfort.

(pp. 96–7)

We shall see that Crusoe ultimately reverts to the darker view of his situation but, after his repentance, he seldom fails to recognize that his *Island of Despair* proceeds from a state of mind, whereas in his journal it is the name of a place. He can now articulate the processes of projection that colour his surroundings. Though the footprint throws him into a panic he is quick, as narrator, to account for the distorting effects of his fear:

I came Home . . . but terrify'd to the last Degree, looking behind me at every two or three Steps, mistaking every Bush and Tree, and fancying every Stump at a Distance to be a Man; nor is it possible to describe how many various Shapes affrighted Imagination represented Things to me in.

(p. 154)

If Defoe was not familiar with Theseus's speech on the 'shaping fantasies' of poets, lovers and madmen he was certainly aware of the tricks played by the mind on perception;[10] and it is in the light of this awareness that he uses physical setting, throughout *Robinson Crusoe*, as a sort of litmus-paper test of his hero's spiritual condition. The island captures Crusoe's inner feelings as deftly as the parrot.

Robinson Crusoe has its roots (as has often been remarked) in several distinct literary traditions, foremost among which are spiritual autobiography and the travel book. Though Defoe is widely known as the father of the English novel this claim is a paradoxical one, for it was precisely his avoidance of the seemingly fictitious that distinguished his work from the host of romances and novellas produced before his time. Because he meant to pass off his first narrative as a true story Defoe did his best to mimic the materials and procedures of a travelogue. But in overall form *Robinson Crusoe* owes a great deal, as George Starr has conclusively shown, to the then popular genre of the religious confession, with its standard progress from fall to repentance, from newfound grace to renewed tribulation.[11] It is, of course, in the nature of this mixed heritage that Crusoe should switch his attention from God to cassava root but – although the confessional pattern predominates here as nowhere else in Defoe's narratives – there is some force in the point made by a contemporary critic who, framing an imaginary dialogue between character and author, had Crusoe complain:

> when you bring me again to a Sense of the Want of Religion, you make me quit that upon every Whimsy.[12]

Certainly the novel's many seams sometimes prove a source of strength, and the treatment of Crusoe's fluctuating moods presents a case in point. Here, what spiritual autobiography puts asunder Defoe joins together, and psychology is surely on his side. Acquired some time after her master's conversion Poll supplies one of many welcome reminders that not all has been rosy in Crusoe's regenerate phase.

It would not do, however, to underestimate the feats of fusion that went into the making of the narrative. We have seen how Defoe uses the imagery of imprisonment to link his hero's despair with the concerns of Exodus: he draws at the same time both on the reports of travellers, and on a tradition of moral allegory which he may well have tapped from Bunyan. In the course of his progress, Bunyan's Christian is introduced to a man who sits in a dark room, murmuring, 'I am what I was not once':

CHR. *Well, but what art thou now?*

MAN I am *now* a Man of *Dispair*, and am shut up in *it*, as in *this* Iron Cage. I cannot get out; O *now* I cannot.

CHR. *But how camest thou in this condition?*

MAN . . . I have so hardened my heart, that I *cannot* repent.[13]

Like Mr Fearing whom Christian encounters later on his journey, stuck as always in the mud – for he has a '*Slough of Despond* in his Mind, a *Slough* that he carried every where with him, or else he could never have been as he was' – the figure of Despair is insulated from change by his own condition.[14] Crusoe, in just the same way, is cut off from 'all Manner of Opportunities to converse with any thing but what was like my self', because of his 'hardned Life' (pp. 131–2).

Defoe's debt to the various accounts of Alexander Selkirk has always been recognized, but the close correspondence between Crusoe and the castaway's spiritual ups-and-downs has not received its due of critical attention.[15] Woodes Rogers, the captain responsible for rescuing Selkirk after his self-inflicted spell of four years on Juan Fernandez, lays considerable stress on the initial period of depression suffered by the mariner:

> He diverted and provided for himself as well as he could, but for the first eight months had much ado to bear up against melancholy, and the terror of being left alone in such a desolate place.[16]

Crusoe's blue period is of much the same duration for, although his release from the captivity of sin takes place in his tenth month on the island, the train of events leading to his conversion – the miraculous sprouting of the corn, the earthquake, his dream of the avenging angel, and his illness – dates back to his seventh. Equally pertinent is the description Rogers supplies of the way Selkirk overcame his melancholy by reading from the Bible, praying and chanting psalms. 'He was a better Christian while in this solitude', he adds, 'than ever he was before, or than, he was afraid, he should ever be again'.[17] According to Rogers, Selkirk was saved from utter desolation by the renewal of his faith and by the company, also, of his kids and cats with whom 'he would, now and then, sing and dance'.[18] Richard Steele in his version of the story, gathered from conversations with Selkirk after his return, adopts the same emphasis: he distinguishes between the *isolato*'s periods of 'dissatisfaction' and 'delight', attributes his triumphs over despair to 'Force of Reason, and frequent reading of the Scriptures', and enlarges on his impulsive urges for society.[19] But Steele is at his most germane when he explains how Selkirk's change of heart altered his outlook towards the island:

> I forgot to observe, that during the Time of his Dissatisfaction, Monsters of the Deep, which frequently lay on the Shore, added to the Terrors of his Solitude; the dreadful Howlings and Voices seemed too terrible to be made for human Ears; but upon the Recovery of his Temper, he could with Pleasure not only hear their Voices, but approach the Monsters themselves with great Intrepidity. He speaks of Sea-Lions, whose Jaws and Tails were

capable of seizing or breaking the Limbs of a Man, if he approached them: But at that Time his Spirits and Life were so high, and he could act so regularly and unconcerned, that meerly from being unruffled in himself, he killed them with the greatest Ease imaginable.[20]

The accounts of Selkirk show not only how much Defoe took from actual experience but how well he grafted on the literary conventions that extend the range and finesse of his sources. We have seen how Selkirk's importation of terror is diversified in numerous ways throughout the text. The means by which Defoe expands on the 'unruffled' spirits which led Selkirk to a new understanding with his environment remain to be examined.

So long as he is the prisoner of his *Island of Despair* Crusoe remains fairly static, never venturing beyond a few hours' hike of his fortified dwelling. Confinement is his punishment for unconfined desires, and his exodus from bondage remains purely metaphorical until, with his recovery and conversion complete, he sets out for the first time to explore. Moral progress is now manifest in the journey he takes into the interior. Moving through ever richer country he is surprised, at the close of his second day, by a Pisgah-like view of his future domain:

At the End of this March I came to an Opening, where the Country seem'd to descend to the West, and a little Spring of fresh Water which issued out of the Side of the Hill by me, run the other Way, that is due East; and the Country appear'd so fresh, so green, so flourishing, every thing being in a constant Verdure, or Flourish of *Spring*, that it looked like a planted Garden.

(p. 99)

The date is mid-July and by any reckoning Crusoe is north of the equator, so the reference to foliage as fresh and as green as that of *Spring* (the italics are Defoe's) underlines his sense of a landscape unspoilt by the Fall, an idea made virtually explicit by the 'planted garden' that supplants his earlier impression of wilderness. On the walk made before his conversion Crusoe notices a scene untouched 'since the Creation' but his recognition is comparatively casual: the overt delight he now takes in the prospect before him serves as an indication of his renewal. In the terms of Pope's paradoxical 'scene of Man', Crusoe wins an insight, for the moment, into nature's hidden order:

> A mighty maze! but not without a plan;
> A Wild, where weeds and flow'rs promiscuous shoot,
> Or Garden, tempting with forbidden fruit.[21]

Defoe sees to it, of course, that the surfaces of realism are kept intact. Like any explorer, Crusoe worries over his co-ordinates (if the valley stretches north, the brook runs due east), but there is no mistaking the allegorical features of his map. The melons and clustering vines are observed with a freshness of detail that suggests they may have been taken straight from Hakluyt:[22]

> in this Part I found different Fruits, and particularly I found Mellons upon the Ground in great Abundance, and Grapes upon the Trees; the Vines had spread indeed over the Trees, and the Clusters of Grapes were just now in their Prime, very ripe and rich.
>
> (p. 99)

But the composition as a whole belongs to the machinery of fable. Crusoe is in the position of Bunyan's Christian, rewarded at length by the Delectable Mountains, some time after he catches his first glimpse of their uplifting terrain:

> and behold at a great distance he saw a most pleasant Mountainous Country, beautified with Woods, Vineyards, Fruits of all sorts; Flowers also, with Springs and Fountains, very delectable to behold.[23]

Only once he has escaped from the dungeon of Giant Despair does Christian reach these hallowed slopes, there to refresh himself with the fountains and fruit.[24] But although Crusoe's progress follows the main lines of this episode we have only to turn back to the text to see how Defoe throws Bunyan's pasteboard setting into vivid relief.

Before he has picked more grapes and limes than he can possibly carry (he resolves, however, to come back for the rest) Crusoe sounds the signature-tune of his happy island:

I descended a little on the Side of that delicious Vale, surveying
it with a secret Kind of Pleasure, (tho' mixt with my other
afflicting Thoughts) to think that this was all my own, that I
was King and Lord of all this Country indefeasibly, and had a
Right of Possession; and if I could convey it, I might have it in
Inheritance, as compleatly as any Lord of a Mannor in *England*.

(p. 100)

Although he seems to show the awareness of some guilt in
commenting on the furtive nature of his pleasure, Crusoe clearly
experiences no real difficulty in reconciling this new dispensation
with his urge for sway. He will later present his authority as
providential, and so close the gap between Adam's stewardship
and that of a feudal lord. Though his afflictions still persist, they
are now contained by parentheses – which points to his success in
controlling the grief caused by his other (if lesser) ruling passion,
his thirst for human society. On one occasion he volunteers a
reason for this, explaining that his companionly urges are more
than compensated by his closeness to God or by what amounts to
much the same thing, introspection:

when I began to regret the want of Conversation, I would ask
my self whether thus conversing mutually with my own
Thoughts, and, as I hope I may say, with even God himself by
Ejaculations, was not better than the utmost Enjoyment of
humane Society in the World.

(pp. 135–6)

Even in context this explanation appears somewhat strained. But
Defoe does, in fact, manage to make his hero's release from
solitude fairly convincing. We are led to feel, after his conversion,
that Crusoe is no longer the embattled loner staring into the void.
The comfortable assurance with which he confides his experience
contributes to the impression, but this holds true, of course,
throughout. Defoe's immediate means are more abstract: he has
his hero gaze at the sea, and ponder the mysteries of genesis. In
defiance of his subjective imprisonment Crusoe is soon spelling
out his belief in the kinship of all creatures, and considering his
place in the divine plan:

What is this Earth and Sea of which I have seen so much,

whence is it produc'd, and what am I, and all the other Creatures, wild and tame, humane and brutal, whence are we?

Sure we are all made by some secret Power, who form'd the Earth and Sea, the Air and Sky; and who is that?

Then it follow'd most naturally, It is God that has made it all: Well, but then it came on strangely, if God has made all these Things, He guides and governs them all, and all Things that concern them; for the Power that could make all Things, must certainly have Power to guide and direct them.

(p. 92)

'Where are you?', and 'How come you here?': in context Poll's cries have an almost metaphysical ring for they carry over from the rhetorical mode of Crusoe's meditations. Locke in a famous section of his *Essay* had asked whether a brainy parrot would count as a human. Defoe may well have been influenced by the passage but Poll plays her part in an account of human identity that is essentially novelistic.[25] While she draws Crusoe into relation, as do the many other pets who come into focus after his repentance, she serves also to sharpen his yearning for the distinctively human – in his dream Crusoe will transform her voice into that of a person calling. The goat found in the cave performs much the same function. After likening the wretched animal to a moribund man ('just making his Will, as we say, and gasping for Life, and dying indeed of meer old Age', p. 178) Crusoe wryly entertains the thought of sharing its dumb acceptance,

I could have been content to have capitulated for spending the rest of my Time there, even to the last Moment, till I had laid me down and dy'd, like the old Goat in the Cave

(p. 180)

and recovers his fighting spirits the sooner. Animals and objects keep Crusoe's spectre of exclusion at bay, and help him to affirm a sense of self.

After the conquest of his solitude Crusoe, like Silas Marner, develops an almost childlike trust in the goodness of creation. Indeed, the Fall seems not to enter into account in either his thoughts on the origin of the world, or his viewing of the island as a 'planted garden' on the excursion that shortly ensues. A gain in confidence is immediately reflected by the style of his life. He sets out to explore, and decides to prolong his trip over several days, happy for once to sleep under the sky. On returning to his old quarters which (placed in the lee of an escarpment, pp. 58–9) have served till now both as a shelter and lookout, he decides he can do without his elaborate system of defences, and so cuts a door through the rock of his cave. His comment on this occasion is telling:

> as I had manag'd my self before, I was in a perfect Enclosure, whereas now I thought I lay expos'd, and open for any Thing to come in upon me; and yet I could not perceive that there was any living Thing to fear.
>
> (p. 103)

Once his terrors are dispelled Crusoe is eager to spread his energies over the land and put down roots. In rapid succession we learn of the way he doubles his stock and grain, perfects his skill at making pots and bread, and – almost in a spirit of revelry – builds a second dwelling for himself. So resourceful does he prove that, in the course of a few months, he practically recapitulates the stages of economic advance Defoe was to set out in his general history of trade.[26] In keeping, moreover, with his belief that he contributes to a hidden order, the boundaries between the natural and artificial realms begin to recede. Taken from the woods Poll learns to speak. Wild cats mate with the tame, and the stakes of his enclosure send out fresh shoots. For a while the notion of rebirth, figured in the coincidence of his birthday and landing, carries dramatic weight.

Conversion supplies one turning point in the narrative, the footprint another. The moment the mysterious mark appears all the old demons come trooping back. Bitterly regretting the passage he has carved out of his shelter Crusoe throws up yet a further ring of defence, 'so monstrous thick and strong, that it was indeed perfectly impassable' (p. 161); but no matter how impregnable his fortresses are – and he retreats into a series of them – Crusoe never feels safe. In ever narrowing horizons the wilderness reasserts its constrictive pressure until he half decides to root up his fields in case their presence should give him away. Looked at from a little distance, his programme for survival seems like a suicide plan.

That there is an element of hysteria in his actions Crusoe is ready to acknowledge. He is equally concerned, however, to stress that his darker view of nature is founded in fact. The footprint turns out, accordingly, to be the token of a world that has suffered the Fall. It is a chastened Crusoe who refers to a 'Nature entirely abandon'd of Heaven', or to 'Creatures . . . sentenc'd to Absence from himself' (pp. 170, 210). These remarks are occasioned, it is true, by the Carib tribe who visit the island to celebrate their rites; the second of them by Crusoe's grim discovery of leftovers from a cannibal feast. But with an irony that almost certainly derives from Montaigne, Defoe twice turns the tables on Europe.[27] He has Crusoe argue, first, that the horrors of the Inquisition easily outweigh pagan cruelty (p. 244). Later, he brackets exotic and familiar forms of barbarity when Friday, naïvely inquiring whether the three Englishmen on the beach are to be eaten, learns that as victims of a mutiny they will be murdered (p. 251). It is noticeable, too, that although Crusoe has no qualms about putting Friday through a homespun catechism, he often gets himself into doctrinal scrapes. When, for example, his bright pupil questions why an omnipotent God should permit evil he pretends, to begin with, not to hear and then fumbles badly for a reply (p. 218). Again, when pondering why the new world should have been denied the means to redemption he is forced back on an uneasy championship of faith against reason (pp. 209–10, 219).

Ultimately the darker world disclosed by the footprint works as a foil to offset the radiance of belief. Crusoe points to this conclusion when he observes that he was blessed by the benign insouciance instilled by his conversion:

> my Satisfaction was perfect, though my Danger was the same; and I was as happy in not knowing my Danger, as if I had never really been expos'd to it . . . How infinitely Good that Providence is, which has provided in its Government of Mankind, such narrow bounds to his Sight and Knowledge of Things, and though he walks in the midst of so many thousand Dangers, the Sight of which, if discover'd to him, would distract his Mind, and sink his Spirits; he is kept serene, and calm, by having the Events of Things hid from his Eyes, and knowing nothing of the Dangers which surround him.
>
> (p. 196)

As the gap between island and idyll widens, Defoe finds a practical way of bridging the actual and ordained. Built up into something of a philosopher-king, Crusoe becomes an executive of the order he celebrates. The better to dispense justice to his world, he appoints himself *governor* or *generalissimo*, and by means of shrewd stage-management interrupts and then reforms the natural course of events. When occasion demands, he will people his domain with an imaginary garrison, or act the part of his aide. And so, after subjecting the mutineers to a harrowing assault course, he exults, perhaps consciously, in his Prospero-like role:

> We could hear them call to one another in a most lamentable Manner, telling one another, they were gotten into an inchanted Island; that either there were Inhabitants in it, and they should all be murther'd, or else there were Devils and Spirits in it, and they should all be carry'd away, and devour'd.
> (p. 266)

But to Crusoe himself, after all, the island has appeared in much the same light. It is because he continues to have a hard time keeping his sense of order intact that the moral drawn from this phase of his life remains central (p. 159). There is little to fear, other than fear itself.

3 Defoe's Wilderness:

The image of Africa in *Captain Singleton*

Over a hundred and fifty years before Verney Cameron made the first recorded journey through equatorial Africa, a similar crossing, from east coast to west, was undertaken by Defoe. The passage in question occupies about one-third of *Captain Singleton* (1720) where it comes by way of diversion in a narrative largely given over to the hero's piracies. Everyone agrees, however, that it is the continental slog that supplies the liveliest part of Singleton's adventures, and a recent critic has referred to his trip as 'the most remarkable and imaginative trek in the whole history of the eighteenth-century English novel'.[1] In fact the episode holds historical interest of a more direct kind, for it represents not only one of the earliest fictional treatments of Africa but probably the most important of its period. Of course, though sharply lit in places, Defoe's picture of the continent is for the most part vague. Its prevailing tonalities are correspondingly sombre.

At the start of his venture Singleton sets the scene with a few slashing strokes:

> We were now landed upon the continent of *Africa*, the most desolate, desart, and unhospitable Country in the World, even *Greenland* and *Nova Zembla* it self not excepted.
>
> (p. 58)[2]

While superlatives continue to betray the mythical basis of his vision, he proceeds to people his ultimate wilderness with tribes 'barbarous and brutish to the last Degree' (p. 58). Apart from materials gathered from his broad reading in travel literature, Defoe relied on a blend of conjecture and hearsay in projecting his image of Africa. Rather like Swift's enthusiastic geographers who embellish the blank spaces on their maps with 'savage-pictures', he seems to have recognized that he was free to invent so long as he steered clear of well-documented features such as famous rivers or the settlements on either seaboard, for the route devised for Singleton's party, as Scrimgeour has pointed out, keeps scrupulously to regions that were almost wholly uncharted.[3] Operating, again, in the twilight zone between fact and fiction, Defoe appears to have allowed himself some degree of latitude in his adaptation of sources. When, for example, he has his east-coast tribe of sunworshippers mistake the explorers for beings 'who came from the Sun, and that could kill them all, and make them alive again' (p. 83), he almost certainly draws on a passage from Hakluyt describing an encounter with American Indians.[4] Defoe fabricated and transplanted wholesale but at the other extreme (and mainly where mercantile issues were at stake) he fell back on first-hand report. He was later to name his informant as a certain Mr Freeman and to identify him with the character of the Englishman-gone-bush who puts in an appearance towards the close of Singleton's journey. On the history of this mysterious and even Kurtz-like figure, a profile of whose activities emerges from the records of the Royal African Company, this chapter will throw fresh light. But the chief aim is to examine the assumptions and energies which underlay Defoe's presentation of the scarcely inked continent; and the first step in this direction is to place the expeditionary interlude in its context.

Singleton's trek is an undoubted asset, but several critics have seen in it the symptom of a digressive tendency that saps the strength of the text as a whole. 'At the transitional points', John R. Moore remarks of the novel, 'the story veers uncertainly, like a sailing vessel about to change its course' – to which he adds, 'when Defoe was uncertain what story he meant to tell, he could make sad work of it'.[5] Perhaps the African journey contributes to the impression of piecemeal construction mainly because it comes after Singleton's piratical leanings have been advertised (pp. 29–31, 36). Clumsy story-telling always deserves a frown, but there is a good case for claiming that *Captain Singleton* represents one of the more intellectually coherent of comparable narratives. Episodes that appear random at first sight fall into place once we credit Defoe with thematic aims and recognize that he is concerned, primarily, with the question of what constitutes the *primitive state*, and by way of corollary, with what constitutes redemption from it.

The phrase is one that Singleton applies to himself when facing starvation in Portugal during his early teens. 'I being then almost reduced to my primitive State', he writes and immediately describes his first taste of foreign parts, 'I knew no body, and could not speak a Word of their Language' (p. 4). Defoe specialized in the lives of the abandoned, but nowhere does he stress the debilitating effects of loss with quite such force as in his treatment of Singleton's calamitous childhood. Although much of his hero's career was modelled on that of Captain Avery, Defoe altogether made up, as Richetti has noted, the upbringing that leaves his young tyro 'not so much outside society as outside any coherent being of his own'.[6] Sold for twelve shillings at the age of two, Singleton, like Moll Flanders, is passed from hand to hand, 'dragged about' as he puts it, and effectively orphaned many times over. After his good Gipsy foster-mother happens 'in Process of Time to be hang'd' (p. 2) he is taken in by the Parish until his right to such provision is successfully contested. Moll is taught the accomplishments of a lady but, apart from his brief spell under the beadle, Singleton comes by no education whatever. All he recalls of his schooling is patronage of the sort recorded later by Blake in 'The Chimney Sweeper': 'the Minister of the Parish used to talk to me to be a good Boy; and that tho' I was but a poor Boy, if I minded my Book, and served God, I might make a good Man' (p. 3). In consequence, although he grows up at the heart of a Christian nation, Singleton develops into the very type of an indigenous heathen. When called a heretic by the Lieutenant of his third ship, the Portuguese carrack, he is saved the trouble of feigning bewilderment, 'I knew nothing about Religion, neither *Protestant* from *Papist*, or either of them from a *Mahometan*' (p. 9). With some alarm he imagines himself arraigned before the Inquisition lacking the knowledge even to supply a *yes* in the right places, a daydream that enlivens his frequent claim to being 'a Boy entirely ignorant of Religion' (p. 9). So well known is he as a pagan on board the Portuguese boat that the crew allow him to be 'no *Turk*' only after he has stripped and submitted to examination (p. 10).

The ground of Singleton's identity is intransigently physical and Defoe might have underlined his cultural estrangement still further had he not required a literate narrator. As it is, he frequently reminds us that his pirate hero feels no particular allegiance to the country of his birth. It is true, almost invariably, of stories set in exotic places that a desire for homecoming spells out homage to the mother culture. In *Heart of Darkness* Marlow triumphs over Kurtz when he coaxes him into the steamer that heads downriver. In *Lord of the Flies*, characters take sides over the priority to be given to hunting or keeping alight the beacon. Or, again, in Herzog's *Aguirre*, political and cultural severance is implied by the decision to follow the waterway into the hinterland. Defoe adapts this feature of the travel story to his own use when he shows that Singleton is never less at home than when he gets there. After his return from Africa he dwindles (like his stock) until a pretext for fresh adventure suggests itself. When he comes home for good he is forced – as the price of his villainy – to keep himself permanently disguised: with the help of a moustache and some strange clothes he passes for Greek but not a single word of English dare he risk in company. In short, Singleton remains an alien; but in one respect his case proves exceptional. While never an Englishman in England, he at no point discloses a preference for settling elsewhere. When he comes across countryside of exceptional resource in Madagascar he cannot bring himself to decide either to stay or to go. The choice is left to his Portuguese companions who determine to head for Europe, and he dismisses his dilemma with a shrug: 'I had no home, and all the World was alike to me' (p. 43). Defoe points, by these means, to the vacant and listless character that dictates Singleton's footloose career.

It is conventional in the adventure story for the hero to experience a sense of release on venturing beyond the bounds of polity. In Singleton's case this moment comes when, as a punishment for mutiny, he and a group of the Portuguese crew are set down on the coast of Madagascar and left there to fend for themselves. But, once again, the personality of the hero prescribes a deviation, for – as Defoe immediately proceeds to show – his castaway already belongs to the *far* side of the border between wildness and civility. 'I was now to enter', Singleton remarks of his newfound freedom, 'a Part of independent Life'; but then he observes,

> a thing I was indeed very ill prepared to manage; for I was perfectly loose and dissolute in my Behaviour, bold and wicked while I was under Government, and now perfectly unfit to be trusted with Liberty.
>
> (p. 14)

Since no institution has helped him surmount the 'State of

Original Wickedness' into which he was born, Singleton is devoid of 'all Sense of Honesty or Religion' (p. 8), and thus already a part of the lawlessness which awaits him beyond the frontier.

Defoe brings a range of devices to bear in order to register the depth of his hero's depravity. He introduces, for example, a series of unsavoury racial stereotypes which he puts to use as a yardstick. After classing the Portuguese as the lowest-ranking nation in Christendom,

> a Nation the most perfidious and the most debauch'd, the most insolent and cruel, of any that pretend to call themselves Christians, in the World
>
> (p. 7)

he has his English renegade admit, 'I was exactly fitted for their Society' (p. 7). It comes as no surprise to find that Singleton rates the people of Madagascar a great deal worse. Yet even while supposing them to be cannibals he again concedes kinship, this time with a wry joke at the expense of himself and his mates:

> I told him I was not so afraid of that, as I was of starving for want of Victuals; and as for the Inhabitants being *Cannibals*, I believed we should be more likely to eat them, than they us, if we could but get at them.
>
> (p. 16)

Homeless Singleton may be, but on leaving Europe he can at least enjoy the status of a heathen among heathens, and in his element he remains so long as his adventures last. They come to an end when he repents – which he does, of course, though with a perfunctoriness scarcely equalled in Defoe. It is significant that his first inkling of grace should take the form of heartfelt thanks that he was not born a pagan (p. 74).

Though the episodes of the novel are diverse they respond to a simple pattern. For, whatever his part, Singleton continues to live, as his name suggests, the life of an outsider. So it is that after exchanging the existence of outcast for castaway, he opts for the most anti-social of professions by turning pirate. Of all Defoe's creations Singleton is by a long way the most appalling. He boasts his lack of compassion, revels in violence, and has even to be reminded that his business on the high seas is bounty rather than bloodshed (p. 266). But by including elements of buffoonery Defoe frequently distracts the reader from the moral ugliness of his hero. Singleton proves disarming when he passes himself off as 'very dull' (p. 4), or conveys his dependence on the suavely shrewd Quaker William with a humour that looks forward to Jeeves and Bertie: 'I would fain have had Friend *William*'s Advice . . . but he always put it off with some *Quaking* Quibble' (p. 188). The jokes are strategic. In his pirate, Defoe found an image of the natural man, and the comic palliatives allow him to charge his portrayal with all the voracity he had ascribed to the instinctual life in the opening lines of *Jure Divino*:

> Nature has left this Tincture in the Blood,
> That all Men *would be Tyrants* if they cou'd:
> If they forbear their Neighbours to devour,
> 'Tis not for want of *Will*, but want of *Power*.[7]

Where constraint wears thin, nature breaks out, as in the life of an Avery or Singleton. If it was from the materials of the rogue tale that Defoe refined his idea of the 'primitive state', he certainly took care to extend the theme when it came to his choice of setting.

A close link between alien cultures and the untutored soul was taken for granted during the Enlightenment. Even the sceptical Hobbes, who bypassed all recourse to Eden or the Fall, had hypostatized his theory of the natural state by referring to the existence of primitive peoples instead. Only very shortly after delivering his famous account of man's native condition – a life 'solitary, poor, nasty, brutish, and short' – does he point to 'many places, where they live so now', citing in particular the 'savage people' of America whom he supposes to subsist with 'no government at all'.[8] Listing a range of cultural achievements elsewhere, he goes on to ask: 'all which supposed away, what do we differ from the wildest of the Indians?'.[9] Whatever might be said of America in this context was all the more applicable to Africa. Commenting on the European view of the Dark Continent during this period, van Wyk Smith notes the recurrence of disutopic paradigms, and quotes a passage from the *Atlas Geographus* (1711–17) by way of sample:

> The Caffres are a sort of libertines, who inhabit from Mozambique to the Cape of Good Hope, live promiscuously

without ceremonies, like our Adamites, and wallow in lust and sensuality . . . They live by war and rapine, and feed on the flesh of their enemies and friends, using their skulls for drinking cups . . . In short . . . they are the most *nasty* and *brutish* of all reasonable creatures.[10]

The casual borrowings from Hobbes in the last clause show just how instinctive was the reflex to embody – in the portrayal of a distant people – ideas deriving from some essentially abstract notion of man's natural state. Although a little less easy to detect, the same principle is at work in the descriptive gloss to Africa supplied by Defoe for the *Atlas Maritimus* (1728). Blacks are repeatedly presented here as 'brutal' and 'savage', terms that are used interchangeably with 'wild' and 'unpolish'd'; and the continent itself identified with *nature* since all that it generates in the way of produce is 'without the Helps of Art, without Cultivation or Manufacture'.[11] Although a strong abhorrence of the primitive is common to many traditions, Hobbes, once again, appears to be the presiding influence. Defoe knew very well that there was agriculture in Africa but, almost as a nervous tic it seems, he clings to the guidelines laid down by the philosopher in his famous definition of the natural state: 'In such condition, there is no place for industry; because the fruit thereof is uncertain: and consequently no culture of the earth; no navigation, nor use of the commodities that may be imported by sea . . . no arts'.[12]

Throughout his long and voluble career, Defoe held conflicting views about *Leviathan*, but there is no doubt that his debt to it is an important one.[13] If Hobbes's view of the natural state was darker than he was willing at times to accept, he could rest content, at least, with the idea that it reflected the condition of man during the nadir of his history, the period after the Flood.[14] When Robinson Crusoe ponders human nature, it is to the Creation and Fall that he turns his thoughts: in his state of grace he sees the island as a 'planted garden'; and the footprint later impresses an understanding of original sin.[15] When Singleton, on the other hand, is confronted with the 'vast howling Wilderness' (p. 96) that Defoe situates at the heart of Africa – a region which he supposes entirely unvisited – his imagination is carried forward to the 'End of Time', and such reflections as he makes on the origin of his surroundings prove deeply ambivalent. The Creator placed fish in the great central lake, 'for to be sure no human Hands ever put any in there, or pulled any out before' (p. 107); but the waste land also contains creatures that appear to emanate from the Devil – witness the monster with 'a hellish, ugly, deformed Look and Voice', a snake-like dragon of which Singleton remarks, 'we did not know what Business Satan could have there, where there were no People' (p. 129). Apart from these few uneasy peeps at genesis, time in Africa begins for Defoe with the Flood. If he wishes to stress the emptiness of the inner desert he writes 'never Man set his Foot [there] since the Sons of *Noah* spread themselves over the Face of the whole Earth' (p. 129). And when he insists on the untamed ferocity of the animals his party meets, he resorts again to the same image of devastation:

> For as I firmly believe, that never Man, nor a Body of Men, passed this Desart since the Flood, so I believe there is not the like Collection of fierce, ravenous, and devouring Creatures in the World.
>
> (pp. 105–6)

Defoe presents the face of Africa as struck in a scowl that reflects, forever, the wrath of God. In other of his writings he could entertain the idea of a primitive innocence corrupted by exposure to the West.[16] When it came to Africa, however, his view was such as to imply that no change could be a change for the worse.

Captain Singleton is the darkest of Defoe's fictions and perhaps for this reason the one in which his reliance on Hobbes is most pronounced. In *Leviathan*, man opts out of his natural state by renouncing his 'right of nature' – the power he has to fulfil his wants – and contracting instead for the rule of law. Contract enables the exchange of strife for peace; and it is precisely this process of transformation that Defoe examines at a variety of levels in *Captain Singleton*. He begins with the castaways who, although they represent a 'mutinous Rabble' (p. 22), sink their individual differences in a public constitution which they recognize to be indispensable to survival (p. 25). Natural right is curtailed still further when they agree to pool their gold finds so as to guard against conflict (p. 156); and the corporate nature of their enterprise directs that even the shelter they build against the rainy season be designed to a strictly communal plan (p. 120).

The growth of social consciousness among Singleton's troop of desperadoes goes some way to dramatizing an idea that Defoe had voiced in his *Review*:

> if twenty Men born in the dark, and that had never known Men or things, were set on Shore in an Island, where they had no body to imitate, and nothing to do but to live; the first thing they would apply to by the Light of Nature after Food, would be to settle Government among them.[17]

The innate desire for social order is a basic tenet of *Leviathan*; and what Hobbes had prescribed as the most fundamental article of natural law – the right to defend peace, even if necessary with force – is repeatedly invoked by Singleton as the *Law of Arms* and put into effect the moment his party encounter an African tribe.[18] The first spear to be thrown on this occasion provides the pretext (long-awaited) for closing ranks and opening fire; hostilities end only once sufficient prisoners are seized to make up a complement of porters. Hobbes had acclaimed as universal the principle that obligations incurred in wartime were binding,[19] but Singleton is reluctant to attribute a grasp of natural law to his captives, whom he keeps shackled on the grounds that they are 'fierce, revengeful and treacherous':

> for which Reason we were sure, that we should have no Service from them but that of meer Slaves, no Subjection that would continue any longer than the Fear of us was upon them, nor any Labour but by Violence.
>
> (p. 66)

Here, however, Defoe seems to question Singleton's judgement. The tribe's chief, dubbed the 'Black Prince', earns the status of noble savage by stepping into the role of mediator and showing his appreciation of contract:

> he made Signs to me, that if I would let one of the Prisoners go to his Town, he should bring Provisions, and should bring some Beasts to carry our Baggage. I seemed loath to trust him, and supposing that he would run away, he made great Signs of Fidelity, and with his own Hands tied a Rope about his Neck,

offering me one End of it, intimating, that I should hang him, if the Man did not come again.

(p. 75)

With elaborate ceremony the porters then swear to be faithful in exchange for protection and food from the European party, but only after the first leg of the journey is over does Singleton win enough confidence in them to abandon his makeshift system of handcuffing. The tribesmen never fail to keep their part in the bargain, allowing Defoe to score a small point against subjugation – a point later to be amplified in the plea for clemency that Quaker William makes on behalf of the mutineer slaves found aboard a drifting vessel:

> I had much ado to keep my Men from cutting them all in Pieces. But *William*, with many Perswasions prevailed upon them, by telling of them, that it was nothing but *what*; *if they were in the Negroes Condition, they would do, if they could*; and that the Negroes had really the highest Injustice done them, to be sold for Slaves without their consent; and that the *Law of Nature* dictated it to them; that they ought not to kill them, and that it would be wilful Murder to do it.

(p. 191, my italics)

Here, once again, Defoe falls back on Hobbes who had proposed, as a rule of thumb for determining natural law, the maxim: '*Do not that to another, which thou wouldest not have done to thyself*'.[20]

Defoe celebrates the fruits of social contract at every available turn. He makes it clear that the expedition owes its success to a code that reduces the 'Hazard of any Difference' among its individual members (pp. 115–16); and the same benefit conspicuously derives from the various covenants formed with local peoples, since by their means conflict is, again, frequently averted. When it comes, however, to presenting relations among the blacks themselves Defoe falters. Typically, his first reaction is to conjure up hordes of savages living in the state of nature. Writing in this vein he is free with the Hobbesian adjective 'brutish' (pp. 25, 58); and correspondingly sceptical of any capacity for pacific, social existence: 'a Parcel of Creatures', Singleton exclaims of the Madagascans, 'scarce human, or capable of being made sociable on any Account whatsoever' (p. 26). Observations of this kind are tossed off throughout, but whenever Defoe settles to description a different picture emerges. Far from revealing wild abandon his tribesmen incline, during these spells, to ant-like servility, and with the exception of the Black Prince, whose negritude is always on the point of washing off, all trace of individuality dissolves in rigid marshalling. What sustains this presentation is the dream of an ideal labour force, and so long as it prevails the narrator's fear and disdain are kept in check. The motif of treachery recurs, however, with the account of a tribe that stages an attack during a truce (pp. 91–3). But if Defoe seriously intended here to pick up the earlier hint that savages are beyond the reach of law, he fails, for his repeated observations of indigenous tokens of peace – oaths to the sun, poles driven into the ground – imply a culture in steady possession of contract. Contradictions multiply and every reading leads to a dead end, for, although quite ready to assume that to live beyond Western polity was to live without social order, Defoe found himself baffled in his attempt to imagine that contradictory thing, a tribe of tigers. When it came to substantiating his notion of the natural state his automatic recourse was, in any case, to individual Europeans.

Hobbes had noted the essentially egalitarian impulse underlying his philosophy, and in so far as Defoe allows Africa to enter into his celebration of social contract, he closes the gap between the tribesmen and his explorers; the observance of natural law limns out, slowly but surely, the features of a common humanity. He reverts, however, to his earlier insistence on the remoteness of primitive peoples, with the appearance of the forlorn 'White Man' in the depths of the continent. The inset story of this lonely figure partly recapitulates and partly reverses that of Singleton. He presents, in the first place, another example of the outcast, for it is after his unfair dismissal from the Royal African Company that he sets up as a freelance trader in the region of Sierra Leone, only to be kidnapped by a series of tribes until he ends three hundred miles inland 'entirely at the Mercy of the Negroes' (pp. 151–2). But whereas Singleton progressively triumphs over his disabilities, submitting to the 'Articles' of his commune, apprenticing himself both to the learned gunner ('Knowledge was the first step to Preferment', p. 69) and to the clever cutler (pointedly referred to as the 'Artificer' or 'Artist'), the fortunes of his compatriot are downhill all the way.

To his inquiry into what happens to a man deprived of religious instruction, and to his probing into the lives of those born outside Western society Defoe now adds, by way of rider, an investigation into what happens to the man stripped of relation to his culture; and his answer could not be less equivocal. There is a primitivism for which the bronzed body in far-away places serves as an outward sign; but the Englishmen's physique, hairy and horrible from exposure, enunciates quite another theme:

> He was a middle-aged Man, not above 37 or 38, tho' his Beard was grown exceeding long, and the Hair of his Head and face strangely covered him to the middle of his Back and Breast, he was white, and his Skin very fine, tho' discoloured, and in some Places blistered and covered with a brown blackish Substance, scurfy, scaly, and hard which was the Effect of the scorching Heat of the Sun; he was stark naked, and had been so, as he told us, upwards of two Years.
>
> (p. 148)

To fill in the rest of the picture Defoe requires only a few broad strokes. Far from debating the pros and cons of a return to society, the White Man speaks of his life among the tribesmen (who appear to cater to his every need) as 'the most wretched Condition that ever Man was reduced to' (p. 149). And when asked why he takes no trouble either to clothe or to arm himself, he replies 'that to him that had so often wish'd for Death, Life was not worth defending' (p. 152). His rescue brings on such transports of joy that he trembles for days on the verge of tears and piously refers to the explorer's arrival as his *Deliverance*. With a haircut and shave his rehabilitation is under way, and with the gift of an outfit his self-esteem evidently rekindles, for he is inspired to fashion himself ('most artificially', p. 151) a leopard-skin cap.

In the section on Africa in his *Atlas Maritimus* (1728), a work started three years after *Captain Singleton*, Defoe returns to his account of the Englishman-turned-native, adding a few fresh details ('yellow hair'd, almost red') and some lurid adjectives ('despicable', 'scrophulous', 'frightful') before concluding:

> In a word, not the Fable of *Orson* the Brother of *Valentine*, could represent a wild Man more to the purpose, than Mr *Freeman* appear'd to them, (for that was his Name).[21]

Defoe's facts are seldom free of fiction, but even if we discount as legend 'the Journey of the Thirteen Portuguese before they met with [him]' there is no doubt as to the identity of the Wild Man.[22] John Freeman's dismissal and recrimination for arbitrary conduct is mentioned in a history of the Royal African Company by K. G. Davies;[23] and the archives of this infamous institution contain not only the correspondence over his period of service at Sherbo (1702–6) but several reports of subsequent adventure up to his death in Sierra Leone five years later. Defoe's acquaintance with Freeman may well date from the spell the officer spent in London, defending his dereliction of property at Sherbro when under attack by the French, for the account given in *Captain Singleton* is more flattering than was the judgement of his governors. But, in any case, since Defoe acted as a publicist for the Company, held large shares in it, and was on close terms with one of its most powerful directors, he would certainly have kept abreast of news, and in all probability read the letters coming in from Africa.[24]

In his fictional portrait of the European-gone-bush it is on the literal aspects of wildness that Defoe insists. What he really pictures, as his later reference to the tale of Valentine and Orson makes clear, is the classical case of an *enfant sauvage* fostered by beasts – a man with coarsened skin, and hair grown to the waist.[25] But apart from his appearance and thoroughly depressed state of mind the English outcast remains in other respects the perfect gentleman:

> We found his Behaviour the most courteous and endearing I ever saw in any Man whatever, and most evident Tokens of a mannerly well-bred Person, appeared in all things he did or said; and our People were exceedingly taken with him. He was a Scholar, and a Mathematician; he could not speak *Portuguese* indeed, but he spoke *Latin* to our Surgeon, *French* to another of our Men, and *Italian* to a Third.

(p. 149)

The magnetism and distinction are reminiscent of Kurtz, but there is never a word of unsound methods. Yet when we turn to Defoe's model we find that the evidence of wildness is all on the moral plane.

Tale-telling seems to have been a perennial occupation among colonial officials in Africa, and there is some reason to take the charges that led to Freeman's dislodgement as manager at Sherbro with a pinch of salt. Quite apart, however, from the complaints that he abandoned an island to the French or often cursed the Company, vowing 'he came not over to defend or Fight for [its] Interest', the testimony to Freeman's misconduct certainly mounts up. At different times he is accused of embezzling diet-money by keeping his men on short commons, of dealing – against prescription – with freelance traders or the Dutch, of underhand hoarding and downright theft. More telling perhaps, a junior member seconded to his station instantly returned, alluding darkly to the manager's 'unlawful ways'. After his dismissal and year in London, Freeman resumed trade at Sherbro in opposition to the Crown, but despite his boast that no one enjoyed such an 'Interest among the Natives as himself', blurted out in the course of a pathetic appeal for re-employment, he seems to have met with little success. There can be no reason to doubt the sober asides that now sparsely punctuate the flow of company business. We hear of 'Mr Freeman and his gang' preparing to convert ships, or 'reflecting scandalously' on their rivals in an attempt to win over former colleagues. One defects; but Freeman is forced to shift the scene of his ambitions:

> He dares not be seen in Sherbro River – he is gone to Serraleon and builds houses tho' Ready dayly to be murdered by ye Country people for his base behaviour.

No details are supplied, but there is mention later of Freeman's setting fire to a tribal settlement. The rest of his life is covered in three sentences, each separated by over a year:

> Mr Freeman has lost his interest in the river . . .
> Mr Freeman has several small vessels going to decay . . .
> Mr Freeman died ye 3rd of December.

He was barely survived by his chief accuser who succeeded him at Sherbro. His name does not appear among the corporation's dead.[26]

Although a rascal in the eyes of the Company there seems, in retrospect, little to choose between Freeman as truant and officer. Slavery was the chief business at Sherbro, and in the letter of appointment setting forth the manager's duties, detailed instructions for the branding of Negroes shortly follow on the rules for morning prayers.[27] In addition to selecting and assigning slaves, a task that involved him in winning the favour of local chiefs, Freeman was expected to explore openings for the more orthodox channels of trade. It was with this aim that he led an expedition for ivory far into the interior during his managerial days; and it is almost certainly the report of this trip that Defoe retails in his *Atlas* (he cites Freeman as his source) in a passage that almost exactly parallels one of the most vivid in *Captain Singleton*.[28] Though the fictional version represents one of the few occasions on which Singleton concentrates on his surroundings, its chief interest lies in what it reveals of Defoe's self-induced blindness. The paragraph opens with an evocation of a vast, desolate plain, strewn with elephant bones – the scene that greets the party as they approach the heart of the continent. With great skill Defoe plays off time against space, small against ever larger units so as to impart a suggestion of the sublime:

> For a Day's Journey before we came to this Lake, and all the three Days we were passing by it, and for six or seven Days March after it, the Ground was scattered with Elephants Teeth, in such a Number, as is incredible; and as some of them may have lain there for some Hundreds of Years, so seeing the Substance of them scarce ever decayes, they may lye there for ought I know to the End of Time.
>
> (p. 106)

It is a thrilling moment and a poignant one, for the diminishing perspective intensifies the frailty of Singleton and his men, who on entering the central desert have seen before them 'nothing but present Death' (p. 97). But as the paragraph gathers pace the exactly felt atmosphere of a setting and juncture gradually yields to an interest in exploitable value, an interest, that in view of the explorer's situation has, moreover, no dramatic dividend to offer:

> As to Number, I question not but there are enough to load a thousand Sail of the biggest Ships in the World, by which I may be understood to mean, that the Quantity is not to be conceived of.
>
> (p. 106)

The same form of words occurs in the *Atlas*, but if the 'thousand ships' still partly function as an index of wonder, the effect proves fleeting for in the following clause Defoe is already parcelling up the desert,

> as they lasted in View for above eighty Miles Travelling so they might continue as far to the right Hand, and to the left as far.
>
> (p. 106)

And by the next sentence he is well launched in the gas of a sworn appraiser,

> this was particularly remarkable to me, that I observed the whole Scull was as good Ivory as the Teeth, and I believe all together weighed at least 600 Weight.
>
> (p. 106)

It is symptomatic of Defoe's outlook that he should in the course of a single page reduce the field of vision from infinity to little more than a grain of sand. The habit of mind that regularly makes the word 'good' a synonym for 'valuable' betrays an allegiance to the mercantilism so widespread during his time. Defoe was unquestionably a part of that ethos which more august spirits determined to shun.[29]

'To tell the Truth', the narrator in *A New Voyage Round the World* (1725) remarks of his more learned crew, 'our *Doctors* themselves . . . were so taken up in the Traffick for Gold; that they had no Leisure to think of any Thing else.'[30] Though the voyage is meant to be exploratory this later text is blighted by Defoe's Midas-like touch: all discoveries must tend, the narrator urges, 'to the Advantage of Trade'; and the success of the venture itself is gauged in terms of profit.[31] The *idée fixe* enters *Captain Singleton* but fortunately in less programmatic guise. Part of the intention here, Peter Earle shrewdly observes, is 'to demonstrate to readers the possibilities and gains to be had from Africa'; this does not deter Defoe from making over half his book to piracy, never an encouraging subject to traders, or from developing his central concern with *the primitive state*.[32] Indeed, he attempts to clamp his obsession to the thematic chassis of his runaway tale. Trade is given a redemptive status equivalent to that of education, or social contract. It has, as the White Man explains, the power to reclaim wilderness, within or without:

he had been all Night revolving in his Mind what he and we all might do to make our selves some Amends for all our Sorrows; and first he said, he was to let me know, that we were just then in one of the richest Parts of the World, tho' it was really otherwise, but a desolate, disconsolate Wilderness; for says he, there's not a River here but runs Gold, not a Desart but without Plowing bears a Crop of Ivory.

(p. 154)

By smuggling in the notion of cultivation Defoe elevates scratch-mining to a remedial art; the aura surrounding the passage derives otherwise from Isaiah's Messianic paean: 'The wilderness and the solitary place shall be glad for them; and the desert shall rejoice, and blossom as the rose' (35:1). Proof of the potency of the White Man's tonic is given by his subsequent recovery from despair. Over his two years of wishing for death he has lost all interest in gold, as he has in weapons (pp. 152, 155): his renewed acquisitiveness comes accordingly as the mark of returning health. For his avidity he pays later with his life, since it is after losing the fortune he has amassed from mining that he dies of a broken heart, but here again Defoe averts his gaze, deliberately overlooking the opportunity for a cautionary tale against greed: 'Life', as he wrote elsewhere, 'should be progressive and increasing.'[33]

Trade was for Defoe the divinity of a secular religion, and he apostrophized it variously as the patron of arts, mother of industry and genius of learning.[34] His prose often takes on the declaratory quality of a psalm when he turns to its celebration:

Trade carries the very soil away, and transposes the World in Parts; removing Mountains, and carrying them over the Sea . . . Their Rivers are throng'd with Shipping like a Wood; their Naval Stores are inexhaustible.[35]

It is not uncommon to find him applying the same figure to spiritual and commercial development. In his *General History of Discoveries* he advances the idea that riches were planted in distant places to act as a challenge to man after the Flood:

The World was to him like a rough Diamond, that has its intrinsic Value in itself; but the Outside conceal'd the Inside, and it was for him to polish it that its lustre might appear.[36]

In the tract he wrote on Peter the wild boy, paraded in London during 1726, he reflects:

> The Soul is plac'd in the Body like a rough Diamond, which requires the Wheel and Knife, and all the other Arts of the Cutter, to shape it, and polish it, and bring it to shew the perfect Water of a true *Brilliant*.[37]

As well as to Mammon, Defoe looked for salvation to the Puritan God of his upbringing; and in *Captain Singleton* where trade vies with Quaker William as the chief redemptive influence, his two religions are at war. Over the issue of slavery, conflict comes to a head. William condemns the institution when he boards the slave-ship; Singleton and he then pocket a huge sum from the sale of slaves. Defoe inherited the Dissenter's tender conscience towards servitude and in an early satire, *The Reformation of Manners*, hit on a memorable phrase when he attacked those who 'Barter Baubles for the Souls of Men'.[38] But he knew also that the transatlantic traffic in slaves provided the base-line of all international trade, and the recognition made him alter his tune. In the course of a lucid exposition of the triangular route he rejoices in the trinkets of exchange:

> Whatever can be said for a Trade, that is the Essence of our Colonies – The Support of our Sugar and Tobacco Works, that brings much Home, and carries little out; that Exports nothing but what we can spare, and brings Home nothing but what we cannot be without – That sets our Poor to Work, for Manufactures, Employs our Shipping, and extends our Dominions; That carries out our Woollen to *Africa*, carries Slaves to *America*; That barters Gold for Glass-Beads, and the Riches of *Africa*, for the Baubles of *Europe*, may be said for this Trade.[39]

It is no accident that Robinson Crusoe's adventures follow the sequence of the main route of trade: he sails down to Guinea as a merchant; crosses the ocean in a Portuguese slaver; turns planter in Brazil until, inspired by his need for cheap labour, he determines to undercut the prices fixed by *asiento* and sets himself up, like Mr Freeman, as a freelance trafficker. The ship in which he comes to grief has been specially fitted out for slaves. But if it was the triangular route that stirred Defoe's creative impulse it was to prove a dangerous stamping-ground for his imagination. Although bitterly resenting his own enslavement, Crusoe ascribes his shipwreck – which he reads as a punishment – exclusively to the bourgeois vice of imprudence, and never reflects, after his repentance, on his shady dealings in the trade. The omission was glaring even by the standards of contemporary readers, one of whom complained:

> having fix'd his Plantation . . . [Crusoe] sets out upon new Adventures . . . bound to the Coast of *Guinea* to buy Slaves . . . yet he neither then nor afterwards found any check of Conscience in that infamous Trade of buying and selling of Men for Slaves; else one would have expected him to have attributed his *Shipwreck* to this very Cause.[40]

Perhaps Defoe's unconscious mind was active where his eyes were sealed, but of his insensibility there can be no doubt. His *Essay upon Projects* includes a scheme for the importation of two hundred slaves; and in the pamphlet he wrote for the Royal African Company he argues against the freelance trade on the grounds that a monopoly would reduce the price of each and every head.[41] The pursuit of wealth had hardened his gaze. It was a blind spot at the centre of his vision that turned the heart of Africa into Singleton's unpeopled waste.

4 Melville's Happy Valley:
Typee in a literary context

Melville is among those great American writers who, sensing an absence of rhetorical convention, consciously set out to find and claim a literary inheritance of their own. In consequence *Typee*, his first book, though written during the eighteen-forties, is founded so firmly in traditions of the previous century that it revives a series of earlier texts dealing with exploration, and goes some way, indeed, to unfolding a critical record of the main landmarks in related literature before the appearance of *Moby Dick* (1851). Much less of a stylistic mosaic than the later masterpiece, *Typee* (1846) preserves the even surfaces of a realistic, first-person narrative and reads like a more polished version of *Robinson Crusoe* (1719), a text to which it reveals a deep and often acknowledged debt.[1] In place of a lunging interior voyage in the track of a slippery whale, what we are given, under cover of Tommo's story, is a rationally conducted commentary on the nature of man. But the homogeneity is less real than apparent for the novel straddles traditions that are essentially disjunct. It is symptomatic that we should find in the course of a few pages a reference to Rousseau's *Confessions* (1781) rubbing shoulders with an allusion to *Rasselas* (1759) (pp. 179, 183). While Rousseau appears paramount in matters of ideology (the word is wholly appropriate) Melville shows himself equally versed in the procedures of Augustan satire: switches of perspective challenge the prevailing optimism, and the narrator's flow of assimilative energy is perplexed from time to time by a darker tone.[2] Modes of address vary too. When Tommo is overtaken by one of his 'inquiring, scientific moods' (p. 245) narrative is suspended to allow for the inclusion of essay material, mainly of an ethnographic kind. Story-telling alternates with this more sombre recounting of fact.

Typee is, indeed, a closely autobiographical work. After a gruelling six months aboard the *Acushnet*, Melville and a friend jumped ship at Nukahiva, one of the Marquesas islands, and made their way inland until they found themselves in the valley of the Taipis, a virtually unvisited tribe notorious for cannibalism. The treatment they received at their hands was hospitable, but after ten days the friend went off in search of medical aid for his companion's swollen leg, never to return; and Melville made his escape little over a fortnight later. To these events the narrative is faithful, and while Melville certainly extended the lapse of time in his story and appears to have exaggerated the primitiveness of the community he was practically the first European to penetrate, he was keen to stress the documentary aspect of his fiction; and accordingly sketched in the geography and historical background to his venture as well as vouching in a preface for its truth.[3] When *Typee* first appeared it was as part of John Murray's 'Home and Colonial Library', a series given over to non-fiction which already boasted Darwin's *Voyage of the 'Beagle'* (1839).

It is altogether consistent, then, that Melville should call attention in *Typee* to his activity as an explorer. He relates his excursion to the early voyages of Mendaña and Quirós and, more frequently, to the experiences of Cook who had put in at the Marquesas long enough to affirm that its inhabitants were the finest people he had encountered in the South Seas (pp. 37–8, 44, 244, 310).[4] Here again Melville places himself at the apex of an eighteenth-century tradition, for it was the sixties and seventies that saw not only the reopening of the Pacific to Western eyes but the rise of a scientific mode of geophysical and ethnographic enquiry which, if not altogether disinterested, presented at least a marked contrast to the raw mercantilism of the preceding era. Owing largely to European rivalry over the consolidation of colonial territory, the first half of the eighteenth century had, in any case, amounted to a relatively uneventful period as far as exploration was concerned. History could offer little to compete with Captain Singleton's adventures or Crusoe's peregrinations in the Gobi desert, and readers in search of the exotic had for the most part to turn to collections of earlier voyages when they had done with Defoe. But the gap between fiction and history which narrowed as the century advanced was effectively bridged by Melville who, when it came to writing novels of exploration, had his own experience on which to rely. He had behind him, also, the example of a new kind of travelogue, relatively organized, more discursive and minute. In *Typee* the influence of such reading is clear from the frequent digressions on topics such as the preparation of *tappa* or *poee-poee*; and by the time of *Moby Dick* the informative, scientific impulse had assumed such prominence as to vie with narrative. But Melville's inset descriptions, even at their least successful, are quite unlike Defoe's fussy shows of fact. Perhaps it was because his stories *were* substantially true that Melville could afford to be so much freer in imparting fictive shape.

Literary influence that is crucial seldom declares itself in a congruency of plots. *Typee* shares with *Robinson Crusoe* a three-stage narrative – a movement from separation through adventure to return – but Melville's more significant debt is to Crusoe's Janus-faced island. The appropriation of this motif is telling for it points to a marked divergence of concern. In *Robinson Crusoe* the hero's shifting states of mind are more important than they are in *Typee*. Melville is less occupied with objectifying the inward tendencies of his hero than with dramatizing the conquest of subjective distortion. Where Defoe holds up the island, with its alternating aspects of paradise and wilderness, as a mirror to his hero's spiritual condition,[5] Melville advances the same options in the spirit of a scientific hypothesis. In a colourful paragraph at the novel's start he lays out the opposed stereotypes of Polynesian life and encourages his reader to guess which picture is the truer:

> The Marquesas! What strange visions of outlandish things does the very name spirit up! Naked houris – cannibal banquets – groves of cocoanut – coral reefs – tattooed chiefs – and bamboo temples; sunny valleys planted with bread-fruit-trees – carved canoes dancing on the flashing blue waters – savage woodlands guarded by horrible idols – *heathenish rites and human sacrifices*.
> Such were the strangely jumbled anticipations that haunted me during our passage from the cruising ground. I felt an irresistible curiosity to see those islands . . .
>
> (p. 37)

In line with this typecasting are the reputations accruing to the two principal tribes of the region: while the Happars supposedly enjoy a monopoly of the virtues, the Typees, tucked away in the depths of an inland valley, collect every dark aspersion. The fiction serves both as a goad to Melville's polemic and as a source of suspense that drives the narrative. 'Typee or Happar?', the question re-echoes through the early chapters of the story, and in accordance with his sharply contrastive expectations, Tommo retails two versions of the landscape, the one romantically idyllic,

> Down each of these little valleys flows a clear stream, here and there assuming the form of a slender cascade, then stealing invisibly along until it bursts upon the sight again in larger and more noisy waterfalls, and at last demurely wanders along to the sea
>
> (p. 59)

and the other grotesque and gothic,

> My thirst was gone, and I fairly loathed the water. Starting to my feet, the sight of those dank rocks, oozing forth moisture at every crevice, and the dark stream shooting along its dismal channel, sent fresh chills through my shivering frame.
>
> (p. 96)

As Tommo and Toby descend into the fearsome chasms that lie between the coastal mountains and the interior they are 'plunged into despair' (p. 95) and their apprehension is heightened when they discover a footpath that spells out some imminent encounter. Melville most aptly relates their feelings of discomfort at this moment to Crusoe's discovery of the footprint (p. 85), and the allusion follows shortly on a paragraph steeped in the imagery and even the language of Defoe:[6]

> The whole landscape seemed one unbroken solitude, the interior of the island having apparently been untenanted since the morning of the creation; and as we advanced through this wilderness, our voices sounded strangely in our ears, as though human accents had never before disturbed the fearful silence of the place.
>
> (p. 84)

Melville uses his setting here to register mood. Tommo's anxiety over his leg, and the sense of isolation engendered by it, are made palpable in the lowering atmosphere he introduces into a scene untouched 'since the morning of the creation'. A similar subjectivity is signalled later when Tommo, rendered helpless by his pain and now entirely dependent on his porter, pronounces the *main* path through the valley to be as impenetrable 'as the recesses of a wilderness' (p. 139). Tommo's obscure hurt serves several thematic ends (his reliance on Western skills being one of them)[7] but its richest pay-off is as a symbol of a general debility. When we see him enter the virtually unfallen realm of the Typees as a cripple limping into paradise, Melville appears for the moment to be attempting something like Defoe's allegorical treatments of original sin:

> one of my legs was swelled to such a degree, and pained me so acutely, that I half suspected I had been bitten by some venomous reptile, the congenial inhabitant of the chasm from which we had lately emerged. I may here remark by the way – what I subsequently learned – that all the islands of Polynesia enjoy the reputation, in common with the Hibernian isle, of being free from the presence of any vipers; though whether Saint Patrick ever visited them, is a question I shall not attempt to decide.
>
> As the feverish sensation increased upon me . . . I chanced to push aside a branch, and by doing so suddenly disclosed to my view a scene which even now I can recall with all the vividness of the first impression. Had a glimpse of the gardens of Paradise been revealed to me, I could scarcely have been more ravished with the sight.
>
> (p. 90)

It becomes increasingly clear, however, that Melville's concern is with a secularized version of the Fall. Just as the chasms which separate the coastal regions of the island from *terra incognita* mark the gulf between primitive and civilized man, so the 'venomous reptile' spells out the spiritual degradation of the intruder in comparison with the indigene. Its coils, indeed, are more accurately identified as the notorious chains of Rousseau. Melville is out to celebrate the 'state of nature' (p. 45), and the words put into Tommo's mouth '*Typee mortarkee*' ('Typee good', p. 116) supply the right answer to the novel's recurring question, for the unknown tribe, because they are less spoilt, turn out to be even more benign than the Happar. Told that the 'penalty of the Fall presses very lightly upon the valley' (p. 265) we regard the tribesmen as survivors from a privileged realm.

Once Tommo has recovered from the bout of despair into which
he falls after the departure of his friend, his leg begins to heal and
he allows himself for the first time to enter into the life of his new
environment. It is to mark this important transition that Melville
introduces an allusion to *Rasselas*:[8]

> if ever disagreeable thoughts arose in my mind, I drove them
> away. When I looked around the verdant recess in which I was
> buried, and gazed up to the summits of the lofty eminence that
> hemmed me in, I was well disposed to think that I was in the
> 'Happy Valley', and that beyond those heights there was
> naught but a world of care and anxiety.[9]
> (p. 179)

Melville seems to have been deeply impressed by Dr Johnson's
fable of the restless Abyssinian prince who escapes from the
mountain-girt paradise which is his birthright in order to explore
the world – only to return, however, to his 'Happy Valley'
chastened and relatively content. The lesson of *Rasselas* is revived
in *Typee* by the figure of Marnoo, a Marquesan paragon who
decides he is better off at home after a taste of Western life; and in
Moby Dick Queequeg supplies a variation on the same pattern for,
having set out to see the world, the Polynesian heir feels so
disabled by it that he shrinks from ever facing his people again.[10]
What principally lays *Typee* open to Johnson's influence is the way
the story revolves around two escapes, the first from the *Dolly*, the
second from the tribe. Tommo jumps ship because he finds life on
board unbearably restrictive, but once settled in the 'Happy
Valley' it is not long before he steps into the shoes of Rasselas,
bemoaning the 'narrow limits' of his 'narrow valley', even to the
point of wishing himself back on the decks he has earlier described
as detestably 'narrow' (pp. 307, 316, 69). Melville canvasses
Tommo's discontent with his own society more fully than he does
his dissatisfaction with life among the Typees, but his hero's
second escape exists in a state of tension with his first and out of
this tension, as we shall in due course see, some of the fullest-
bodied writing in the novel arises. An Augustan form contains,
and finally gives maturity to, the generous flow of primitivist
sentiment.

Whereas Defoe is often happy to allow inconsistencies to lodge
together, nothing is more characteristic of the Augustan
enterprise than energy brought to bear on squaring up the

disparate in an attempt to render issues distinct and whole. The activities essential to such an undertaking are built into the heroic couplet – the matching up of ideas for comparison, the disclosure of sameness in apparent antithesis or of difference in accepted identity – and they find a particular extension in the topos of travel. The visitor in a strange place evokes two fields of vision; for as Pope amusingly observes of the grand tour made by his young 'Aeneas':

> Intrepid then, o'er seas and lands he flew:
> Europe he saw, and Europe saw him too.[11]

Since there is no greater boon to the satirist than a standpoint that shows up the time-worn and commonplace as seemingly arbitrary, the view from outside-in was particularly favoured by early eighteenth-century writers. In *Windsor-Forest* (1713) Pope congregates 'feather'd' Indians on the banks of the Thames in order to call attention to 'Our Speech, our Colour, and our strange Attire';[12] and through the eyes of a couple of Persian explorers in Paris, Montesquieu in his *Lettres Persanes* (1721) makes the customs of his society appear uncovenanted and outlandish. A similar distanced view underlies Swift's devastating account of colonial annexation in *Gulliver's Travels* (1726):

> a crew of pirates . . . set up a rotten plank or a stone for a memorial, they murder two or three dozen of the natives . . . Here commences a new dominion acquired with a title by *divine right*.[13]

And it is in the same vein that Melville presents the 'piratical seizure' of Tahiti by the French in *Typee* (see Chapter III and Appendix, p. 334). More central, however, to Swift's concerns is the two-way traffic in vision that sets the claims of man as a natural and as a social being in opposition as we turn from the magnified needs and importunacies of Gulliver to the intricate but heartless organization of the Lilliputians, or hover between the more complex abstractions embodied in the Houyhnhnms and Yahoos. Shifting scales and unexpected perspectives have always played an important part in general satire, and the travelogue has, in consequence, often proved an asset to it. Partly owing to this alliance, no doubt, the equation between travelling and self-

discovery was sufficiently well established by the second half of
the century for Sterne to observe in *A Sentimental Journey* (1768)
that the chaise in which he sat at Calais was agitated not by the
road but by the feverish movements of his pen; his next activity in
the stationary remise, his seduction of the widow from Brussels,
counts as a further exploration; but it soon becomes clear that the
real business of the sentimental traveller is reverie, the excitation
of an unremitting flow of thought and feeling. It follows from this,
of course, that the traveller might as well stay put, a conclusion
that Sterne has no intention of shirking: 'I am of opinion, That a
man would act as wisely, if he could prevail upon himself to live
contented without foreign knowledge or foreign improvements'.[14]

For writers associated with the Enlightenment it was the
metaphysical dividends rather than the substance of exploration
that generally counted. Johnson drew the idea of *Rasselas* from
Jerome Lobo's first-hand account of the Abyssinian custom of
confining royal children in a mountain fastness, but his moral tale
is given only the sketchiest geographical location;[15] and when,
indeed, he was later introduced to James Bruce who had an
unprecedented knowledge of the region he affected boredom,
remarking afterwards that he had not perceived 'any superiority
of understanding'.[16] The Scottish laird was, in fact, probably the
last explorer to retain a certain Augustan diffidence towards the
status of his mission. In his *Travels* he records his jubilance on
reaching the source of the Blue Nile, a goal he had nurtured for
seven years, but with wry humour immediately quotes the remark
of his less Quixotic companion – 'you had much better leave that
bog and come into the house'.[17]

In *Rasselas* (1759), in many respects the summation of the
tradition we have been examining, Johnson addresses himself to
the question of what constitutes man's greatest happiness. This is
the criterion that guides the Abyssinian prince in his 'choice of
life', and his only constraint is the insuperable fact that one option
will necessarily exclude others, for 'no man can, at the same time,
fill his cup from the source and from the mouth of the Nile' (p. 79).
Nature, indeed, as the poet Imlac observes, 'sets her gifts on the
right hand and on the left' (p. 78), and the prince's choice is
greatly vexed by the consideration that the essential issues are too
comprehensive or engrossing to be surveyed at all steadily:[18]

To the mind, as to the eye, it is difficult to compare with

exactness objects vast in their extent, and various in their parts. Where we see or conceive the whole at once we readily note the discriminations and decide the preference: but of two systems, of which neither can be surveyed by any human being in its full compass of magnitude and multiplicity of complication, where is the wonder, that judging of the whole by parts, I am alternately affected by one and the other as either presses on my memory or fancy?

(p. 74)

In the terms of this metaphor, to explore is to create distance and so facilitate the comparison of objects that baulk the observer close at hand. Without some degree of reflective detachment, the implication is plain, no moral activity is possible. The immediate choice that confronts Rasselas is between his 'prison of pleasure' (p. 126) and the outside world, but his dilemma touches on a series of related oppositions – between riches and poverty, precept and practice, celibacy and marriage, Africa and Europe, freedom and confinement, to name a few. These antinomies take on increasing definition as Rasselas' experience accumulates and he balances, in company with the reader, one example against another; but in accordance with the principle that 'when wrong opinions are entertained . . . they mutually destroy each other and leave the mind open to truth' (p. 74), Johnson shows himself less concerned to legislate than to break down hasty judgements. The debate on the relative merits of the retired life provides a case in point and, perhaps because it flows so instantly from the prince's circumstances, dominates much of the action. While planning his flight from the Happy Valley Rasselas notices 'new competitors for imprisonment' (p. 3) gathering at the palace gates. The same irony informs Imlac's story of how he absconded from his merchant family in response to the thrill of the sea: 'when I cast my eye on the expanse of waters my heart bounded like that of a prisoner escaped', exclaims the poet, soon to protest his hatred of 'barren uniformity' once on it (pp. 22–3). His history caps Rasselas' progress, for having won entrance to the Happy Valley and resigned himself 'with joy to perpetual confinement' there, Imlac makes off with his pupil in order to escape its 'perpetual vacancy' (p. 35). His tale serves, however, merely as a prelude to the account of the apostate hermit who spends his days in such a dither of conflicting hopes that his future is easily foretold: 'in a few years [he would] go back to his retreat, and, perhaps, if shame did not restrain, or death intercept him, return once more from his retreat into the world' (p. 58).

The hermit's career keeps coming full circle but Rasselas, although he returns to the Happy Valley, goes back to a different life. In another context, Johnson once remarked that 'every man who works is confined . . . you know the notion of confinement may be extended, as in the song, "Every island is a prison" '.[19] Properly sceptical of his urge for novelty and freedom Rasselas has learnt, in sum, to 'commit [himself] again to the current of the world' (p. 93). It becomes clear on his return that the imaginative distance at which he has set his former mode of life provides a measure of the difference between pleasure and happiness. Johnson's understanding of this distinction rests on the Aristotelian view that sensual gratification does not cater to the needs of the distinctively human, rational soul: 'man . . . has some desires distinct from sense which must be satisfied before he can be happy' (p. 6). It is for this reason that the Happy Valley fills Rasselas at last with distaste for all the 'recurrence of its luxuries', as does its unflattering counterpart, the Arabian seraglio whose inmates entertain 'no ideas but of the few things that were within their view' (pp. 126, 104). Rasselas' venture begins with the recognition, 'I have already enjoyed too much, give me something to desire'; and it ends with a resumption of duty that promises to absorb, if only in part, his troublesome energies and relieve his 'hunger of imagination' (pp. 8, 85). For Johnson, as for Milton and Coleridge, Mount Amhara represents an earthly paradise but one sufficiently incomplete to serve as a foil for a greater good.[20]

Prominent among the many systems of thought that come under review in *Rasselas* is the primitivism expounded by Rousseau. Johnson summarizes the arguments of the *Discours sur l'origine et les fondements de l'inégalité* (1754) and parodies the abstract declaratory style of the *philosophe* in the chapter headed 'The happiness of a life led according to nature' (pp. 58–60). There is a decided irony here, for while Johnson believes that it is, indeed, through the expression of his nature that man attains happiness, he supposes, as Imlac explains, that it is through the redemptive institutions of society that man most nearly surmounts the fallen state. Rasselas' counsellor, however, holds civilization to blame for human misery and argues that man has only to rely on precepts 'infused at nativity' and 'observe the hind of the forest, and the linnet of the grove' in order to recover his natural inheritance. Johnson loathed Rousseau but his account is fairly faithful to the gist of the Second Discourse.[21] What it fails to convey is the curiously Calvinist insistence on the degradation of man that seems to have led Rousseau to subvert the traditional confidence in institutional amelioration and to discount, in particular, the idea that virtue can be won from a mutinous psyche in a recalcitrant world. The discourse opens with the assertion that society has so changed human nature as to have obliterated all trace of the divine image in man. Knowledge, however, of the 'real foundations of human society' can only come from an understanding of the original state, and the philosopher has accordingly to reconstruct 'the celestial and majestic simplicity impressed by the divine Author' before he can prescribe man's 'real wants, and the fundamental principles of his duty'.[22] In setting about this task Rousseau necessarily comes into conflict with Hobbes, and the nature of his disagreement proves peculiarly revealing, for he maintains with much brilliance that the primitive state depicted in *Leviathan* is the projection of civilized man's depravity, that the greed and strife attributed to the hypothetical, natural man are, in fact, the product of the thinker's own diseased condition:

> In reasoning upon the principles which this author hath laid down, he ought to have said, 'the state of nature, being that in which the care of our own preservation is the least prejudicial to that of others, was consequently the best calculated for peace, and the most agreeable to mankind.' But he advances the direct contrary, in consequence of having improperly admitted into the care of savage man's self-preservation, the gratification of a variety of passions, which owe their rise to society, and which have rendered laws necessary.[23]

In the course of his essay Rousseau suggests, more than once, that thought is itself a symptom of man's corruption; and his procedure, in essence, is to sweep aside Hobbes's premises and build instead on his faith in the benevolence of creation.[24] But although he prides himself, perhaps paradoxically, on the purely intellectual nature of his speculation, Rousseau shows himself ready at times to draw on evidence pertaining to primitive tribes, and in this connection identifies the Caribbeans as the 'people

who have as yet least of all deviated from a state of nature'.[25] He
may well have been influenced by the reports issued, in regular
Relations, by Jesuit missionaries some of whom surmised that the
Indians might be free of original sin.[26] It seems likely that he, in
his turn, reinforced the impressions made on French explorers by
the South Sea islanders in the next decade; in Diderot's rhapsodic
Supplément au voyage de Bougainville (1796), at least, his presence is
conspicuous.

Of Melville's debt to Rousseau in *Typee* there can be no doubt.
Quite apart from an important reference to the *Confessions* which
we shall come to later, two inset essays (Chapters 17, 27), the first
offering a comparison between the tribe and 'more enlightened'
communities, the second a survey of the islanders' mode of life,
reveal a close acquaintance with the argument of the *Discourse on
Inequality*. It is not simply that Melville is so often carried away by
his enthusiasm that he exceeds his empirical authority or that the
more detailed observations filtered through his narrative
sometimes contradict the principles he enunciates as an essayist,
but that his emphasis shows a conscious alignment with
Rousseau's analysis. He follows the philosopher in diagnosing
property and self-esteem as the root causes of evil, and holds up
the anarchism of the Typees as a model of the true *polis*:

> how came they without the aid of established law, to exhibit, in
> so eminent a degree, that social order which is the greatest
> blessing and highest pride of the social state?
>
> (p. 271)

Like Rousseau again, he attributes the harmony of island life to an
innate code:

> It is to this indwelling, this universally diffused perception of
> what is *just* and *noble*, that the integrity of the Marquesans in
> their intercourse with each other, is to be attributed.
>
> (p. 272)

Since the expression of their goodness is unconstrained, the
Typees display a whole catalogue of assets: 'perpetual hilarity'
(p. 181), 'unanimity of feeling' (p. 274), 'honesty' (p. 271),
'charity' (p. 271), physical beauty, perfect health and gentleness.
More frequently, however, Melville defines the Marquesan

virtues by supplying a list of cancelled Western vices, a technique that has always come in handy in describing the golden age.[27] So, for instance, we are told,

> the heart-burnings, the jealousies, the social rivalries, the family dissensions, and the thousand self-inflicted discomforts of refined life, which make up in units the swelling aggregate of human misery, are unknown among these unsophisticated people.
>
> (p. 180)

And at one point we are treated to a page-long inventory of negatived ills ('no cares, griefs, troubles . . . no quarrelling, no contention', pp. 181–2) which, even if its component items are fairly easily deduced, probably enjoys the distinction of being the most thorough in existence. It is when Melville contraverts the deepest springs of suffering, conferring on the Typees not only a total absence of sexual jealousy, but liberty of conscience, a sceptical attitude towards the supernatural, and virtual equality between the sexes and social ranks, that the text begins to look doctrinaire. Unsurprisingly, his negation of sexual jealousy bears a tell-tale resemblance to Rousseau's.[28]

Though Melville's philosophical bias declares itself most plainly in the novel's interludes of discursive prose, he shows a wonderful talent for enclosing meaning in the anecdotal and descriptive details of his narrative.[29] It is through such sleight of hand that the directions of the novel are made clear from the first. Shortly after Tommo places the blame for the unpleasantness aboard the *Dolly* on the Captain's abuse of authority, he describes the provisioning of the ship in such a way as to implant the idea that natural goodness is continually being done to death:

> The owners, who officiate as caterers for the voyage, supply the larder with an abundance of dainties. Delicate morsels of beef and pork, cut on scientific principles from every part of the animal, and of all conceivable shapes and sizes, are carefully packed in salt, and stored away in barrels; affording a never-ending variety in their different degrees of toughness, and in the peculiarities of their saline properties. Choice old water too, decanted into stout six-barrel-casks, and two pints of which is allowed every day to each soul on board; together with ample

store of sea-bread, previously reduced to a state of petrification, with a view to preserve it either from decay or consumption . . .
(pp. 56–7)

In sharp contrast to the stale, deck-bound crew are the naked Marquesans, introduced a few pages earlier, whose dancing heads as they swim towards the ship materialize from garlands of coconuts, so that here we see the reverse exchange of food into flesh:

> As I leaned curiously over the side, endeavouring to solve their mysterious movements, one mass far in advance of the rest attracted my attention. In its centre was something I could take for nothing else than a cocoanut, but which I certainly considered one of the most extraordinary specimens of the fruit I had ever seen. It kept twirling and dancing about among the rest in the most singular manner, and as it drew nearer I thought it bore a remarkable resemblance to the brown shaven skull of one of the savages. Presently it betrayed a pair of eyes . . .
> (p. 47)

Melville would have owed the idea for this scene to a remarkable chapter from Fenimore Cooper's *The Prairie* (1827) in which a Pawnee scout, carefully concealed among foliage, gradually assumes animate form in the eyes of two observers. The shaven head of the Indian is variously taken for a pile of leaves, a stone, and a coiled-up snake, before a 'pair of dark, glaring, and moving eyeballs' refuse to be overlooked.[30] Cooper devises the episode to dramatize frontier attitudes towards the Pawnees, whom one of the observers proceeds to characterize as 'a violent race . . . difficult to define or class, within the usual boundaries of definitions'.[31] Melville turns the metamorphosis to his own account, creating his noble beings out of an idyllic setting so as to forge a powerful emblem of the natural man. From there it is an easy step to imaging the island's inner valley as an Eden. Glimpsed from the coastal ridge the 'gardens of Paradise' enfold a community whose 'summer garb of Eden' lays bare the 'naked simplicity of nature', an embodiment of all the West has lost (pp. 90, 135, 247–8):

Stripped of the cunning artifices of the tailor, and standing forth in the garb of Eden – what a sorry set of round-shouldered, spindle-shanked, crane-necked varlets would civilized men appear! Stuffed calves, padded breasts, and scientifically cut pantaloons would then avail them nothing, and the effect would be truly deplorable.

(p. 248)

In a text where *physis* is given precedence over *nomos* it seems right that the incarnate idea should do most of the work.

In *Typee* the narrator tacks between the islanders and the civilized West. He looks out, that is to say, as well as looking in, but in so far as he gazes through the spectacles of Rousseau, the one prospect is as dark as the other is bright. Across this simple scheme there is played, however, a further tonal contrast resulting in a more intricate design, a chequer-work more in keeping with the multiple perspectives relished by the writers of Augustan satire, and truer to Melville's own experience. In determining to escape from his 'Happy Valley' as he has earlier escaped from the whaler, Tommo opens a positive as well as negative aspect to each of his domiciles. He succeeds for the most part in accounting for the changes in feeling that lead to his flight from Nukahiva without reneging on his championship of the Typees; but the shift is one that involves him in some subtle modulations of attitude, some finely conducted comedy of misapprehension, and leaves him still with a residue of inconsistency.

At the start of the novel Tommo yearns for a taste of the 'verdant scenery' which he glimpses from the deck of his 'detested old vessel'; shortly before the end he rejoices ecstatically in the 'flashing billows' of the surf breaking upon a beach (pp. 69, 328). In either case it is a sense of constriction that prompts Tommo to relocate his horizons. His first inkling of entrapment in the valley comes after Toby has been foiled on his first attempt to reach the harbour for medical supplies. That it is a Happar rather than Typee weapon that stops him, further gives the lie to the idea that the two tribes are all good and all bad. But myths die hard and while it is clear that the 'horrible character' imputed to the Typees is 'wholly undeserved', the sense of restricted freedom greatly darkens the character of the Happar: 'we were hemmed in by hostile tribes . . . we could not hope to pass . . . without encountering the effects of their savage resentment' (pp. 148, 154). It is at this juncture that Tommo's attendant, Kory-Kory – variously described as gaoler and friend – tries to convince his charge that it would be altogether unreasonable to think of flight. But his picture of the island as a paradise so utterly fails to take personal freedom into account that it amounts to a travesty, and leaves Tommo with a headache:

> 'Ah! Typee mortakee! – nuee, nuee mioree – nuee, nuee, wai – nuee, nuee poee-poee – nuee, nuee kokoo – ah! nuee, nuee kiki – ah! nuee, nuee, nuee!' Which literally interpreted as before, would imply, 'Ah, Typee! isn't it a fine place though! – no danger of starving here, I tell you! – plenty of bread-fruit – plenty of water – plenty of pudding – ah! plenty of everything! ah! heaps, heaps, heaps!' All this was accompanied by a running commentary of signs and gestures which it was impossible not to comprehend.
>
> (p. 155)

This is not Eden but the land of Cockaigne as depicted by Breughel; and when Kory-Kory reports on the afterlife, later in the novel, the same shortcomings are evident:

> the realms of bliss, and bread-fruit – the Polynesian heaven – where every moment the bread-fruit trees dropped their ripened spheres to the ground, and where there was no end to the cocoanuts and bananas: there they reposed through the livelong eternity upon mats much finer than those of Typee; and every day bathed their glowing limbs in rivers of cocoanut oil.
>
> (p. 238)

Kory-Kory's paradise is too replete to allow for aspiration, which is why, on the principle that 'a bird in the hand is worth two in the bush' (p. 239), he is ready to admit that he prefers the life he enjoys in the present. What fully engages Tommo, however, is the myth of the chieftain who sails to the next world in his warboat. His sympathies are with the 'immortal spirit yearning after the unknown' and the heaven he pictures is, after the manner of the Island of Love in Camoens' epic, the reward for strenuous exertion.[32] Envisaging the next world in its approach rather than

in his possession Tommo, like a true explorer, sets the magic land-
fall in the offing:

> I see thy canoe cleaving the bright waves, which die away on
> those dimly looming shores of Paradise.
>
> (p. 239)

By including a full range of heavens Melville accounts for his hero's
increasing languishment in an earthly paradise.

But if all the delights of Typee fail to rid Tommo of his 'anxiety
to escape from a captivity' (p. 200), Kory-Kory has another string
to his bow: the dangers of traversing the territory of the savage
Happar. Over and above the irony afforded by this inversion of
the stereotype, there is the comic symmetry of Western and
Marquesan modes of denigration to attend to. But the scene in
which Kory-Kory impresses his listener with the rampant
cannibalism of the Happar offers still more, for in the course of a
desperate attempt to convey his meaning the Typee apologist
nibbles at the inside of Tommo's arm. His confusing antics as he
switches, without ever quite losing himself, from the role of
commentator to agent seem, indeed, to undo any hard and fast
distinction between the neighbouring tribes:

> Thus far he explained himself by a variety of gestures, during
> the performance of which he would dart out of the house, and
> point abhorrently towards the Happar valley; running in to us
> again with a rapidity that showed he was fearful he would lose
> one part of his meaning before he could complete the other; and
> continuing his illustrations by seizing the fleshy part of my arm
> in his teeth, intimating by the operation that the people who
> lived over in that direction would like nothing better than to
> treat me in that manner.
>
> (pp. 154–5)

Despite Kory-Kory's vehement denials, Tommo's suspicions of
Typee cannibalism persist. First reawakened by a dark thought as
they sit down to a dish of pig with their hosts ('a baked baby, by
the soul of Captain Cook!') his fears on this occasion are firmly – if
rather knowingly – allayed:

> When the taper came, I gazed eagerly into the vessel, and

recognized the mutilated remains of a juvenile porker! 'Puarkee!' exclaimed Kory-Kory, looking complacently at the dish.

(p. 145)

His fears remain inactive for some time to come, for Tommo, in resigning himself to the pleasures of the 'Happy Valley', relegates evil to an outer sphere ('beyond those heights there was naught but a world of care and anxiety', p. 179), and virtually exchanges the images of Typee and Happar. Toby's failure to reappear temporarily brings back the original prejudices leading him to brand his captors as 'nothing better than a set of cannibals' (p. 172), but he adapts little by little to the rhythms of Typee life, and is soon revelling in its erotic opportunities. He is quick to shed his sailor's uniform and at feasts takes part in the dancing stripped to the waist. In a series of idyllic scenes he reports on his courtship of the beautiful and often naked Fayaway who, by special dispensation from taboo, joins him in his boat. As they drift across the sheets of water Tommo's integration seems altogether complete.

But although he overcomes his own taboos to the point of nerving himself to eat raw fish, Tommo absolutely refuses to submit to any tattooing of his face; and it is this reserve of loyalty to his Western identity that proves to be the watershed in his developing relationship with the Typees. As social pressure mounts, his resistance grows until he determines to escape. The old Typee image is now reinstated in force, and Melville deliberately points to the way his hero's outlook has come full circle, for at the height of the scene in which Tommo receives positive proof of the tribe's cannibalistic rites it is again Kory-Kory who steps forward to exclaim 'Puarkee! puarkee!', this time over a mess of human bones (p. 316).

Though the disclosure does much to pave the way for Tommo's departure it is not allowed to interfere seriously with his polemical defence of the islanders. Melville returns to the task he addresses in the novel's opening refrain 'Typee or Happar?' – his rebuttal of the depreciatory images that suit the book of both colonialist and missionary:

entering their valley, as I did, under the most erroneous impressions of their character, I was soon led to exclaim in amazement: 'Are these the ferocious savages, the blood-thirsty cannibals of whom I have heard such frightful tales! They deal more kindly with each other, and are more humane than many who study essays on virtue and benevolence, and who repeat every night that beautiful prayer breathed first by the lips of the divine and gentle Jesus.'

(p. 274)

Typee takes its place in a debate on the rights and wrongs of the Western presence in the South Seas, a debate – later to be joined by Ballantyne – in which Melville sides with Kotzebue against Darwin.[33] The fervour with which the narrator takes up the cause of the islanders leads to occasional inconsistency. After a spirited treatment of cannibalism in the vein of Montaigne's famous essay, the practice is twice given out as being confined in the Pacific to the bodies of slain enemies alone (pp. 180–1, 278); yet Tommo discovers a European head among the relics at the Ti, and Marnoo's warning, 'you get well, he kill you, eat you, hang you head up there' carries full weight (pp. 309, 319). On the whole, however, the paradox of imprisonment in paradise leads Melville into remarkably little contradiction, for he hits on a simple resolution to the problem of why his hero chooses to escape from a life that engrosses the greater part of 'the virtues of humanity' (p. 274).[34] That Tommo refuses to have his face tattooed points to certain stubborn limits of identity: his situation presents a case of 'One Law for the Lion and Ox is Oppression'.[35]

On first meeting Marnoo, the Marquesan who has turned his back on the West, Tommo is deeply humiliated to find himself ignored by this dashing visitor who rivets the attention of every Typee. Noting his fit of pique, Tommo comments ruefully on the voracity that underlies all heroic temper:

These were my feelings at the moment, and they were prompted by that glorious principle inherent in all heroic natures – the strong-rooted determination to have the biggest share of the pudding or to go without any of it.

(p. 195)

His diagnosis evidently extends, in part, to Marnoo too, for it turns out that the 'Polynesian Apollo' has carefully planned his show of disregard:

> At this declaration of the exalted opinion I had formed of him,
> he appeared vastly gratified, and gave me to understand that he
> had purposely behaved in that manner, in order to increase my
> astonishment.
>
> (p. 199)

The episode is given considerable emphasis not only by Tommo's
indication that such experience is common to civilized life
(p. 195), but by the contrast it offers to the unassuming and
unassertive manners of the islanders which frequently come in for
comment. Tommo singles out 'unanimity of feeling' (p. 274) as
the most admirable trait of the Typees, and twice dilates on the
absence of quarrels or disputes among them, adding on the second
occasion:

> [they] were bound together by the ties of strong affection. The
> love of kindred I did not so much perceive, for it seemed
> blended in the general love; and where all were treated as
> brothers and sisters, it was hard to tell who were actually
> related to each other by blood.
>
> (p. 276)

Again, it is in marked contrast to any bevy of belles at a public
resort that the Typee girls are said to be quite without 'envyings of
each other's charms' (p. 182). Taken together, these scattered
remarks and scenes imply that it is principally self-esteem that
causes the divide between primitive and civilized man. And when,
with a further hint of self-mockery at his vanity, the narrator
analyses his horror at the thought of facial tattooing, this decisive
issue, too, is tied to the same theme:

> What an object he would have made of me! . . . I was fairly
> driven to despair; nothing but the utter ruin of my 'face divine',
> as the poets call it, would, I perceived, satisfy the inexorable
> Mehevi and his chiefs.
>
> (p. 294)

But however wry he may be at his own expense, the narrator
makes it clear that it is the force of 'heroic nature' that endows
Marnoo with special appeal. (We are even told that 'the natural
quickness of the savage had been wonderfully improved by his
intercourse with the white men', p. 199.) Nor is there any

mistaking the 'strong-rooted determination' that fuels Tommo's adventures, leading him to exhaust horizon after horizon. The restlessness that prompts him first to turn his back on the *Dolly* and later to regret the lack of sophisticated company, even to welcome the sight of a naval uniform, is itself, it seems, a necessary condition of civility (pp. 156, 328).

The Augustan convention of contrary perspectives, so deeply written into the structure of *Typee*, provides a critique of the novel's more overt primitivism. It discourages readers, for one thing, from supposing that they are at bottom as sweet-minded as the islanders; and when the narrator remarks, towards the close, that his subsequent experiences on board a man-of-war have 'nearly overturned all [his] previous theories' (p. 274), he comes close to withdrawing his ideology altogether. His debt to Rousseau is, in any case, less to the rhetorician of the First Discourse than to the speculative thinker of the Second who identifies *amour-propre* – the psychological correlate to the various material causes of civilized man's misfortune – as the force responsible for tearing apart the social fabric in the last and most attractive phase of primitive life.[36] In sum, Melville relies on the Rousseau who, rather than counselling despair in the face of a hopeless future, celebrates the virtues that he strategically confers on the past – the Rousseau who bends the wish 'to go back' into constructive aims addressed to the present.[37] In the last analysis it is the high premium attached to the most immediate qualities of everyday existence – to sensation and to feeling – that underwrites Rousseau's complicated salvage operation on the primitive; and it is precisely in this connection that Melville chooses to make his debt explicit, when he gives substance to the privileged existence of the Marquesans by pointing to that state of physical exhilaration memorably evoked in the *Confessions*:

[The Typees'] continual happiness . . . sprang principally from that all-pervading sensation which Rousseau has told us he at one time experienced, the mere buoyant sense of a healthful physical existence.

(p. 183)

In the passage in question Rousseau recounts how, after declaring himself the devoted slave of Mme de Warens, he set out on foot across the Alps to seek his fortune:

I walked gaily on my way with my pious guide and his lively companion. No misadventure disturbed my journey. I was as happy physically and mentally as at any time in my life. I was young, vigorous, healthy, fearless, and full of confidence in myself and others. I was enjoying that short but precious moment in life when its overflowing fullness expands, so to speak, one's whole being, and lends all nature, in one's eyes, the charm of one's own existence. . . . Every object I saw seemed a guarantee of my future happiness. I saw in my imagination a country feast in every house and wild game in every meadow, bathing in every river and fishing from every bank; delicious fruit on every tree and voluptuous assignations in its shade; bowls of milk and cream on the mountain-sides, everywhere the delights of idleness, and peace and simplicity, and the joy of going one knew not where.[38]

The whole paragraph might serve as an epigraph to *Typee* for it not only marks out that meeting-ground of the primitive and sophisticated which is so central a concern of the text, but deals in the same coupling of exploratory excitement and sensual luxuriance that gives Melville's first work its distinctive blaze. There is, however, one difference in emphasis. From the moment we are introduced to the 'gay and dapper young cock' (p. 36) cooped aboard the *Dolly*, we are prepared for the many romps and bathing scenes that add up, in view of the date, to a remarkably radiant plea for the joy of sexuality. The language and attitudes belong for the most part to the eighteenth century,

> I happened to pop upon Mehevi three or four times when he was romping – in a most undignified manner for a warrior king – with one of the prettiest little witches in the valley
>
> (p. 259)

but the Victorian novel would have to wait for Thomas Hardy before it could match Melville's candour.

5 Captain Ahab and the Albatross:

Moby Dick in a period context

Only the whale puts an end to the *Pequod*'s circuit of the oceans and nothing stops the narrator, who introduces himself as *Ishmael*, from ranging over history. *Moby Dick* is global in its scope and to this feature, more than any other, it owes the aura of timelessness which many fascinated critics note. In his study of the novel Charles Olson, for example, writes of Melville:

> He had the sea of himself . . . It enabled him to draw up from Shakespeare. It made Noah, and Moses, contemporary to him. History was ritual and repetition when Melville's imagination was at its own proper beat.[1]

And D. H. Lawrence was moved by the brooding presence of the past in the book to compare American literature to a transplanted tree that instead of coming new 'ran more swiftly into age'.[2] The temporal layering of *Moby Dick* is partly a reflection of the bravura with which Melville, drawing on a host of disparate influences, fashioned a literary idiom for himself; but it is also a device tuned to the novel's special concerns. Melville knows what he is about when he christens the wind whistling through New Bedford *Euroclydon* after the north-easter that blasted St Paul in his boat off Crete (p. 34): he is leading up to a subject and setting that are 'antemosaic', or even 'pre-adamite', in short to a realm that he will determinedly present as 'the unwarped primal world' (pp. 582, 530).[3] The immanence of the primeval is a recurrent theme in novels dealing with exploration, but the stratified text of *Moby Dick* is exceptionally well suited to its treatment. Ishmael's delvings into the past are inspired, as much as his voyage, by 'an everlasting itch for things remote' (p. 30), and his narrative, in both its allusiveness and tessellated texture, sails as far from stylistic norms as the *Pequod* beyond the New England horizon. So successful, indeed, is Melville at passing himself off as the contemporary of Noah and Moses that his links with his age have suffered from relative neglect.[4] Yet to isolate what is most distinctive of his period in *Moby Dick* (1851) is to move, by degrees, towards the novel's centre.

Melville originally made his name as an explorer, and shortly before the publication of his masterpiece ruefully remarked that he would continue to exist for his public as the 'man who lived among the cannibals'.[5] Set in the South Seas, his first two novels, *Typee* (1846) and *Omoo* (1847), show an obvious kinship with the travel book.[6] Although a self-advertising fictionality sets *Moby Dick* apart, one of its most striking features, a curious juxtaposing of narrative and discursive material, clearly reflects a crisis that overtook travel writing in the early half of the nineteenth century. In a history of the Royal Geographical Society, Ian Cameron comments on the growing scientific impulse in this period that went a long way to transforming the 'descriptive narrative' favoured by earlier explorers:

> . . . no-one could doubt the commitment to science of an eighteenth-century explorer such as Cook. It would, however, be fair to say that in the early nineteenth century men like Humboldt and Ritter did bring about a change in the concept of what geography was about. Before them its essence had been descriptive narrative. After them, its essence was detailed investigation in a number of specialized disciplines – botany, for example, or hydrography, geology or geomorphology.[7]

Perhaps the best single example of the change is provided by *Aspects of Nature* (1808), the widely influential travelogue in which Humboldt attempted, without full success, to keep personal narrative separate from sections of 'scientific elucidation'.[8] Later in his career, while surveying the writings of explorers, he accounted, with evident regret, for the bifurcation he had done much to foster. Turning to the example of travels from the early Renaissance he observes:

> They had the unity which every work of art requires: everything was connected with an action, *i.e.* subordinated to the journey

itself . . . This attractive unity of composition is necessarily wanting in the greater part of modern travels, and especially in those undertaken for scientific purposes; in these, what is done yields precedence to what is observed; the action almost disappears under the multitude of observations.[9]

Humboldt's position is an instructive one. For while he celebrates the ideal of a unified sensibility – praising Columbus for the way he 'teaches us anew that the creative imagination of the poet exists in the Discoverer' – he insists on the inductive foundations of all knowledge: 'there is nothing stable and certain but facts'.[10] Schiller thought he had put in a decisive stroke when he remarked of the explorer, 'his mind is that cold, dissecting kind that wants all nature to be shamelessly exposed to scrutiny'; but his strictures hardly meet the case.[11] Humboldt dismantles, it is true, and readily admits his inability to integrate, but his overriding aim, as he repeatedly states, is to instate a more inclusive order. His ideal, he observes in the preface to *Cosmos*, is 'to discern physical phenomena in their widest mutual connection, and to comprehend Nature as a whole, animated and moved by inward forces'.[12] Tantalized by discrete and partially assembled fragments, Humboldt rejoices in a pantheism typical of the Romantic literature in which his sensibility was grounded.

Many explorers in Humboldt's wake laboured under an obligation to be scientific, and Melville was among them. An empirical impulse, already apparent in the ethnography that punctuates *Typee*, becomes more pronounced and at the same time more self-conscious with *Moby Dick*. The interspersed chapters on whales and whaling are part of an attempt to supply the definitive account of a creature which from either a 'scientific or poetic' point of view 'lives not complete in any literature' (p. 181). Only thinly disguised as Ishmael, Melville adds first-hand experience to his gleanings from the authorities and we find him poised in this role between the modern scientific journalist and the seventeenth-century writer of anatomies. Unlike Sir Thomas Browne who, as Lytton Strachey remarks, was inductive 'just up to the point where the examination of detail ends, and its co-ordination begins', Melville assembles 'substantiated facts' with an eye to such imposing tasks as a 'systematization of cetology' (pp. 156, 181).[13] Unlike the scientific journalist, on the other hand, he submits the job of fact-gathering to a good deal of ironic play. If the sub-sub-librarian who hoards quotations about whales falls short of 'veritable gospel cetology' for lack of system, even the experts, comically nicknamed Coffin, Sleet or Fogo Von Slack, come in for their share of debunking. Ishmael is determined to address the whole man to the whole whale and while the longest run of referential chapters deals in anatomy of a literal kind – carcasses are sliced, shredded and inspected from every angle before Moby Dick hoves in view – the ultimate verdict is that the beast defies all analysis: 'Dissect him how I may, then, I but go skin deep; I know him not, and never will' (p. 486). It is in the same spirit that Ahab tramples on his quadrant and curses Science, exclaiming 'with thy impotence thou insultest the sun!' (p. 634). But if Melville dwells on the limits of empirical knowledge, he is also ready at times to expose belief to a reductive materialism. The tendency of Ishmael's brisk lecture to Queequeg on 'the rise and progress of primitive religions' is that self-denial breaks 'the obvious laws of Hygiene and common sense', and that supernatural awe is born of 'undigested apple-dumpling' (pp. 125–6). These views do not stop Ishmael, however, from professing himself a member of the 'great and everlasting First Congregation' in which all men splice hands (p. 128), and his frequent intimations of sympathetic accord with the universe constitute, as we shall see, one of the poles in the novel's dialectic movement. What Melville evidently had in view was a text sufficiently comprehensive to include Leyden jars and cycloids as well as Faustian pacts, a text moreover that would not only encompass imagination and science but witness their skirmish. The claims he makes for organic unity are not really founded (p. 380), for though the novel's expository parts are often among its most vivid and even thematically dense, there is much that is tacked on by mere expedience. Only intermittently is the reader aware of a synthesis that matches the privileged moments in which for Ishmael 'fact and fancy, half-way meeting, interpenetrate, and form one seamless whole' (p. 623).

Corresponding exactly to what some later psychologists would name the 'oceanic feeling', Ishmael's moments of mystical illumination are frequently associated with sunlight falling on a mild, swell-swept sea.[14] Melville evokes these moods superbly but always with a degree of critical reserve. In the chapter headed 'The Gilder' from which the last quotation comes, he goes out of his way, for example, to indicate what Ishmael's vision of coherence excludes:

> when beholding the tranquil beauty and brilliancy of the ocean's skin, one forgets the tiger heart that pants beneath it; and would not willingly remember, that this velvet paw but conceals a remorseless fang.
>
> (p. 623)

Similarly, in the famous passage from 'The Mast-Head', it is the thought of coming unstuck and crashing down that puts an end to the account of what every tyro in the crow's-nest feels on gazing into the depths and losing touch with the boundaries of self:

> every strange, half-seen, gliding, beautiful thing that eludes him; every dimly-discovered, uprising fin of some undiscernible form, seems to him the embodiment of those elusive thoughts that only people the soul by continually flitting through it. In this enchanted mood, thy spirit ebbs away to whence it came; becomes diffused through time and space; like Cranmer's sprinkled Pantheistic ashes, forming at last a part of every shore the round globe over . . . But while this sleep, this dream is on ye, move your foot or hand an inch; slip your hold at all; and your identity comes back in horror.
>
> (p. 214)

The admonitory note is sounded again when Tashtego slips into the balmy spermaceti filling the well he has dug from the head of the *Pequod*'s first catch:

> had Tashtego perished in that head, it had been a very precious perishing . . . Only one sweeter end can readily be recalled – the delicious death of an Ohio honey-hunter, who seeking honey in the crotch of a hollow tree, found such exceeding store of it, that leaning too far over, it sucked him in.
>
> (p. 445)

Melville is determined to renounce all love of easeful death but, from a letter written to Nathaniel Hawthorne while at work on *Moby Dick*, it is clear that he was susceptible to the feelings that he begins by relegating sternly to Romantic poetry:

In reading some of Goethe's sayings, so worshipped by his votaries, I came across this, '*Live in the all*.' That is to say, your separate identity is but a wretched one, – good; but get out of yourself, spread and expand yourself, and bring to yourself the tinglings of life that are felt in the flowers and the woods, that are felt in the planets Saturn and Venus, and the Fixed Stars. What nonsense! Here is a fellow with a raging toothache. 'My dear boy,' Goethe says to him, 'you are sorely afflicted with that tooth; but you must *live in the all*, and then you will be happy!' As with all great genius, there is an immense deal of flummery in Goethe, and in proportion to my own contact with him, a monstrous deal of it in me . . .

P.S. 'Amen!' saith Hawthorne.

N.B. This 'all' feeling, though, there is some truth in. You must often have felt it, lying on the grass on a warm summer's day. Your legs seem to send out shoots into the earth. Your hair feels like leaves upon your head. This is the *all* feeling. But what plays the mischief with the truth is that men will insist upon the universal application of a temporary feeling or opinion.[15]

Melville looked on Hawthorne as a teller of dark truths: 'even his bright gildings but fringe and play upon the edges of thunder-clouds', he had recently observed in his celebrated essay on the novelist.[16] But even if we suppose that his friend required some preparation for Ishmael's benign moods, there is no mistaking the scepticism that Melville displays towards *Ineinsbildung*, the one-making which amounted to a central tenet of faith among the early German Romantics.[17]

In a compelling survey of early nineteenth-century thought from his study *The Wheel of Empire*, Alan Sandison boldly compares political with epistemological theory and proposes a relation between the rise of imperialism and changing notions of *sensibilia*. He outlines Hegel's idea that the subject recovers selfhood in absorbing the object, and shows how it gradually gave ground in the period to the view that the ego constitutes itself by *resisting* the external world. He goes on:

Awareness of the rupture between subject and object and a yearning for reunion is, of course, one of the chief characteristics of Romantic writing. 'What is called Romanticism in England and on the Continent is . . . the concern for the reconciliation of subject and object, man and nature, consciousness and unconsciousness'. But though the crisis in which the 'imperial' writers . . . find themselves is basically Romantic, centred as it is in an intense awareness of this dissociation, they no longer really believe in the possibility of reconciliation. Theirs is a papiermaché grail: it is without intrinsic worth and with a purpose that is purely and confessedly psychological. No longer was there any possible prospect of that matter-spirit continuum which according to Albert Guerard is the proper object of the Romantic experience . . . In a sense what they sought now was less reconciliation than 'victory'.[18]

These conclusions have an obvious bearing on *Moby Dick*, for the two opposing attitudes towards nature which Sandison adumbrates here correspond to those which Melville dramatizes in the figures of Ishmael and Ahab. Where Ishmael sets out to discover the external world, Ahab pits himself against it; where the narrator assimilates, the hero looks for triumph. But while, taken together, Ishmael and Ahab may be seen to illustrate Keats' distinction between 'men of genius' and 'men of power', or the clash between Goethe's 'live in the all' and Fichte's contrary injunction to posit and then oppose a non-ego, in neither does the stereotypical trait wholly dominate.[19] Melville is more concerned to examine than propound and, to this end, Ishmael shows himself aware of the way his pantheistic intuitions threaten his utilitarian self, and Ahab partly revives the tendencies that he has gagged to make room for the 'creature he creates' (p. 272). We are alerted, moreover, to the destructiveness that inheres in either ideal. The fate of Narcissus awaits those who try to embrace the human image reflected off the surface of a far from benevolent ocean (p. 26); but, conversely, a hostile attitude towards the world entails perpetual war with the self. Issuing from an invisible source, a flickering irony plays over the heads of both narrator and hero. So defenceless is negative capability that Ishmael comes close to joining the quest that represents a negation of his own. 'A wild, mystical, sympathetical feeling was in me; Ahab's quenchless feud seemed mine', he is once moved to remark (p. 239); and only narrowly does he escape embroilment in the self-consuming vortex made by the sinking *Pequod* (p. 724). Ahab, on the other hand, whose mission begins in stark parody of Ishmael's enchanted merging – 'his torn body and gashed soul

bled into one another; and so interfusing, made him mad'
(p. 248), increasingly finds himself, for all his vaunted autonomy
of spirit, a creature of ivory appendages, a pawn of the material
world. So it is that Melville throws two opposing shibboleths of his
period into dynamic relation and, in the midst of frenzied action,
quietly registers the result.

The attitudes that Ishmael and Ahab display towards the
universe emerge, it hardly needs saying, in their feelings for Moby
Dick. The White Whale takes its emotional colouring from the
perceiver, and there is no suggestion of whitewashing when both
Starbuck and the genial Captain of the *Enderby* who has lost his
right arm to it, insist that the violence of the beast proceeds from
instinct rather than the malice imputed to it (pp. 220, 564). The
sane thing on losing a limb to an exceptionally aggressive whale,
the Captain confides, is to steer clear and preserve the others
(p. 563). To Ahab, however, who feeds on the vengeance he
nurtures, the whale appears as a mere front for a universe which
he imagines to be malignly disposed towards man:

> some unknown but still reasoning thing puts forth the
> mouldings of its features from behind the unreasoning mask. If
> man will strike, strike through the mask!
>
> (p. 220)

His terror and loathing of the 'dumb brute' are to some extent
self-directed, for the whale, as well as providing him with an
emblem of the cruelties of existence, serves as a dumping-ground
for the fury that rages in his breast. His campaign otherwise
resembles the magic rite of damaging some easily grasped image
in order to hit out at some less touchable ill:

> That intangible malignity which has been from the beginning;
> to whose dominion even the modern Christians ascribe one-half
> of the worlds; which the ancient Ophites of the east reverenced
> in their statue devil; – Ahab did not fall down and worship it like
> them; but deliriously transferring its idea to the abhorred white
> whale, he pitted himself, all mutilated, against it.
>
> (p. 247)

Yet since the many grievances which Ahab has 'piled upon the
whale's white hump' (p. 247) beg the question of his own

culpability, we are left free to conjecture that the 'reasoning thing' behind the unreasoning mask is the reflection of his own malign intent, and the conjecture is certainly reinforced by the frequent equations of the hunter and the hunted: Stubb's dream of Ahab with a humped back as well as white leg (p. 177); Ahab's own rallying cry, 'he heaps me' (p. 221), and his later complaint of being 'humped' with weariness (p. 684). It would be a naïve reader who supposed the evil that Ahab wars on in the whale divorceable from his own demonic energies. The view of Ahab as St George taking on the dragon is given the lie, in any case, by the stress Melville places on his hero's self-laceration.

The monomania around which Ahab assembles his factitious identity represents an assault upon the world in general, concentrated though it is upon a particular whale, and out of this enmity he manufactures his object of terror. For Ishmael, however, as Melville goes to some pains to demonstrate, Moby Dick comprises an entirely contrary if equally bleak set of resonances that are summed up in the fact of whiteness (p. 253). Chief among these is the feature that Ishmael comes to last in his anatomy of the 'colorless, all-color': the notion that the albino stands in relation to type as do the primary qualities of an object to its secondary, subjectively assumed ones:

> consider that other theory of the natural philosophers, that all other earthly hues – every stately or lovely emblazoning – the sweet tinges of sunset skies and woods; yea, and the gilded velvets of butterflies, and the butterfly cheeks of young girls; all these are but subtle deceits, not actually inherent in substances, but only laid on from without; so that all deified Nature absolutely paints like the harlot, whose allurements cover nothing but the charnel-house within; and when we proceed further, and consider that the mystical cosmetic which produces every one of her hues, the great principle of light, for ever remains white or colorless in itself, and if operating without medium upon matter, would touch all objects, even tulips and roses, with its own blank tinge – pondering all this, the palsied universe lies before us a leper . . .
>
> (p. 264)

Ishmael's ultimate horror is of a universe which, once peeled of the aspects imparted by the observer, proves inert and blank, impossible, in the last analysis, to assimilate. Because his instinct is to reach out and incorporate the external world, he is stunned by the prospect of an opaque ego. His quest continues to be fuelled, nevertheless, by his hunch that 'certain significance lurks in all things' (p. 549).

Ahab needs no such assurance, for he asks no more of his world than that it throw back his image. Gazing at the golden doubloon, which will eventually go to him as the first member of the crew to sight Moby Dick, he is delighted to read, written small in each of its emblems, an allegory of his own grandeur and strength, a discovery that leads him to reflect:

> that, too, is Ahab; all are Ahab; and this round gold is but the image of the rounder globe, which, like a magician's glass, to each and every man in turn but mirrors back his own mysterious self.
>
> (p. 551)

While Ishmael continues to be haunted by the featureless and unknowable, whether in the shape of a gigantic squid without 'perceptible face or front' (p. 366), the eyeless forehead of that 'hooded phantom' the sperm whale itself (pp. 30, 486), or death or other of the enigmas which he wreathes in cancelled adjectives ('untried', 'unshored', 'unneared' and so on, p. 617), he remains as eager to overcome separateness as he is swift to detect it. 'I am quick to perceive a horror, and could still be social with it', he confesses in the first sketch of his character (p. 30). Ahab, on the other hand, looks to the external world only for confirmation of the identity he has created by fiat. Not for his eyes are the strange hieroglyphics that craze the skin of whales (pp. 399–400); and when he does catch sight of the arcana tattooed on Queequeg's body, the secrets of which will be sealed forever on his death, he turns away, immediately harking back to his leitmotif, 'Oh, devilish tantalization of the gods!' (p. 612).

Melville portrays Ishmael and Ahab in opposition, but both figures, together with the quests they represent, are founded in Romantic individualism. Ahab's assault on Moby Dick manifests his rebellion against a hostile and repressive order; Ishmael's pursuit of the whale is the token of his determination to embrace a reality too daunting to be contained by man in his social aspect:

unless you own the whale, you are but a provincial and sentimentalist in Truth. But clear Truth is a thing for salamander giants only to encounter; how small the chances for the provincials then? What befel the weakling youth lifting the dread goddess's veil at Sais?

(p. 438)

In keeping with this conceit of himself Ishmael associates the 'slavish shore' with delusion, the 'intrepid effort' exacted of the independent mind with the open sea (p. 149). When Ahab protests against procrustean pressures it is to insist rather on the stature sacrifice has brought him:

Starbuck is Stubb reversed, and Stubb is Starbuck; and ye two are all mankind; and Ahab stands alone among the millions of the peopled earth, nor gods nor men his neighbours! Cold, cold – I shiver!

(p. 697)

Solitariness is for them both a necessary condition, whether of insight or self-exaltation, and it is to assert their singleness that they each selectively draw on the imagery of exploration. This use of exploratory metaphor appears, indeed, to be particularly characteristic of Romantic literature. Since for the Augustans the truths that matter most are those that endure and remain available to common understanding, the explorer typically serves in their fiction as a distant observer who can reflect with relative impartiality on his home culture or, through his encounter with alien people, isolate what is least accidental in human nature. For the Romantics, however, the idea of exploration holds a largely contrary set of significances. It is, for example, precisely the disparity between vision and common sense ('the spontaneous consciousness natural to all reflecting beings') that Coleridge, in a famous chapter from *Biographia Literaria*, chooses to translate into spatial terms:

The first range of hills that encircles the scanty vale of human life is the horizon for the majority of its inhabitants. On its ridges the common sun is born and departs. From them the stars rise, and touching them they vanish.[20]

So far the topology is that of *Rasselas*, but instead of turning to the world that lies beyond the mountains, Coleridge fixes on a realm far above the heads of the 'multitude below': cloud-begirt ascents and undiscovered springs 'which few have courage or curiosity to penetrate' make up the territory proper to the philosopher-poet. Coleridge's extended metaphor belongs to the start of a nineteenth-century tradition which associates remote and inhospitable regions with the search for truth. In writers as diverse as Browning, Ibsen, Olive Schreiner and Nietzsche the tradition remains current and seems to pass into irony only with Virginia Woolf's mock-heroic presentation of Mr Ramsay's quest for Z.[21] The passage from *Biographia* – a work that Melville acquired in 1848 – would certainly have played its part in entrenching a common literary resource.[22]

Melville champions intransigence in *Moby Dick*, but by no means uncritically. He counts the cost of Ahab's commitment to an absolute by disinterring, from time to time, the qualities that have fallen prey to his monomania. He relies, too, on the contrast offered by Ishmael who, since his quest for truth is founded in the urge to assimilate, continually seeks to overcome the separateness which nourishes the hero of his narrative. In short, Ahab's exclusivity is challenged throughout by the celebration of sympathy; and it is here that Melville reveals an important debt to Coleridge whom he singles out not as philosopher or critic, but as a poet of 'noble merit' (p. 256). This influence first becomes apparent when Ahab, lamenting the loss of his organic attachment to nature in a chapter entitled 'Sunset', provides what amounts – if we allow for a little dramatic emphasis – to a brief precis of 'Dejection: An Ode':

> Oh! time was, when as the sunrise nobly spurred me, so the sunset soothed. No more. This lovely light, it lights not me; all loveliness is anguish to me, since I can ne'er enjoy. Gifted with the high perception, I lack the low, enjoying power; damned, most subtly and most malignantly! damned in the midst of Paradise!
>
> (p. 226)

Not only does Ahab present himself as failing to respond to the beauty of the external, twilit scene but he blames his failure on an intellectual sophistication that has choked his spontaneous being, on something comparable to the 'abstruse research' that has suspended the poet's 'shaping spirit of Imagination'.[23]

It is to *The Ancient Mariner*, however, the work in which Coleridge most insistently probes the sacrifices entailed by isolation, that Melville looks for a model of his central thematic conflict. The 'wild Rhyme' comes up in connection with the albatross that Ishmael introduces into his catalogue of white things – here the bird has a function quite independent of the poem, serving, like the white whale, as an emblem of an unnearable reality that entices and overawes (p. 255). But later, as we shall see, Melville uses the symbol very much as Coleridge does. So many wild readings have attached to Coleridge's bird that one half expects to see 'shooting albatross' glossed as eighteenth-century slang for taking heroin, but in fact its significance is quite firmly defined by the context of the poem. Not until it appears are the crew of the ice-bound boat relieved of their morbid fears and the isolation that besets them:

> And through the drifts the snowy clifts
> Did send a dismal sheen:
> Nor shapes of men nor beasts we ken –
> The ice was all between.
>
> The ice was here, the ice was there,
> The ice was all around:
> It cracked and growled, and roared and howled,
> Like noises in a swound!
>
> (lines 55–62)[24]

Onto the setting the mariners project their terror of the beasts that are nowhere to be seen, and through some deftly implied sense distortion Coleridge renders their isolation individual as well as corporate; for the actual sound of the ice, a harsh cracking, is fed into the echo-chamber of a single swooning consciousness where it emerges ever less distinct and yet more menacing: consonants are increasingly muffled while verbs grow more predatory in the progression, 'cracked and growled, and roared and howled'. At this point the albatross gently materializes and to such effect that it not only requickens the mariners' instincts for cheer and companionship, welcomed, as it is, as a fellow soul and treated as a guest –

It ate the food it ne'er had eat,
And round and round it flew   (lines 67–8)

And every day, for food or play,
Came to the mariner's hollo   (lines 73–4)

but also succeeds in forging a link with the blanked-out universe
that lies beyond the ice as surely as moonbeams penetrate the fog:

Whiles all the night, through fog-smoke white,
Glimmered the white Moon-shine.   (lines 77–8)

In killing the bird the Mariner destroys the spirit that enkindles
both the exuberant departure of the ship and the marriage feast
(the two are spliced together at the poem's start) and in its place
he reinstates the self-enclosing 'land of mist and snow' (line 134),
a spirit from which proceeds to dog the voyage.

    It seems, at any rate, to have been a reading along these lines
that led Melville, not long after his allusion to *The Ancient Mariner*,
to introduce the chapter headed 'The Albatross' in which, while
presenting the *Pequod*'s first contact with a passing boat, he
develops a related conjunction of themes. Ishmael reports how at
the mere mention of Moby Dick all attempts to communicate
across the intervening stretch of sea founder. The ships are
mysteriously drawn apart and the Captain of the *Goney* (or
Albatross) drops his speaking-tube into the water. This idea of
cancelled relationship is pursued in the next chapter, 'The Gam',
where we learn that Ahab's obsession has caused him to forego the
custom in wide practice among whaling crews of exchanging
places and news on a chance meeting. The positive emphasis
given to the 'gam' is telling:

For not only would [the crew] meet with all the sympathies of
sailors, but likewise with all the peculiar congenialities arising
from a common pursuit and mutually shared privations and
perils.

                                                        (p. 318)

Ahab is prepared to delay for no longer than it takes to acquire the
'information he so absorbingly sought' (p. 317). In cutting across
the cordial institution – from which Melville generalizes to all

instincts for 'friendly and sociable contact' – he as good as kills the albatross.

Like *Robinson Crusoe*, Coleridge's poem is the offspring of a marriage between spiritual autobiography and the travel book. The Mariner's progress from impiety to penitence and regeneration illustrates the lesson he impresses on the Wedding-Guest towards the close:

> He prayeth well, who loveth well
> Both man and bird and beast.　　　　(lines 612–13)

Looked at from this angle the poem unfolds, as Robert Penn Warren pointed out, a moral fable that represents the notion of 'the one life', so central to the 'conversation poems'.[25] Though hardly just, it is at least appropriate that the Mariner, in view of the rejection of nature's accord implicit in his violent act, should experience the extremes of ostracism and self-imprisonment; appropriate too that a gesture of pure generosity towards creation, his blessing of the water-snakes, should restore him to grace. The fable, however, is patently at odds with the poem's universe. Coleridge himself called attention to the monstrous disproportion between the Mariner's suffering and his crime; and it is clear that the 'one life' is celebrated in the poem as a myth in defiance of an absurd world rather than as an item of belief.[26] For this reason it would seem, the Wedding-Guest after attending to the moral that gave rise to 'All Things Bright and Beautiful' takes his leave *sadder* and *forlorn*; and the Mariner himself, despite his regeneration, remains a haunted and deracinated being, passing 'like night, from land to land' (line 586), easily mistaken for one of the dead even while he speaks:

> I fear thee, ancient Mariner!
> I fear thy skinny hand!
> And thou art long, and lank, and brown,
> As is the ribbed sea-sand.　　　　(lines 224–7)

When Melville borrows this image to describe Ahab at the instant he begins his chase, an instant darkened by a recognition of what his vengeance will entail, he draws on a Mariner whose curse remains irremovable:

when all these conceits had passed through his brain, Ahab's brow was left gaunt and ribbed, like the black sand beach after some stormy tide has been gnawing it, without being able to drag the firm thing from its place.

(p. 492)

Melville's debts to the poem are, in fact, manifold. His description of foam-flakes (p. 311), blinded eyes (p. 461), of a tongue-tied, painted crew (p. 313) or of the skeletal *Delight* (p. 679) are all steeped in Coleridge's vivid imagery, while the machinery of the 'wild Rhyme' – particularly the use of well-attested phenomena for supernatural effect – proves equally invasive. More important, however, is the way the poem provides an index to the exploration of Ahab's offence against the precept of *living in the all*.

In the course of its exactly scheduled passage the *Pequod* crosses the path of many ships, and on more than one occasion the crew have cause to cast back 'lingering glances' (p. 628); but it is on meeting the *Rachel* that Ahab's violation of the gam is really made to tell. The boat's name recalls the prophecy of Herod's massacre of the innocents (p. 671), and with reason, for it is with 'iciness' that Ahab refuses the Captain's request that he join the search for his missing twelve-year-old boy, and the scene raises not only the spectre of the son and newly-wedded wife whom he has already, in effect, 'widowed' by leaving behind forever (p. 683), but also the fate callously meted out to Pip. Indeed Stubb, the hard-headed mate who has refused to rescue Pip a second time from the ocean, in case he should lose a whale, provides the measure of his Captain's ruthlessness when he protests against the decision to turn a deaf ear to the *Rachel*'s plea.

That Melville can register so severe an appraisal without surrendering Ahab's claims to sympathy is largely owing to the way he succeeds in suggesting the intensity of his hero's distress. The contrast between the Captain's 'Grand-Lama-like exclusiveness' (p. 591) and the capacity for social merging that Ishmael exemplifies in his 'marriage' with Queequeg and later voices in his rhapsody at the try-works (pp. 84, 532), runs through Ahab's character itself and assumes, little by little, the form of a rift in the human psyche. Ishmael, who begins and ends his narrative by presenting himself as an outsider, and most movingly recalls his childhood terror of isolation (p. 33), is only too well acquainted with the state to which Ahab aspires. His yearnings

for union ('let us all squeeze ourselves into each other', p. 533) are
based on his knowledge of separateness, as he himself indicates on
overcoming his recoil from the 'soothing savage':

> I began to be sensible of strange feelings. I felt a melting in me.
> No more my splintered heart and maddened hand were turned
> against the wolfish world.
>
> (p. 83)

Ahab, conversely, gradually admits to the sociable nature that he
keeps for the most part suppressed, even if his admission
sometimes takes the form of cursing 'mortal inter-indebtedness'
(p. 601). Shortly before the chase begins in earnest he experiences
a sensation of kinship with his setting characteristic of Ishmael,
and to mark his access of feeling, after dropping a tear into the
ocean, sums up the life he has spent on deck:

> the desolation of solitude it has been; the masoned, walled-town
> of a Captain's exclusiveness, which admits but small entrance
> to any sympathy from the green country without.
>
> (p. 683)

The small outlet represents, for the present, the Ishmael-like
relationship he has formed with the crazed Pip from whom he is
able to 'suck most wondrous philosophies' (p. 667). But the 'cords'
and 'heart-strings' (p. 659) by which Ahab feels himself attached
will prove as destructive to the boy as the harpoon line which has
twice dragged him into the sea; his plight is clearly linked with
that of newly-born whales unlucky enough to fall into the path of a
harpooner:

> Starbuck saw long coils of the umbilical cord of Madame
> Leviathan, by which the young cub seemed still tethered to its
> dam. Not seldom in the rapid vicissitudes of the chase, this
> natural line, with the maternal end loose, becomes entangled
> with the hempen one, so that the cub is thereby trapped.
>
> (p. 498)

Generation and bonding are often used in *Moby Dick* to epitomize
the relational but this last brutal image is given a particular
psychological resonance in context, for Ishmael, in describing an

assault upon a school of breeding whales, associates the sight of calves gathered in an 'innermost fold' – where they suckle safely in transparent water at a great depth – with what he identifies as a centre of serenity within himself:

> And thus, though surrounded by circle upon circle of consternations and affrights, did these inscrutable creatures at the centre freely and fearlessly indulge in all peaceful concernments; yea, serenely revelled in dalliance and delight. But even so, amid the tornadoed Atlantic of my being, do I myself still for ever centrally disport in mute calm.
>
> (pp. 498–9)

The logic of this metaphor provides for the further sense that what is practised upon whales is practised upon the self, and accordingly supplies a rationale for the many images of self-inflicted violence that crowd the text. Thus it is that Ahab's 'eternal, living principle' is devoured by his willed identity, by the 'very creature he creates' (p. 272), or that Starbuck warns in vain, 'Ahab beware of Ahab' (p. 605). On the theme of self-immolation Ishmael extemporizes for two chapters at a time, skipping from whales cooked by their own light and calf-heads eaten by 'bucks', to letters on the suppression of cruelty to ganders written with quills, till he comes to rest on cannibalism among fish (pp. 392–6). He flirts, too, with a rhetoric of self-cancellation – with 'endless ends', and 'uncatastrophied fifth-acts' (pp. 606, 616); and delights in tail-in-mouth constructions:

> both chasing and being chased
>
> (p. 491)

> Is heaven a murderer when its lightning strikes a would-be murderer?
>
> (p. 651)

> yesterday I wrecked [the compass which today] would feign have wrecked me
>
> (p. 655)

> Who's to doom, when the judge himself is dragged to the bar?
> (p. 685)

Ishmael sees Ahab's signature everywhere, and the generalizing habit is particularly appropriate to a narrator whose most distinctive trait is the urge to dilate. The contrary tendency appears in Ahab whose 'ever-contracting, dropping circle ashore' (p. 592) typifies a process of concentration that is both bodily and mental. Into the straits of a narrowing resolve his energies flow 'deepeningly contracted' after his accident (p. 248), and so fretted is he with purpose that by the time of the chase he has grown humped and bowed as well as haggard (p. 684). Melville repeatedly describes Ahab as *eaten into* by his obsession, and the metaphor is kept alive by the limb made of polished jawbone that seizes its chance, on one occasion, to tear at his flesh (pp. 590, 592). As the voyage progresses we pick up the clues which show Ahab increasingly mastered, for all his boasted freedom, by the object of his hatred: he surrounds himself with ivory accoutrements, screws himself into the deck; and, manifest in Fedallah, his evil genius goes down at last pinned to the back of the whale.

Ishmael finds a source of serenity at the centre of his being; how, then, are we to regard the war Ahab makes on his world? In *Typee* Melville celebrates the natural innocence of the South Sea islanders and identifies aggression as a symptom of life in the West; in *Moby Dick*, however, it is the behaviour of Ahab and his men that he offers as a token of the natural forces that ruffle the surfaces of civility:

> Long exile from Christendom and civilization inevitably restores a man to that condition in which God placed him, *i.e.* what is called savagery. Your true whale-hunter is as much a savage as an Iroquois. I myself am a savage, owning no allegiance but to the King of the Cannibals; and ready at any moment to rebel against him.
>
> (p. 358)

Important among the other savages that Ishmael enlists in his undercover enquiry into human nature are the sperm whales; and the variety of impulse they display is as mixed as the conduct of the *Pequod*'s crew. In a whole school there is equal evidence of pugnacity and delight, and in describing sexual jealousy among the bulls, Ishmael comes close to suggesting that intensities are matched at either extreme:

As ashore, the ladies often cause the most terrible duels among their rival admirers; just so with the whales, who sometimes come to deadly battle, and all for love.

(p. 503)

The idea that antinomies are natural and necessary is developed further in the account of the whale cemetery in the Arsacides where the sight of vines clinging to the huge skeletons for support triggers off the reflection: 'Life folded Death; Death trellised Life; the grim god wived with youthful Life, and begat him curly-headed glories' (p. 574). The motif of 'warp and woof intermixed' is sounded earlier in the famous passage evoking the vision of the drowning Pip, and there again the emphasis falls on the ambivalence of creation: the 'unwarped primal world' is at once both 'joyous' and 'heartless' (p. 530). By way of a closing emblem, Melville has Ishmael make a lifeboat of the coffin of his friend.

'The King of Cannibals' has many counterparts in nature, but even the self-destruction that seems a consequence of wilful perversion is paralleled by a creature of the deeps. While Queequeg murders the sharks, the sharks murder each other but also themselves:

They viciously snapped, not only at each other's disembowelments, but like flexible bows, bent round, and bit their own; till those entrails seemed swallowed over and over again by the same mouth, to be oppositely voided by the gaping wound.

(p. 395)

Ahab belongs to a world in which even the instinct of self-preservation is blind.

When the Ancient Mariner imparts his final lesson he endorses his hymn of praise to the 'one life' by invoking a divinely ordained creation:

> He prayeth best, who loveth best
> All things both great and small;
> For the dear God who loveth us,
> He made and loveth all.   (lines 614–17)

Moby Dick which Melville described to Hawthorne as 'a wicked book' hints at a darker genesis.[27] Whaling men, whales, the underworld of the sea, even the Orient revive in varying degree 'the ghostly aboriginalness of earth's primal generations' (p. 308); but in the chapter on whale fossils Ishmael is taken back still further – 'to that wondrous period, ere time itself can be said to have begun; for time began with man' (p. 582). Writing almost a decade before *The Origin of Species* (1859), Melville wryly extrapolates from the traditional biblical landmarks on venturing beyond the human realm. We are reminded that the whale survived the Flood without the help of Noah, the ice age too (pp. 589, 582); and that a recently unearthed skeleton, thought in Alabama to be that of a fallen angel, belonged in fact to an ancestor of the modern whale, to 'one of the most extraordinary creatures which the mutations of the globe have blotted out of existence' (p. 582). Against Leviathan, Melville counterpoints Zeuglodon; but where Job is convinced by his monster of an omnipotent, controlling presence, Ishmael is merely thrown back on his feelings of awe:

> I am horror-struck at this antemosaic, unsourced existence of the unspeakable terrors of the whale, which, having been before all time, must needs exist after all humane ages are over.
>
> (p. 582)[28]

An explorer to the end, Melville deferred to no system. A fully-fledged theory of evolution was still to appear, but he shows himself familiar with the two chief components that went into its making. Through his scientific reading he was well acquainted with the notion of mutation among the species; and from his remarkable description, in *The Encantadas*, of the huge tortoises of the Galapagos – perhaps the very ones that stimulated Darwin's account of a modifying environment – it is clear that he had pondered deeply on the struggle for survival.[29] He presents the giants as emblems of 'indefinite endurance', himself as a paleontologist pouring over the rockface of their battered shells, each fissure and abrasion capable of disclosing untold secrets of descent. Less fancifully, he comments on the creature's habit of engaging in headlong conflict with every obstacle in its path:

> Their stupidity or their resolution was so great, that they never went aside for any impediment. . . . At sunrise I found [one] butted like a battering-ram against the immovable foot of the

foremast, and still striving, tooth and nail, to force the
impossible passage.[30]

This is Ahab all over. The '*all* feeling' which counteracts his
implacable drive was still to regain a sanction from nature, and
would do so only once a clearer picture emerged of the way the
diverse species joined in a common ancestry. For Melville,
however, the suspicion of flummery was not enough to cut off a
valuable resource.

6 Conrad Dismantles Providence:

Deserted idylls in *An Outcast of the Islands*

With the grim sequel to his present misfortunes already told in Conrad's first novel, a half-disillusioned Almayer at the close of *An Outcast of the Islands* (1896) vents his disappointment by rounding on the universe,

> Where's your Providence? Where's the good for anybody in all this? The world's a swindle! A swindle!

The abuse he hurls at the heavens is checked at length by a stammered reply:

> My dear fellow, don't – don't you see that the ba– bare fac– the fact of your existence is off– offensive . . . I– I like you – like . . .
>
> (p. 367)[1]

The speaker is a dying naturalist specially brought in for the novel's coda, and he punctures the 'quarrel with Providence' by insisting on Almayer's part in the order he vilifies. His enigmatic words trail into silence, but the trappings of his profession combine with details of the tropical setting (insects stream into a smoking flame) to impart a strong evolutionary bias to his utterance. The decisive gloss to his remark comes in *Falk* (1903) when Conrad characterizes his man-eating hero, almost an emblem of the will to strive, as a creature who perpetually gives 'cause for offence'.[2]

While the ending of *An Outcast of the Islands* highlights a pervasive concern with the loss of order and exhibits the tonal range of a narrator who moves between pathos and resilient irony, it also makes a claim to a wider relevance than attaches to the

113

novel's colonial themes.[3] Through it Conrad relates his local
portraiture to a metaphysical issue which he took to be of
overriding importance to his age: he belonged, after all, as Ian
Watt has recently suggested, to the first generation who had
pressing reason to doubt 'the traditional view of man's flattering
eminence in the history, as well as the design, of the cosmos'.[4] He
was haunted, as has frequently been pointed out, by the vision of a
lost human significance. Many passages from his correspondence
fill out the often cited declaration from *A Personal Record*, 'I have
come to suspect that the aim of creation cannot be ethical at all'.[5]
Under the tutelage of astrophysics as well as the life sciences
Conrad entertained a 'severely scientific' view of the universe
which set moral constructions at nought.[6] The contrast between
the halo of conviction surrounding human activity and the dismal
truth prescribed by the cold light of reason fascinated him, and he
often images a chaos opening up beyond the shifting mists of
illusion as in this representative extract from his letters to
Cunninghame Graham:

> Of course reason is hateful – but why? Because it demonstrates
> (to those who have the courage) that we, living, are out of life –
> utterly out of it. The mysteries of a universe made of drops of fire
> and clods of mud do not concern us in the least. The fate of a
> humanity condemned ultimately to perish from cold is not
> worth troubling about. If you take it to heart it becomes an
> unendurable tragedy. If you believe in improvement you must
> weep, for the attained perfection must end in cold, darkness and
> silence . . . Faith is a myth and beliefs shift like mists on the
> shore; thoughts vanish; words, once pronounced, die; and the
> memory of yesterday is as shadowy as the hope of to-morrow.[7]

The bearing of these ideas on Conrad's first novels has not, I
believe, been fully brought home. Recurrent themes such as
patronage, imprisonment and projection, which have come in for
separate treatment (and often been taken as disjunct), revolve in
context round a concern with the disappearance of a rational
order transcending the self.[8]

In both *Almayer's Folly* (1895) and *An Outcast of the Islands* (1896)
Conrad foregrounds the collapse of various personal fictions and
in doing so invokes the breakdown of wider systems of belief.
When Almayer learns that his lifelong dream of returning, rich, to

Europe with his daughter has never coincided with his daughter's wishes he finds the 'whole universe unsettled and shaken'.[9] An earlier moment of truth, the foundering of his commercial prospects at Sambir, inspires the outburst that closes *An Outcast*. In the case of Almayer's patron, Tom Lingard, who succeeds in realizing his fantasies to the extent of presiding as an 'Arcadian' law-giver over a river that he has grown to regard as his own, it is the betrayal of Willems, his other protégé, that precipitates the profound insight into chaos that his sense of decency proves powerless to dispel:

> there remained nothing but the sense of some immense infamy – of something vague, disgusting and terrible, which seemed to surround him on all sides . . . Was there, under heaven, such a thing as justice? He looked at the man before him with such an intensity of prolonged glance that he seemed to see right through him, that at last he saw but a floating and unsteady mist in human shape. Would it blow away before the first breath of the breeze and leave nothing behind?
>
> (p. 265)

Conrad's words to Cunninghame Graham are recalled by the imagery here as they are by an earlier comment on Lingard's glimpse of a reality beyond the 'limits of the universe strictly defined by those we know':

> There is nothing for us outside the babble of praise and blame on familiar lips, and beyond our last acquaintance there lies only a vast chaos; a chaos of laughter and tears which concerns us not; laughter and tears unpleasant, wicked, morbid, contemptible – because heard imperfectly by ears rebellious to strange sounds.
>
> (p. 198)

The pattern persists. Babalatchi, the sly counsellor who engineers the Arab take-over of Sambir, briefly surrenders to the same vision on receiving news of Omar's death, but the bitter cry that rises to his lips, 'as profound as any philosophical shriek', is muffled by his triumph and he turns once more into 'the puller of wires' (p. 215).

Against this varied range of crises there stand out the two

failures of trust that make up the story of the novel's central figure, the outcast himself. Before he brings ruin on himself by taking money off his employer, Willems revels in his prospects of success. The adulation of his wife and her half-caste family feed his self-esteem, but he rejoices chiefly in the promise of a trading career that will sweep him onward to the bright if hazy 'goal of his ambition' (p. 11). He is jolted out of his life of acquisition, however, when Hudig sacks him for 'borrowing' money without permission, and a shame bred of his enormous pride instantly eats away the fabric of his social presence:

> For the first time in his life he felt afraid of the future, because he had lost his faith, the faith in his own success.
>
> (p. 31)

He sees himself stripped of past and future, a naked being recoiling from 'the presence of unknown and terrible dangers'.

Conrad dramatizes this climax in his hero's existence by introducing a scene that holds the key to much of the novel's symbolic action. After falling out with his family Willems takes to his heels until he finds himself at last in the dark beyond the outskirts of the coastal settlement. Escape from 'the temple of self and the concentration of personal thought' is associated with his movement into the wilderness:

> it seemed to him that the world was bigger, the night more vast and more black . . . he went on doggedly with his head down as if pushing his way through some thick brambles.
>
> (pp. 30–1)

The metaphor of departure from the straight and narrow path, sounded in the first sentence and continually returned to, orchestrates an underlying identity between the jungle and the uncovenanted life into which Willems is ejected by his transgression. In *Almayer's Folly* the image of *terra incognita* is applied to the discovery of passion: shortly before her elopement with Dain, Nina (aptly named after Columbus's vessel) roundly tells her father,

> We entered a land where no one could follow us, and least of all you. Then I began to live.[10]

Exploratory imagery in *An Outcast* carries darker associations –
the hinterland of Borneo is more often equated here with absence
than with recovery.

Though Willems is apparently rescued from his plight by
Captain Lingard who shows him the secret entrance to his river
and leaves him upstream in the company of Almayer, his
disorientated condition now finds a correlate in a region that
Conrad was later to describe as 'one of the lost, forgotten,
unknown places of the earth'.[11] It is in this setting that Willems
undergoes his second and more poignant reversal of fortune. He
falls for Aïssa, the beautiful daughter of Omar, who returns his
love. In the heart of the jungle a realm of enchantment opens for
them both, but even as Willems seems set to launch himself on a
life that holds truer riches than his previous career, he suffers a
loss of nerve. Aware that he has scant resources to balance against
his dependence on Aïssa, he struggles against total surrender,
clinging pathetically to his old, threadbare self. Without escaping
the antagonism and betrayal entailed by his devotion he finds his
love poisoned at source. But the charged ironies of his situation
lead to insight. At the moment that he sidesteps the murderous
kriss wielded by Aïssa's father, he looks beyond the immediate
context of his vexed affairs to perceive a world ridden with conflict
and doubt:

> It was the unreasoning fear of this glimpse into the unknown
> things, into those motives, impulses, desires he had ignored,
> but that had lived in the breasts of despised men, close by his
> side, and were revealed to him for a second, to be hidden again
> behind the black mists of doubt and deception. It was not death
> that frightened him: it was the horror of bewildered life where
> he could understand nothing and nobody round him; where he
> could guide, control, comprehend nothing and no one – not
> even himself.
>
> (p. 149)

A failure of serenity robs Willems of both his old identity and his
new. Piloting Abdullah's men up the secret channel, he plays the
key role in ousting his patron at Sambir, and one consequence of
his betrayal is that his hatred of Aïssa grows. Reviling the images
of his lost life (pp. 338–9) and cursing himself at the same time for
his newfound desire, he ends as his own worst enemy and, sensing

this, Lingard abandons him to his own devices on the upper reaches of the river. There until his violent death he and Aïssa endure a tormented state of mutual isolation – 'each the centre of dissimilar and distant horizons; standing each on a different earth, under a distant sky' (p. 334). Although he has cherished the dream of a shared retreat –

> his face brightened with the soft light of dreamy enthusiasm . . . he looked like some ascetic dweller in a wilderness, finding the reward of a self-denying life in a vision of dazzling glory . . .
> 'And then I would have her all to myself away from her people – all to myself – under my own influence – to fashion – to mould – to adore – to soften – to . . . Oh! Delight! And then – then go away to some distant place where, far from all she knew, I would be all the world to her!
>
> (p. 92)

Willems finds at last that Aïssa and he each constitute their own 'deserted island'.[12]

Conrad undermines his characters in order to expose the flawed status of their belief; and the pattern of a willed or received order crumbling under the impact of a sinister reality, or the related coupling of ordinary experience with some darker counterpart, recurs with particular persistence in the early work. That his concern with a changing world view, manifest in his repeated portrayals of blighted hope, should emerge with a special clarity from his second novel has to do, perhaps, with a subtle inversion of his readers' expectations there. Much in *An Outcast of the Islands* suggests a deliberate disaffiliation from the desert-island-idyll set in Eastern seas: the novel's title, its lavish but ambivalent response to an exotic setting, its sustained metaphors of exploration and of the castaway were sure to summon associations mostly of a contrastive kind. Likening the book to Melville's *Typee* (1846) for its 'scenic descriptions of tropical islands', a contemporary reviewer went on to prepare his readers for a 'ruined paradise'.[13] In his turn, Conrad once curtly remarked of *Typee* and *Omoo*, 'I didn't find there what I am looking for when I open a book';[14] but, of course, for many readers it was Conrad's pessimism that proved an insurmountable bar. 'Even genius', wrote a critic in the *Spectator*, 'will not win forgiveness for the repulsive cynicism of the dialogue between Almayer and the

Professor in the last chapter.'[15] Like the botanist's 'bare fact of existence' the evolutionary perspective introduced in the coda gave cause for offence.

There can be little doubt that such responses were foreseen. Conrad supplies one pointer in the novel when he closes a chapter with the sketch of a jaundiced tale, sung repeatedly by the crafty Babalatchi, stage-manager of the *coup d'état* at Sambir:

> It had all the imperfections of unskilful improvisation and its subject was gruesome. It told a tale of shipwreck and of thirst, and of one brother killing another for the sake of a gourd of water. A repulsive story which might have had a purpose but possessed no moral whatever.
>
> (p. 138)

There is a distinction, to be sure, between Conrad's art and that of the one-eyed singer, but the eerie dithyramb does darkly mirror the action of the novel and characterize its tenor. The struggle between the castaway brothers prefigures the rivalry (fomented by Babalatchi) that is to set Almayer and Willems – 'brothers' in the eyes of their honorary father, Lingard – at each other's throats. The notion, too, of murder in the place of expected sanctuary parallels the many homicidal fantasies and acts that stud the idle hours spent along the river's uncrowded banks. Willems's death – to take a single instance – is contemplated by six characters before Aïssa blasts him through the chest.[16] In lieu of a privileged glimpse into the prelapsarian state Conrad presents characters in the throes of internecine violence. Even his image of the rescued castaway is dextrously emptied of solace:

> Those three human beings abandoned by all were like shipwrecked people left on an insecure and slippery ledge by the retiring tide of an angry sea – listening to its distant roar, living anguished between the menace of its return and the hopeless horror of their solitude – in the midst of a tempest of passion, of regret, of disgust, of despair.
>
> (p. 328)

Willems is by any reckoning an unpleasant man, but his story – like Babalatchi's cautionary tale – is given a general significance in line with the remark Conrad once made to Cunninghame

Graham: 'Abnegation – self-sacrifice means something. Fraternity means nothing unless the Cain–Abel business. That's your true fraternity. Assez.'[17]

Much of the force of Conrad's polemic is lost unless we appreciate the context of the desert island genre. Foremost among countertypes, *An Outcast of the Islands* relates to a book like *Typee* in much the same way that William Golding's *Lord of the Flies* (1954) relates to *Coral Island* (1857); and to Ballantyne's novel I propose now to turn since it provides an admirably clear paradigm of the kind.

In a critical work on fiction Barbara Hardy identifies a particular sort of novel in which a 'single and simplified belief . . . excludes much of the varied causality to be found in life', and as an example of such 'dogmatic form' cites *Robinson Crusoe*, a text in which 'action and characters are shaped by . . . a special belief, the belief in Providence'.[18] What holds for Defoe's first novel proves even truer of its much later descendant *Coral Island*, for Ballantyne plots the workings of Providence with the assiduity of an astrologer. A timely prayer accounts for the deliverance of Ralph and his two mates from the fate of the rest of the crew (pp. 6, 10).[19] Supernatural influence can again be detected in Jack's single-handed victory over the bloodthirsty warriors as in Ralph's later escape from a cannibal horde (pp. 147, 201). When a sudden downpour saves the three boys from sentence of death, Providence can be said to kill two birds with one stone; for the tribesmen are so impressed by the timing and violence of the storm that they instantly embrace the Christian faith (pp. 270, 274). While Ralph, like Crusoe, is brought closer to the devout life by his new setting (pp. 19, 27), the island offers up images of a pristine world more consistently than does Defoe's. With an imagination unburdened by knowledge of the South Seas, Ballantyne purveys an 'ancient Paradise' (p. 24) in all the aureate terms of pastoral and his brightly enamelled sketches come equipped with sententious mottoes:

> The sea was shining like a sheet of glass, yet heaving with the long deep swell that, all the world round, indicates the life of ocean; and the bright sea-weeds and the brilliant corals shone in the depths of that pellucid water, as we rowed over it, like rare and precious gems. Oh! it was a sight fitted to stir the soul of man to its profoundest depths, and, if he owned a heart at all,

to lift that heart in adoration and gratitude to the great Creator
of this magnificent and glorious universe.

(pp. 114–15)

The recovery of the unfallen extends to the boys' relationship in
which teasing absorbs the only traces of malice, so that the
narrator can fairly report:

There was, indeed, no note of discord whatever in the
symphony we played together on that sweet Coral Island; and I
am now persuaded that this was owing to our having been all
tuned to the same key, namely, that of *love*!

(p. 103)

So persistent is the idyll that the reader has to be reminded that
the islands are 'very unlike Paradise in many things' before any
action can be got under way (p. 24). Beyond the charmed circle of
the reef there lies a starkly variegated universe that seems to be the
product of a dualistic creation. With such vehemence does
Ballantyne denigrate his Melanesians (all his islanders are black),
that every intrusion into their preserve appears as an advance for
the cause of heaven. And even while the narrator insists on the
horrors of the pagan world, the novel succeeds in suggesting that
evil is accidental and temporary, devoid of proper standing in the
normal universe. Pagan excesses (of a hectic sort) are placed on a
par with natural disasters – the falling rock, the tidal wave, the
menacing cry – those unexpected events that momentarily
suspend the assurance of continuing order, and so interrupt, as
Ralph puts it, the even tenor of their way (p. 138). The reader is
led to understand that when the boys act heroically they simply
lend a hand to the properly benevolent processes of nature.
Whenever they intervene it is on the assumption that they are
merely fishing a spanner out of the works. Even at the height of
the novel's violence Ballantyne presents – perhaps with some
Mozartian or Shakespearean reminiscence – an ocean
wonderfully animated with benign intention:

With a savage laugh, the chief tore the child from her arms and
tossed it into the sea. A low groan burst from Jack's lips as we
witnessed this atrocious act and heard the mother's shriek, as
she fell insensible on the sand. The rippling waves rolled the

child on the beach, as if they refused to be a party in such a foul murder, and we could observe that the little one still lived.

(p. 145)

Once he has quelled the preposterous chief, Jack, needless to say, restores the baby to its mother – thus completing what nature, seemingly of its own accord, began. His little act of rescue looks forward to the novel's most extended episode, the deliverance of Avatea who is saved from a forced marriage and restored to her deserving lover.

To turn from Ballantyne's text to *An Outcast* is to move into a world that revokes all assurance of order. The change makes itself felt even in those descriptive passages that Conrad, for his part, over-modestly called 'mere scenery'.[20] Where Ballantyne delights in the picturesque and – in so far as he aims at thematic ends – stresses the harmonious relationship between the natural objects that he selects, Conrad portrays a wilderness that supplies an immediate analogue to the human scene because of his fidelity to an overriding principle, the individual's struggle for life. This, at least, is a conspicuous feature of that 'sense for the *psychology of scene*' which Edward Garnett singled out as Conrad's most distinctive contribution to the novel.[21] The gift was Conrad's from the start as the following passage from *Almayer's Folly* makes clear:

the big trees of the forest, lashed together with manifold bonds by a mass of tangled creepers, looked down at the growing young life at their feet with the sombre resignation of giants that had lost faith in their strength. And in the midst of them the merciless creepers clung to the big trunks in cable-like coils, leaped from tree to tree, hung in thorny festoons from the lower boughs, and, sending slender tendrils on high to seek out the smallest branches, carried death to their victims in an exulting riot of silent destruction.[22]

The passage follows on Almayer's discovery of his daughter's elopement with Dain, a discovery that shatters the dream that has sustained his life; but although the fate of the hapless trees vaguely foreshadows the decay that awaits Almayer, the scene does not so much conjure up a direct equivalence – our sympathies are, in fact, divided between Nina and her father – as illustrate the conception that in the natural world, at any rate, one creature prospers at the expense of another. When Ballantyne, on the other hand, describes the main valley of his island the scene he conveys, though an entirely uninhabited one, finds its focal point in man – the movements of the narrator's eye are guided by utility and pleasure:

> Some trees were dark glossy green, others of a rich and warm hue, contrasting well with those of a pale light green, which were everywhere abundant. Among these we recognised the broad dark heads of the bread-fruit, with its golden fruit; the pure, silvery foliage of the candle-nut, and several species which bore a strong resemblance to the pine; while here and there, in groups and in single trees, rose the tall forms of the cocoanut palms, spreading abroad, and waving their graceful plumes high above all the rest, as if they were a superior race of stately giants keeping guard over these luxuriant forests. Oh! it was a most enchanting scene, and I thanked God for having created such delightful spots for the use of man.
>
> (pp. 68–9)

Unlike Conrad's giants who at last face, themselves, the starvation on which their triumph depends, Ballantyne's tall and gracefully plumed palms live up to the responsibilities of senior standing with a stateliness that becomes superior rank. Their protectiveness represents one of many tokens of providential design. With its plentiful food, its natural breakwater and balmy air – surf on the distant reef tenders a lullaby to the boys as they settle to sleep under the stars – the island offers a blueprint of the unfallen place. Only once they have ventured out beyond the atoll do Ralph and Peterkin discover that they can no longer take for granted the structure of reliance on which their experience of the island has been founded. When a sudden squall pounces on their makeshift boat, Ralph remarks:

> Peterkin and I were so much in the habit of trusting everything to Jack that we had fallen into the way of not considering things, especially such things as were under Jack's care. We had, therefore, never doubted for a moment that all was going well, so that it was with no little anxiety that we heard him.
>
> (p. 134)

While Ballantyne is ready to admit that unbounded confidence can prove a liability in the fallen world, it is Jack's paternal care of his younger comrades that he is out to celebrate.

Providence is a variable concept, and for the most part a vague one. It tends to be most closely defined when consciousness of suffering or of free will is at a low ebb. It may be interpreted in terms chiefly of material or spiritual reward; it may be construed, again, as centred either on the life of the individual or of the race. Implied by all versions, however, is a sense of security stimulated by a faith in the ultimately ethical nature of the universe; which is to say that while Providence is a theological dogma it proposes itself more immediately as a state of mind, a resource of serenity, what the Stoics knew as *ataraxia*. In Christian thought a range of differing tenets has been animated by the vivid figure of God the Father, a metaphor that goes back to the Sermon on the Mount and the Lord's Prayer. To the roles of creator and law-giver, this convention adds that notion of a solicitous parenthood commemorated in many nineteenth-century hymns. To quote from one example:

> Father-like, He tends and spares us,
> Well our feeble frame He knows;
> In His hands He gently bears us,
> Rescues us from all our foes;
> Alleluia! Alleluia!
> Widely yet His mercy flows.[23]

A cynic might have argued that Providence was no more than a feeling of familial security projected into the sky. Given the force and prevalence of the paternal analogy, it is not surprising that declining faith in a transcendent order should have called the entire issue of psychological dependence in question. This, at least, seems to have been the direction taken by Conrad's imagination when at the start of his career he examined a series of tutelary relationships that reflect the relation of God and devotee.

In his introductory note to *An Outcast* Conrad recalls that his interest in the person who suggested his hero was aroused chiefly by his 'dependent position'.[24] When we meet Willems, however, it is in the complementary role of a panjandrum presiding over the fawning submission of his Sirani wife and hangers-on. In the opening paragraph a grotesque brand of devotional language is

applied to the homage that the odious Willems exacts from the Da
Souza family – 'He loved to breathe the coarse incense they offered
before the shrine of the successful white man' (p. 4). This imagery
gradually widens into an explicit metaphor of Willems's God-like
role:

> he fed and clothed that shabby multitude; those degenerate
> descendants of Portuguese conquerors; he was their
> providence; he kept them singing his praises . . . It is a fine thing
> to be a providence, and to be told so on every day of one's life. It
> gives one a feeling of enormously remote superiority, and
> Willems revelled in it. He did not analyse the state of his mind,
> but probably his greatest delight lay in the unexpressed but
> intimate conviction that, should he close his hand, all those
> admiring human beings would starve.
>
> (pp. 4–5)

The attitudes Willems displays are the least attractive of many
generated on the providential model in *An Outcast*. But while his
assumptions of supremacy reduce those about him to ciphers – he
associates his wife with the parrot and after she has served as an
audience dismisses her with a contemptuous 'Go to bed, dummy'
(p. 9) – the Da Souzas prove to be equally corrupted by their
dependence on him:

> His munificence had demoralized them. An easy task. Since he
> descended amongst them and married Joanna they had lost the
> little aptitude and strength for work they might have had to put
> forth under the stress of extreme necessity. They lived now by
> the grace of his will. This was power. Willems loved it.
>
> (p. 5)

The forces that enable the little anti-hero to 'tyrannize good-
humouredly' over his family are many and diverse – part of the
irony lies in their sheer arbitrariness – but to Willems himself it
appears that his dominant role flows from the 'very nature of
things', and as self-evidently, too, as light from the sun, or
perfume from flowers (p. 3).

In a world in which the institution of *in loco parentis* is taken as
part of a rationally ordained scheme it is easy for Willems to find a
natural sanction for his domestic set-up. Conrad's analysis of the

actual relationships that underlie Willems's patriarchal cloak takes two main directions. It becomes clear in the first place that the social codes which ratify Willems's expression of absolute will leave him locked in sterile self-absorption. In some fine commentary on this phase of the novel, R. Roussel remarks on the self-love that condemns Willems to 'a solipsistic world which makes an authentic life impossible'.[25] Conrad's presentation here may well show the influence of Schopenhauer's key idea that egoism has the effect of insulating the individual from reality.[26] Despite the enormous challenge posed later by Aïssa's beauty, Willems's career ends in a self-conceit as inviolable as that with which it began. He remains a man 'possessed ... by the immovable conviction of his own importance, of an importance so indisputable and final that it clothes all his wishes, endeavours, and mistakes' (p. 327). After he has rejected passion and with it the living world, he moves through a landscape which his egoism has rendered barren:

> Upon the faintly luminous background of the eastern sky, the sombre line of the great forests bounded that smooth sea of white vapours with an appearance of a fantastic and unattainable shore. He looked without seeing anything – thinking of himself. Before his eyes the light of the rising sun burst above the forest with the suddenness of an explosion. He saw nothing.
>
> (pp. 339–40)

When he does use his eyes the jungle merely returns an image of his morbid state:

> Death everywhere – wherever one looks. He did not want to see the ants. He did not want to see anybody or anything. He sat in the darkness of his own making.
>
> (p. 342)

As he becomes increasingly self-enclosed he approaches the fate of those self-defeating egotists whom Schopenhauer memorably characterizes:

> their knowledge remains subject to their will; they seek, therefore, in objects, only some relation to their will, and

whenever they see anything that has no such relation, there sounds within them, like a ground bass in music, the constant inconsolable cry, 'It is of no use to me;' thus in solitude the most beautiful surroundings have for them a desolate, dark, strange, and hostile appearance.[27]

The identity that Willems fashions for himself round the satisfaction of his greed – he marries Joanna only to ingratiate himself further with his employer – leads ineluctably, despite all the reversals and unexpected openings of his subsequent history, to a self-imposed condition of solitary confinement. Abetted by his authoritarian role, Willems ends as the prisoner of his will.

A second aspect of Willems's experience brought into focus by the metaphor of Providence at the novel's start, is his assumption of racial superiority. Although he prides himself on being free of all colour prejudice (p. 35) Willems's sense of importance hinges on the respect he exacts from his mulatto family, and from his situation in the larger colonial context. Willems, as Bruce Johnson shrewdly observes, is the kind of white man who 'falls back on his role as sahib or tuan for all sense of identity, for authority, for moderate success – for all the things he would have to accomplish laboriously among his white peers'.[28] The psychological consequences of Willems's racial patronage only become fully clear when his relationship with Aïssa develops. Passion itself becomes equated in his mind with darkness, until from the ivory tower of his public identity he legislates against his own desires in the name of racial purity:

> He was disappointed with himself. He seemed to be surrendering to a wild creature the unstained purity of his life, of his race, of his civilization.
>
> (p. 80)

> 'The eyes of a savage; of a damned mongrel, half-Arab, half-Malay. They hurt me! I am white! I swear to you I can't stand this! Take me away. I am white! All white!'
>
> (p. 271)

But if in playing God Willems loses his humanity, his creatures also undergo disfigurement. The moment he loses his job and is accordingly dislodged from his position of power, his self-effacing wife reveals an underside of festering rancour. Her eager denunciation of her husband betrays a tell-tale reversal of roles (p. 27) and her brother Da Souza who stands in wait for Willems with a rusty iron bar shows himself already entrenched in the vacated place of authority:

> Do not hurt her, Mr Willems. You are a savage. Not at all like we, whites.
>
> (p. 28)

It is not long before he insinuates that his brother-in-law is a half-breed (p. 29). Among settlers, race and status are so finely intermeshed that in growing assertive, Da Souza inks in his former icon and announces himself white.

While the providential imagery that Conrad applies to Willems is partly mock-heroic (his pretensions to stature are unerringly punctured), it serves also to underline the essentially irrational basis of his authority. It provides a means of articulating the aura so widely attaching to class or to racial dominance in the life and popular fiction of the period. Conrad is in company here with Kipling who, when he offers an 'allegory of Empire' in a short story from *Life's Handicap* (1896), chooses as his central metaphor the all-providing Father. The treatment is characteristically sardonic, for the more successful Naboth proves in easing a benevolent Sahib out of his goods, the more frequently he pleads his devout submission:

> He said I was his father and his mother, and the direct descendant of all the gods in his Pantheon, besides controlling the destinies of the universe.[29]

The same theme, from a very different approach, still informs Paul Scott's Indian tetralogy (1966–75) where the collapse of the Raj is presented in terms of a clash between hieratic and secular conceptions of power.[30] When Conrad returns to this area of concern in *Under Western Eyes* (1911) he shows his young Russian hero struggling to retain a conservative liberalism in the face of Czarist mysticism on the right and a displaced Messianism on the left. For the ruthless President de P— the autocracy of the state is a reflection of an omnipotent God:

the thought of liberty has never existed in the Act of the Creator
. . . revolt and disorder in a world created for obedience and
stability is sin. It was not Reason but Authority which
expressed the Divine Intention. God was the Autocrat of the
Universe.[31]

For the more congenial Mikulin the status quo can be made the
instrument of divinely inspired reform. History for the
revolutionaries, on the other hand – despite their identification of
the church with oppression – also unfolds a providential plan.[32]
Razumov's great temptation is to succumb to such a reading of
events. 'I have the greatest difficulty in saving myself from the
superstition of an active Providence', he confides shortly before
his confession.[33] That he does finally succumb is further witness to
the energies demanded of his independent vision.[34]

In *An Outcast* it is about the figure of Tom Lingard that the
treatment of Providence gathers to a head, and part of the reason
for this is that the old Captain connects with the theme in two
ways. Whereas Willems celebrates an amoral world, building his
career on the maxim, 'where there are scruples there can be no
power', it is precisely firm principles that distinguish Lingard
from the 'unscrupulous, and noisy crowd' (pp. 8, 273). He
upholds a clear-cut code of conduct; but, in addition to that, he is
convinced that right-doing naturally results in material success.
His faith, as the narrator reminds us in a passage of extended
commentary, is both simple and pragmatic:

> In life – as in seamanship – there were only two ways of doing a
> thing: the right way and the wrong way. Common sense and
> experience taught a man the way that was right. The other was
> for lubbers and fools, and led, in seamanship, to loss of spars
> and sails or shipwreck; in life, to loss of money and
> consideration, or to an unlucky knock on the head.
>
> (p. 199)

Lingard, then, is the exponent of an ethical universe. For many,
however, he is also the centre of it. Willems merely heads a cowed
family; Lingard's realm takes in Sambir together with a network
of trade that reaches far up-river, and he wields an absolute
authority over all. What gives him his power is the fortunate
dovetailing of two structures of belief. Though not a religious

man, Lingard derives his confident outlook from the Sunday-school teaching of his native village and from his early contact with the Mission to Fishermen and Seamen. From there, too, derives his impulse to shape stray lives 'under his busy hand' (p. 198). To the Malay community who are only too happy to fall under his despotic spell he represents, at the same time, a magical presence, the *Rajah Laut*, or King of the Sea, a title almost equivalent to that of the semi-divine *Anak Agong* or Son of Heaven whose mystery still tells on Mrs Almayer.[35] Conrad makes it clear that his sovereignty is the product of reciprocally projected traditions. While Lingard plays the part of 'sky pilot', the local people interpret his ledgers as books of magic lore (pp. 198, 299–300).

So dazzled is Lingard by the immensity of his success that he comes to overlook his human frailty. From an instrument of divine purpose he turns into that purpose itself. As is to be expected of the man who has lived 'for years beyond the pale of civilized laws' (p. 235), he evolves some idiosyncratic notions of justice and never wavers in carrying out his resolves. His fiats are received throughout his territory as 'preordained and unchangeable' (p. 235), immutable as Allah's law. Though the narrator holds back, the main lines of a critique of Lingard's character are quick to emerge. We are allowed to glimpse the little red eyes that, glaring out like 'a pair of frightened wild beasts crouching in a bush' (p. 188), betray depths of insecurity behind the swaggering front. More crucially we see that the generosity which is his most remarkable trait often masks a compulsive need for applause, and furthermore that his habit of having his way leads him to place a premium on deference among his acquaintances and friends (pp. 15–16, 32).[36] Lingard remains, all the same, a likeable character and Conrad suggests that he is redeemed not only by the endearing intensities of his Quixotic personality but by his public role. It seems, in a word, that he plays the part of Providence well:

His deep-seated and immovable conviction that only he – *he, Lingard – knew what was good for them was characteristic of him, and, after all, not so very far wrong.* He would make them happy whether or no, he said, and he meant it. His trade brought prosperity to the young state, and the fear of his heavy hand secured its internal peace for many years.

(p. 200, my italics)

The wording of this defence echoes a passage from Alfred Wallace's *The Malay Archipelago* (1869), one of Conrad's favourite books, in which the naturalist concludes an enthusiastic account of 'Rajah' Brooke's rule of Sarawak with the reflection:

> That his government still continues, after twenty-seven years . . . is due, I believe, solely to the many admirable qualities which Sir James Brooke possessed, and especially *to his having convinced the native population, by every action of his life, that he ruled them, not for his own advantage, but for their good.*[37]

Wallace's championship of the adventurer turned *tuan* reinforces the apology for 'paternal despotism' to which he repeatedly returns in the course of his travelogue.[38] Such a system comprises, he readily admits, a violation of his own liberal views:

> we Englishmen do not like despotism – we hate the name and the thing, and we would rather see people ignorant, lazy, and vicious, than use any but moral force to make them wise, industrious, and good.[39]

He excuses himself, however, from applying his principles on the shaky ground that primitive people constitute a special case. The notion of social progress that he proceeds to adduce obviously owes much to the evolutionary sciences:

> There are certain stages through which society must pass in its onward march from barbarism to civilization. Now one of these stages has always been some form or other of despotism, such as feudalism or servitude, or a despotic paternal government; and we have every reason to believe that it is not possible for humanity to leap over this transition epoch, and pass at once from pure savagery to free civilization.[40]

Wallace speaks of a 'struggle for existence' among the Dyaks (that will lead them in due course to 'a more complicated social state') in the same way that he speaks of the 'struggle for life' among animals and plants.[41] A notable feature of his inferences is that he takes the various peoples of Malaysia as the representatives of fossilized stages in his own culture. What sustains his argument is a crude notion of social evolution as at once fixed, single and hierarchical – unsurprisingly he makes free play with various metaphors on 'steps'. In view of the vastly destabilizing effects of evolutionary theory it is ironic that he should fall back on a world picture that amounts to nothing more than the old *scala naturae* translated from space into time. Even when he borrows a metaphor from the life sciences, quaintly using the term 'missing link' to denote the differences between European and local culture,[42] he tacitly relies on a version of the famous chain of being. All movement is uniform and upward and there are to be no leaps. In the last analysis, it is really through a displaced version of Providence that Wallace reconciles himself to the idea of racial hegemony and honorary paternal care.

Although Conrad turns a blind eye to Lingard's native subjects, he follows up every symptom of dependence displayed by his protégés. Once disaster has struck in the form of the Arab take-over of the river, Almayer reproaches his patron for his unreasoning benevolence, bitterly describing himself as one of 'the victims of your infernal charity' (p. 161) but he ends his outburst, all too characteristically, by lamenting Lingard's absence over the period of crisis. The weak will that several critics have observed in Almayer finds a sanction in the subservient stance he adopts towards his manager. About Lingard Almayer's dreams and energies revolve – we learn that he allows his watch to run down whenever the Captain is out of the river – and in him he reposes such trust that when Willems warns of his imminent treachery he takes refuge in the simple consolation that since nothing has gone seriously wrong in the past, nothing ever will (pp. 308, 93). That he should spend the fatal night of Lakamba's assault sewn into a hammock and humped about like a bale of goods underlines the atrophying effect of his habitually passive part in Lingard and Co. The image has its own finality; but the analysis of tutelage is carried further not only through the portrayal of desolation that overwhelms Willems after his betrayal of his benefactor, a loss of self that prompts yet another abject bid for rescue, but through the empty revolt of Willems's and Almayer's wives who, in suffering the loveless marriages engineered for them by their respective patrons, Hudig and Lingard, taste the bitter fruit of casual benevolence. When Willems belatedly discovers that Hudig has married him off to his illegitimate daughter, his comment is conclusive: 'while he worked for the master, the master had cheated him; had stolen his very self from him' (p. 36).

One of the consequences of Lingard's paternal despotism is that his satellites grow reluctant to accept responsibility for what happens to them. Like those equally improvident 'waiters upon Providence', the Durbeyfields of *Tess*, Willems and Almayer favour a fatalistic reading of their histories.[43] 'It wasn't me. The evil was not in me', Willems urges – with all sincerity – when Lingard agrees to see him after his disgrace (p. 273). He convinces himself (and some readers too) that he was *forced* into disloyalty by Babalatchi's schemes; but his pretence is given the lie by the single consideration that he has all along sought to betray Lingard's secret, even at the moment that Lingard has for a second time come to his aid (pp. 18, 43).

The probing of Willems's self-deceit leads Conrad into some of the richest and most innovative writing of the novel. Because Willems is eager to disown all aspects of himself that have led to trouble, he camouflages many of his impulses as external forces acting upon him. His passion for Aïssa accordingly becomes the 'thing that came over me', a 'madness', even possession by the devil. So it is that we witness through his eyes the metamorphosis of his compliant lover into a predator, jailer, murderer and thief (pp. 269–73). Willems distorts reality, however, at the cost of creating a split within himself. In some superbly realized sequences he is shown grappling with his double – in the form, first, of a 'slippery prisoner' over whom he has charge, later in that of a distant figure receding ever further into undergrowth (pp. 78, 145). The idea that sustains the presentation of Willems's breakdown closely parallels the psychoanalytic sense of projection started by Freud with a paper on anxiety neurosis (1894) in which he argues that when the psyche is led into dangerous conflict by a deep, somatic desire it reacts as if it were threatened by an external object[44] – a mechanism he was to illustrate later in the case history of the paranoid Dr Schreber.[45] Appropriately, it is when Willems most vehemently asserts his purity that Aïssa appears most evil; or again, when he most fiercely declaims his innocence that the jungle assumes its darkest aspect (p. 271). To be aware of projection is to take responsibility for oneself.

Willems remains an arrested being: he repudiates the wilderness into which he moves, and his awakened sense of reality is smothered before it quickens into growth. Conrad provides through his uncongenial hero – who alternates between god and underdog, puppet and puppeteer – a twofold exposition of the stunting effects of patronage. Bloated will as much as starved initiative contributes to Willems's incessant defence against the new. Self-imprisonment and projection prove to be his habitual ways of fending off the challenges to an immature soul. Whether he revels in his flattered ego, or fails out of timidity to possess the resources of a freshly disclosed self, the outcome is the same. Conrad's choice of an anti-hero who acknowledges little while being exposed to much enables him to dramatize the gulf between a typically wishful view of life and that irrational world which the novel owes, in part, to nineteenth-century science. In *An Outcast of the Islands* Conrad set out to undermine what Freud was to call 'presumption on the part of man'; and one of his targets, a myth whose detection Freud ascribed to Darwin and his collaborators, was the notion of 'a divine descent which permitted [man] to break the bond of community between him and the animal kingdom'.[46]

Conrad's depiction of his hero's passion for Aïssa has been read as an outright condemnation of sexual love.[47] But it is, rather, Conrad's appreciation of erotic intensity that gives him insight into the way love can represent a dire threat to the ego. His exact identification of sexual desire with the experience of death (pp. 80–1, 141, 152) is in keeping with a recent insistence on the continuity of violence and lust: so Georges Bataille, for instance, opens his *Death and Sensuality* with the question, 'What does physical eroticism signify if not a violation of the very being of its practitioners?'[48] The truculence of Willems's passion is a part, in any case, of the overall stress that Conrad lays on the moral ambivalence of our deep-seated energy, a theme which flows from a perceived disjunction between social identity and the instinctual life. Willems's sensations, variously described as 'deadly happiness' (p. 141), 'idiotic beatitude' (p. 140), and 'delirious peace' (p. 141) express the paradox of a human psyche, the parts of which do not cohere in accordance with some master plan.

Accounting in *The Malay Archipelago* (1869) for a staple of Dyak diet, Wallace remarks that the huge juicy fruits of the Durian are not infrequently also a cause of death:

Poets and moralists, judging from our English trees and fruits, have thought that small fruits always grew on lofty trees, so that their fall should be harmless to man, while the large ones trailed on the ground. Two of the largest and heaviest fruits known, however, the Brazil-nut fruit (Bertholletia) and Durian, grow on lofty forest trees, from which they fall as soon as they are ripe, and often wound or kill the native inhabitants.

After describing the damage inflicted by the spiny cases of the fruit he impresses a sober moral on his readers:

From this we may learn two things: first, not to draw general conclusions from a very partial view of nature; and secondly, that trees and fruits, no less than the varied productions of the animal kingdom, do not appear to be organized with exclusive reference to the use and convenience of man.[49]

Both plots and setting of *An Outcast of the Islands* radiate from a vision of man's eccentric place in the universe, and the lesson drawn by the great naturalist, whom Conrad hailed not only as a pioneer explorer but as a 'profoundly inspired' man, provides a suitable epigraph to the early work.[50]

7 The Hidden Man:

Heart of Darkness, its context and aftermath

Placed between *Youth* and *The End of the Tether* in a volume which Conrad once described as a rendering of the 'three ages of man', *Heart of Darkness* resolves, when scanned, into a composite image of lost innocence.[1] A central evil looms against a range of human hopes and draws depth from the relief. There is the dimming of Kurtz's original idealism, guyed at the central station and reflected at the end in the pale purity of the Intended. There is the clouded naïveté of the 'Harlequin' whose round eyes have grown used to horror; and there are, though of differing sincerity, the pious pretences of the Aunt and of the Company which the narrative bluntly punctures. For Marlow the trip up the Congo marks no less than life's 'culminating point' (p. 51), and what brings his crisis to a head is the recognition of a truth which passes relatively undisguised in the remote setting until it emerges plainly in Kurtz. The grim disclosures that await Marlow at the continent's centre acquire a universal status, and the journey into the interior takes on, in consequence, the character of a psychological progress. That the journey carries the further implication of a return to a primordial past shows that Conrad is intent, once again, on impressing the view, current among many writers in the thrall of evolutionary theory, that man is irrecoverably shaped by his origins, flawed by a darkness welling from his heart.

But while Marlow's story revolves about the brutality of the instinctual life, we are made aware, from the first, of man's capacity to distance himself from his impulses. Action aboard the sea-bound *Nellie* is suspended as the incoming tide swings the yawl about her anchor in the Thames and her resigned pilot retires sternwards to join a listless crew. Then it is that, through the eyes of the bridging narrator, we glimpse Marlow sitting with legs crossed 'right aft':

He had sunken cheeks, a yellow complexion, a straight back, an ascetic aspect, and, with his arms dropped, the palms of hands outwards, resembled an idol.

(p. 46)

Over the immensity of the twilit scene Marlow broods like a Buddha (the comparison is offered three times – pp. 50, 52, 162), and his mood spreads through the group of friends as the narrator dryly observes:

We exchanged a few words lazily. Afterwards there was silence on board the yacht. For some reason or other we did not begin that game of dominoes. We felt meditative, and fit for nothing but placid staring.

(p. 46)

The switch between active and meditative states reappears in Kurtz (who is as much icon as beast once pacified by the current of the African river); and for many readers this interplay would have had behind it the famous distinction drawn by Schopenhauer between the world as will and as idea. Conrad seems to have held, like the philosopher whose work he knew well, that while reality is grounded in the instinctual life, any true representation of it entails a relaxation of the will.[2] Oriental belief is frequently invoked in *The World as Will and Idea* to illustrate the notion of 'pure perception' but Schopenhauer's thinker lifts the veil of illusion to find, not the omnipresent Godhead sought by the Buddhist or Brahmin, but a cycle of energy and pain from which he is only momentarily free. On this view the release that consciousness brings is necessarily fraught with tragic insight; and it is such a notion that Conrad voices in a letter to Cunninghame Graham:

What makes mankind tragic is not that they are victims of nature, it is that they are conscious of it. To be part of the animal kingdom under the condition of this earth is very well – but as soon as you know of your slavery the pain, the anger, the strife – the tragedy begins.[3]

This comment has a particular bearing on *Heart of Darkness* (1899) for it was the Congo, Conrad told Garnett, that put an end to that golden period of his youth when, without a 'thought in his head', he led the life of 'a perfect animal'.[4]

The picture of innocence that unfolds in *Youth* is Marlow's picture of himself on his first long voyage. Here, in place of the *dégagé*, almost sardonic narrator of *Heart of Darkness*, we have a rhapsodic Marlow bent on recapturing the lost sources of his joy – 'Oh Youth! . . . pass the bottle', is the chant of his rite. Self-absorption is the premise of the story through which the youth moves in a cocoon of self-generated assurance, neither minding disaster ('Now this is something like. This is great. I wonder what will happen', he exclaims when the deck blows up about his feet), nor responding to the shadowy world that lies beyond the blaze projected by his high spirits:

> Oh, the fire of [youth], more dazzling than the flames of the burning ship, throwing a magic light on the wide earth, leaping audaciously to the sky, presently to be quenched by time, more cruel, more pitiless, more bitter than the sea – and like the flames of the burning ship surrounded by an impenetrable night.[5]

Though Conrad's appreciation of these energies is more generous, his youthful hero resembles, in his state of blithe encapsulation, Schopenhauer's type of the unregenerate whose vision is blinkered by a *principium individuationis*. Happiness, in this sphere, is 'only the dream of a beggar in which he is a king, but from which he must awake [to] the suffering of his life'; and perception is limited to 'phenomena as separated, disunited' rather than being levelled at 'the inner nature of things, which is one'.[6]

The parallel is telling for it underlines an important feature of *Heart of Darkness* – a tendency to abstract, to assert underlying rhythms and set echoes going. Though this principle may begin with atmosphere, with that 'sinister resonance' which Conrad was at pains to play across the whole, it reaches, as we shall see, into the metaphoric and thematic structure of the work, and constitutes itself finally as that search for kinship which is, in essence, Marlow's quest.[7] One pointer to Conrad's esemplastic concern comes in the striking comparison of Marlow's story-telling to a haze illuminated by an inner source of light. Such a unifying radiance contrasts with the discrete, final sense of the downright sailor's yarn ('the whole meaning of which lies within the shell of a cracked nut', p. 48), and the contrast is given further force by the immediately foregoing account of how Marlow's wanderlust sets him apart from the run of sailors for whom 'home is always with them – the ship' (p. 48). The image lingers, for Marlow reports later that his crisis in Africa 'seemed somehow to throw a kind of light on everything . . . and into my thoughts. It was sombre enough . . . and yet it seemed to throw a kind of light' (p. 51). This numinous glow stands at a remove from the brilliant imagery of flame accorded, in the earlier story, to a younger, still ardent self.

That the hero of *Youth* rejoices in the life of will and remains rooted in the phenomenal world, does nothing to restrict his love of adventure, however. The Far East holds for him, unlike others on his boat, all the 'whispered promise of mysterious delight'; and on arriving there he imagines himself gazing at *terra incognita* through the eyes of 'ancient navigators'.[8] It is, indeed, this romantic, wilful exploration that sets off Marlow's disenchanted view in *Heart of Darkness*. For here the first narrator, when he celebrates the 'great knights-errant of the sea', draws on just the sort of descriptive colour used in *Youth*, his roll of great Englishmen conjuring up something like a firework display over the Thames. In reply to his chauvinism Marlow pictures the *Roman* exploration of *Britain*, incidentally telescoping the proud imperial metaphors of 'torch' and 'sacred fire' into a mere 'flicker' in the passage of time (pp. 47, 49). But even before he receives his answer some irony creeps into the narrator's collocation of glorious deeds ranging

> from the *Golden Hind* returning with her round flanks full of treasure, to be visited by the Queen's Highness and thus pass out of the gigantic tale, to the *Erebus* and *Terror*, bound on other conquests – and that never returned.
>
> (p. 47)

Conrad accentuates the note of mortality struck in the reference to Franklin's Arctic trip by pointing up the lexical clash of the ships' names (in *Youth* the night sky is 'black, black as Erebus'), but he could count also on his reader's familiarity with the gruesome outcome of this expedition – the starvation, and the cannibalism practised by some last survivors.[9] For a moment the lamp of adventure gutters in the dark, oppressive air of *Falk* (1903) whose forbidding hero staves off death in icy latitudes by eating a man he has killed in self-defence.

Marlow's sketch of the Roman settlement in Britain serves as a strategic link between the romantic parade of English explorers and the Belgian occupation of the Congo which provides the chief subject of the novella's first part. It opens up a field for Janus-faced comparisons in which Britain figures both as wilderness and as invading power. Despite the occasional vague word that Marlow puts in for imperialism (on rereading we may be reminded of Mark Antony's 'And Brutus is an honourable man'), the main thrust of his preamble is directed against colonization which he strips down to *realpolitik*:

> It was just robbery with violence, aggravated murder on a great scale, and men going at it blind – as is very proper for those who tackle a darkness. The conquest of the earth, which mostly means the taking it away from those who have a different complexion or slightly flatter noses than ourselves, is not a pretty thing when you look into it too much.
>
> (pp. 50–1)

Although Marlow is speaking here of the Romans it is with a generality that comprehends not only the Eldorado Exploring Expedition who set off into the tropical forest with all the rapacity of 'burglars breaking into a safe' but even the *Golden Hind* returning from the New World with treasure-laden flanks (pp. 87, 47). The other face of the Janus-headed equation, that of Britain as subject nation, crops up again when Marlow, well-launched into his account of the Congo Free State, comments on the depopulation caused by the colonizers: what would happen, he asks, if a body of mysterious, armed men 'took to travelling on the road between Deal and Gravesend, catching the yokels right and left to carry heavy loads for them'? (p. 70). The comparative view – 'truth stripped of its cloak of time' (p. 97) – is the habit of Marlow's outlook, and it is around the issue of exploration that his recurring concern with lost innocence first crystallizes.

What tempts Marlow into seeking immediate employment with the company is the snake-like course of the Congo, glimpsed on a map in a shop window, but his itch for African adventure goes back to the fascination he felt as a boy for the largest blank on his atlas. The magic of this space is, however, a thing of the past; and that 'mysterious delight' which the Marlow of *Youth* associates with unvisited places has altogether vanished with it:[10]

it was not a blank space any more . . . It had ceased to be a blank space of delightful mystery – a white patch for a boy to dream gloriously over. It had become a place of darkness.

(p. 52)

In context the image has particular force for while it sustains the tonal contrasts of the opening, and restates Marlow's rebuttal of the first narrator's rhapsody, it introduces a rhetoric of cancellation, instances of which will range from the comic,

. . . the great man himself. He was five feet six . . .

(p. 56)

. . . he was amazing, and had a penholder behind his ear . . .

(p. 67)

to the sinister,

[he] was making correct entries of perfectly correct transactions; and fifty feet below the doorstep I could see the still tree-tops of the grove of death.

(p. 70)

Marlow's blank map provides a foil as precise as that supplied by the dazzlingly punctilious Accountant, and one yet more comprehensive, for it functions as a symbol of innocence, an innocence full-blooded enough, moreover, to include the assertive aspects of selfhood. To the usual associations of whiteness the empty space adds the spice of invitation. To the dreamer it offers a screen free of interference, and to the adventurer a challenge. Even an explorer as beset by unforeseen hazards as was Stanley on his first crossing of the continent, could find a tonic in the prospect of entering uncharted territory. 'This enormous void', he declaims, 'blank as it is, has a singular fascination for me':

Never has white paper possessed such a charm for me as this has, and I have already mentally peopled it, filled it with most wonderful pictures of towns, villages, rivers, countries, and tribes – all in the imagination – and I am burning to see whether I am correct or not . . . To-morrow, my lad, is the day we shall cry – 'Victory or death!'[11]

Between blind elation of this kind and the contemplative brooding of Marlow there falls the social and psychological experience that finds expression in *Heart of Darkness*.

And in describing the biographical roots of this experience Conrad turns once again to the contrast between his childhood fantasy of the blank map and its sordid realization, almost two decades later, at Stanley Falls:

> Yes, this was the very spot. But there was no shadowy friend to stand by my side in the night of the enormous wilderness, no great haunting memory, but only the unholy recollection of a prosaic newspaper 'stunt' and the distasteful knowledge of the vilest scramble for loot that ever disfigured the history of human conscience and geographical exploration. What an end to the idealized realities of a boy's daydreams! I wondered what I was doing there.[12]

It is clear from the essay 'Geography and Some Explorers', from which this passage comes, that the Congo Free State played a part in Conrad's development comparable in some respects with the French Revolution or the events of 1848 in the lives of previous generations of writers. Spelling out the reality of Leopold's colony, a speaker in a parliamentary debate of 1903 applied, really rather tamely, a remark of Guizot's on the Second Republic: 'it began with Plato and ended with the gendarme'.[13]

When Conrad joined the *Société Anonyme Belge* it was on the understanding that he would be part of an inland exploring party under the leadership of a certain M. Delcommune.[14] The essay on geography shows how his appetite for such adventure had been stirred by an extensive and lifelong reading of African explorers.[15] To this literature *Heart of Darkness*, although it ranks among Conrad's most closely autobiographical works, reveals an important debt, and one that has escaped due attention. The matter is delicate not only because the exact limits of Conrad's experience will never be clear (the *Congo Diary* gives away little) but because the influence proves remarkably far-reaching and tenacious. There are, within short range, a variety of descriptive parallels, a brief list of which would certainly include the shattering account of conditions on a coastal mine placed near the start of Schweinfurth's *The Heart of Africa* (1873),[16] Stanley's lecture to the irritable Barttelot on the necessity for restraint in the tropics, and, from *In Darkest Africa* (1890) again, his recurrent application of sea and beast imagery to the jungle.[17] There are, too, as we shall see, some strong points of resemblance between the personalities of Kurtz and Burton. Further sought but more deeply pertinent, however, are the formal characteristics that *Heart of Darkness* shares with African travelogues of its period.

In his essay on exploration Conrad remarks on the way the scientific spirit of 'militant geography' had largely given place in his lifetime to less disinterested forms of travel; and this change is reflected in a switch towards more popular narrative modes in most travel writing. Even writers like Barth and Schweinfurth who uphold the tradition of Humboldt, make substantial concessions to an audience on the lookout for adventure. And while Schweinfurth often shows himself torn between his avowed aim of demythologizing Africa and an urge to instil suspense, his work, after the lapse of a decade, is singled out as an example of all that is reductive in the scientific mind by Stanley, who boasts of his own success in 'relegating dryness to the maps'.[18] Another contribution to the collapse of empirical austerity in Africa is proposed by Philip Curtin who points out that as routes became more taxing, explorers were 'selected for their ability to make a difficult journey and still survive'.[19]

One upshot of this development was the importation of dynamic plot to the travelogue, and in the case of such popular successes as Burton's *Mission to Gelele* (1864), Schweinfurth's *The Heart of Africa* (1873), and Stanley's *How I Found Livingstone* (1872) or his *In Darkest Africa* (1890) it is essentially the same plot: a journey into the interior leads, at its furthest point, to a climactic meeting, usually with an important personage (the King of Dahomey, Livingstone, Emin Pasha, – in Schweinfurth's case, with the Pygmies) about whom the reader is kept briefed from the first. The climax, furthermore, often brings some horrifying disclosure – cannibalism among the neighbouring tribe to the Pygmies, the Niam-Niam, in Schweinfurth; human sacrifice at Gelele's annual So-Sin custom in Burton; or, failing that, a resource of which Stanley makes the most, a subtle reversal of expectation such as the laconic greeting of Livingstone, or the guarded reception of Emin Pasha of his would-be rescuers. Plots of this kind are not confined to travelogues, of course; and Marlowe's obsessive yet anti-climatic tracking down of Kurtz might convincingly be bracketed with the hunt conducted in

Henry James's *The Aspern Papers* (1888) by the narrator in search
of a mentor's relics, were it not that the African setting raises an
important assumption of the period that gives further life to a
formal comparison. Almost without exception, the explorers
concerned are tempted to regard Africa as a segment of primeval
history miraculously translated to the present.[20]

Even for the level-headed Schweinfurth the more primitive
tribes (and there is a tendency to see the centre of the continent as
their proper home) still cling to 'great mother Nature'; from which
it is a short step to describing Africa as 'the embryo of the most
advanced civilization'. And, for all his debunking, Schweinfurth
parades the Pygmies, when they at last appear, as if they were
mysterious castaways on the evolving globe – 'a living
embodiment of the myths of some thousand years!'[21] Even men as
diverse in outlook as Livingstone and Burton find common
ground in the nostrum of a *living past*. For Burton, East Africa lays
bare 'man's rudimental mind' while for Livingstone the traveller
is 'thrown back in imagination to the infancy of the world'.[22]
Stanley adheres, most persistently of all, to the imagery of
creation. He compares a Pygmy couple met on his route to Adam
and Eve, adding for good measure that they represent 'the oldest
types of primeval man'. Though his idea of genesis is
evolutionary, the Old Testament frequently runs in his head: mist
rising over Lake Albert recalls the description of Chaos, and,
echoing Genesis again, he prides himself on being the first
European to gaze on the Congo basin 'since the waters
disappeared . . . and the earth became dry land'. To the
mysterious immanence of the past Stanley frequently returns,
comparing all life on the continent to an unageing Rip van
Winkle, and Africa itself to the dark stillness of the hours before
dawn.[23]

Coming back to *Heart of Darkness*, we find not only that
Marlow's journey into the interior is shadowed by a figurative
recovery of the past but that his whole approach to Kurtz is
charged by the metaphor. At a first view from the sea, the
landmass of Africa has a nascent look, 'almost featureless, as if still
in the making' (p. 60), and once the central station is put behind,
the comparison resurfaces:

Going up that river was like travelling back to the earliest

beginnings of the world, when vegetation rioted on the earth
and the big trees were kings.

(p. 92)

From then on the primeval aspects of the settings are focused often
enough for phrases such as 'the night of the first ages' to take on an
incantatory quality. Out of the metaphor of time-travel Conrad
develops a trajectory far more conspicuous than that found in any
travelogue, but his aims are principally psychological, and he
avoids the literalism that marks the 'living fossil' theme in much
fiction of his period.[24]

Many novelists proved only too keen, indeed, to trade on a
pseudo-scientific resurrection of the monsters that 'militant
geography' had long since laid. In J. P. Webster's *The Oracle of
Baal* (1896), for example, a Professor and his companion stumble
on the Affri (a band of anthropoids) before reaching a 'cave of
sleep' at the continent's centre, which holds the bones of many
extinct creatures and a monstrous ape. Though in more muted
guise, the idea of a mysteriously preserved past enters *King
Solomon's Mines* (1886) when the explorers find themselves trapped
in the presence of the Kukuana dead, silicified over the centuries
by the dripping roof of their cavern. A more sprightly version of
Haggard's 'hall of death' turns up in Buchan's *Prester John* (1910)
where the rites and regalia of a newly revived cult, dating back to
the Queen of Sheba, are housed in a resplendent grotto. Whether
Conrad was acquainted with this tradition of 'African' novels it is
hard to say, but his debt to the travelogues certainly seems to have
been reinforced by a knowledge of *A Journey to the Center of the Earth*
(1864), the famous fantasy by Jules Verne in which a professor
and his nephew encounter, on their way down a volcano, living
specimens from ever more ancient history – an enraged
ichthyosaurus figuring prominently among the beasts they watch.
Marlow on viewing the coastline only *feels* that he is 'about to set
off for the centre of the earth'; and the 'ichthyosaurus' covered
with glitter is his imaginative reading of a bathing hippo (pp. 60,
86). To his surroundings he responds, it is fair to say, as would any
cultivated Victorian.

What, in fact, distinguishes Marlow as a traveller is the
readiness with which he acknowledges kinship with the African
setting. He makes his journey, as we shall see, the occasion of a

series of insights into the atavistic sources of his own mind. One aspect of this recovery is the affinity he discovers between himself and Kurtz, who has in the course of his regression effectively *reversed*, as Ian Watt puts it, 'the direction of historical evolution'.[25] It is clearly Conrad's intention that Marlow should be seen to find, in his long-delayed meeting with the tantalizing stranger, a fully explicit version of his own buried identity. There is an irony in that what lies in wait for Marlow at the end of his quest proves to be an image of himself. But although such structural feats belong to fiction rather than to the travelogue, similar subtlety is at work in Burton, that most shrewd and brisk of African explorers, who not only highlights the changes he experiences in himself on escaping the bonds of civility, but delights in showing that the excesses of the dark continent are in no way foreign to Europe though they may exist there in camouflaged form. In the opening pages of his *First Footsteps in East Africa* (1856), the account of his journey to the Moslem stronghold of Harar where he passed as an Arab – as he had done earlier in Mecca – Burton gives a diverting account of the way his party, on entering the desert, broke into all the 'joviality arising from a return to Nature'.[26] He quotes a line from Dryden's *Conquest of Granada* celebrating man in his 'free' state, and noting the easy happiness of his Arab companions, wryly remarks that 'it is not only the polished European [who] lapses with facility into pristine barbarism'.[27] He takes up the same topic in a more sonorous way at the start of *Zanzibar* (1872), insisting on the physical exuberance that rewards the man who shakes off 'the fetters of Habit . . . and the slavery of Home'.[28] Marlow, though less of a primitivist and correspondingly less susceptible to the allure of the outward-bound, does at least admit a thrilled response to his surroundings (p. 96). That he keeps his desire in check, refrains, in his own words, from going ashore 'for a howl and a dance' (p. 97) marks the boundary between himself and Kurtz, whose lack of inhibition in this regard may well owe something to Burton. Kurtz is repeatedly associated with 'midnight dances ending with unspeakable rites' (human sacrifices are hinted at), and it is on such an occasion that Marlow nobbles him as he crawls on all fours before a swaying figure with a headgear of horns (pp. 118, 142–3). The scene represents the nadir of atavistic regression for Kurtz, and also for Marlow who revels in the 'boyish game' of tracking down his quarry and, on finding him,

threatens to smash in his head. Marlow revealingly owns that the
beating of the drum became confused, at this point, with the
beating of his heart (p. 142); and it is worth noting here that tribal
dancing seems to have supplied a particularly good touchstone in
the nineteenth century of attitudes towards the primitive. At one
extreme there is Robert Moffat, the missionary, for whom the
sight of dancing blacks raised the spectre of hell-fire: 'There has
been much dancing and singing today', he records on visiting the
Matabele, 'it is a terrible barrier, not to know the language of a
people who are dancing on to everlasting destruction.'[29] For
reasons less doctrinaire Schweinfurth also found the sound
repelling, so much so that he sprinkled the parchment of some
Nubian drums with muriatic acid.[30] Burton, however, seems
never to have missed an opportunity for joining in the revelry. In a
climactic scene from his *Mission to Gelele* he tells how he took part
in the dance that initiated the complex rituals of human sacrifice
at the Dahomey court, both imitating the king's decapitating
gestures, and drinking to his health from a cup made of an
enemy's skull.[31] His account includes the short sketch of a
sorcerer who sways about and presides over the dance with horns
attached to his head.[32] But despite the sensational nature of the
matter he conveys, Burton is careful to sabotage any pat recourse
to moral shock on the part of his readers. If Byron drank from a
skull, why not Gelele? Or, come to that, are the captives and
criminals executed in the state rituals of Dahomey treated with
less dignity than the victims of public hanging in Europe? And is
the Dahomean custom of gluing a cowrie shell with blood onto the
musket stock for each dead foe really any different from the
English practice of decorating soldiers, seeing that it too
'stimulates murder, and excites perpetual jealousies in the
service'?[33] Because of these dry, Montesquieu-like sallies into
comparative savagery, as well as his sensual abandon, Burton
supplies a bridge between the dark continent and a European
audience, and Kurtz functions in the same way.

One indication of Kurtz's representativeness is that proposals
for models of him have never been in short supply. Many
historical figures contributed to Conrad's portrait and Burton,
even if his claims have been overlooked, is surely among them.
Although he seems to have lacked Kurtz's degree of cruelty and to
have left, unlike Stanley, a record quite free of slaughter, Burton
had a reputation for what Livingstone broadly terms 'bestial

immorality' and was more often known as 'the white nigger' than by the tag of 'amateur barbarian' that he gave himself.[34] With Kurtz he shares not only a remarkable range of intellectual gifts but a link also with diabolism that he did much to flaunt.[35] Just as Kurtz is alternately seen as angel and fiend, so Burton was credited by Swinburne with 'the brow of a god and the jaw of a devil', while to the more prosaic Speke he became the man who had 'gone to the Devil in Africa'.[36] His interest in erotica and his lifelong campaign against Victorian prudery (of which his *Arabian Nights* translation was only a part) lie behind his boast that he 'speaks the things that others think and hide'.[37] It was probably the candour with which he expressed his nihilism and lust that turned him, after his death in 1890, into a hero of the *fin de siècle*. Tributes to his physical vitality and profound despair go hand in hand. In language close to some of Marlow's, Swinburne speaks of 'the look of unspeakable horror in those eyes which gave him at times an almost unearthly appearance'.[38] And while Arthur Symons testifies to his 'tremendous animalism, an air of repressed ferocity, a devilish fascination', Frank Harris reassuringly notes that 'deep down in him lay the despairing gloom of utter disbelief'.[39]

Conrad's debt to the explorers turns out, then, to be a complex one. Biographical influence apart, it ranges from specific if unconscious borrowing to a deep abstraction of form. But the travelogues bear on *Heart of Darkness* in still another way. Conrad was addressing an audience whose ideas of Africa and particularly of the Congo were largely moulded by their reading of travel writing, much of which sold very well. During the eighteen-nineties the eyes of Europe were fixed on Central Africa in any case, and Conrad's readers were in some respects fairly well informed. My contention, then, is that Conrad uses certain images with an awareness of the significance they held for a wide public and that, because this significance has in some cases been lost, the full argument behind his exposure of conditions in the Congo no longer shows. Where these conventions come most strongly into play is in the picture of the social evil that accounts for Marlow's lasting disillusion.

While it is true that explorers paved the way for the colonization of Africa, they were often critical of it and responsible to some extent, too, for the campaign against exploitation that began to gather impetus before the publication of *Heart of Darkness*.[40] Even

Stanley, twice in the employ of King Leopold, found it expedient to warn against unscrupulous rule as early as 1890.[41] But the voice of protest was raised first in connection with slavery, long before imperialism took hold in the continent during the eighteen-eighties. And there can be no doubt that the efforts, principally of Livingstone, but also of Cameron, Baker and many others, greatly advanced the move to end slavery in Africa, hastening in particular the decisive treaty with the Sultan of Zanzibar of 1876, which broke the main channels of the Arab trade. So deeply was the public imagination stirred by the abolitionist cause that the European powers were quick to appropriate it as a chief weapon in the moral armament of empire. By far the most notorious case is that presented by the Belgian king who in a spirit of cold cynicism put abroad a smokescreen of pious pretence behind which he manoeuvred himself into private ownership of the Congo.[42] Many were the scientific and philanthropic institutions, including a Society for the Suppression of Slavery (known to Kurtz) through which he rallied support for a goal which he saw entirely in terms of national status and his own gain. He seems to have sensed that the anti-slavery lobby would provide the most effective spearhead in what he advertised as a latter-day Crusade. He certainly knew what he was about when, in his inaugural speech at the first of many international conferences, he re-echoed the words recently engraved in Westminster Abbey on Livingstone's tomb. 'May Heaven's rich blessing', the explorer's legend read, 'help to heal this open sore of the world'; and Leopold's speech ran:

> Before the horrible evil of the slave-trade, which in the interior of Africa claims over 100,000 victims yearly, the citizens of civilized countries must come to an agreement to heal the sore. The headquarters of this humane undertaking might well be situated on Belgian soil.[43]

The first trading stations on the Congo were set up accordingly as ' "pacifying" bases from which to abolish the slave trade', and they were modelled, in theory, on the socialist ideal of the *phalanstères*.[44] Another counter in all the talk (among a circle known to Marlow's Aunt) was the redeemed slave, to be known as the *libéré*.[45]

Marlow's description of his first view of the workers at the company station is justly famous. Without any striving for pathos it unfolds a series of images which are devastating in their precise notation of misery and degradation:

> A slight clinking behind me made me turn my head. Six black men advanced in a file, toiling up the path. They walked erect and slow, balancing small baskets full of earth on their heads, and the clink kept time with their footsteps. Black rags were wound round their loins, and the short ends behind waggled to and fro like tails. I could see every rib, the joints of their limbs were like knots in a rope; each had an iron collar on his neck, and all were connected together with a chain whose bights swung between them, rhythmically clinking.
>
> (p. 64)

For contemporary readers, however, this passage carried, along with its kinetic evocation of feeling, a quite distinct iconographic significance. The chain-gang with an armed escort (who appears here, at the end of the paragraph) was the most basic of the images associated with slavery in Africa. Such a procession was described by every explorer from Mungo Park to Stanley and frequently illustrated in accompanying plates.[46] The fact that the men Marlow sees are required to *work* while in chains, again falls in with the picture of Arab cruelty painted by traveller after traveller – Park, for example, dwelling on the pain caused to slaves in the file by 'walking quick with heavy loads upon their heads'.[47] One of the most wrenching passages in Livingstone's work describes the 'broken-heart' that overtakes, and often kills, those who pass life 'chained together by the neck, and in the custody of an Arab armed with a gun';[48] and this aspect of slavery, too, is reflected in Marlow's mention of the 'deathlike indifference' of the men in the chain. Norman Sherry has suggested that it is very unlikely that Marlow's observations at the company station were drawn from Conrad's own experience at Matadi (there is, for one thing, no word in the *Congo Diary*) and this leaves us freer to speculate on the strategy that underlies a shattering scene.[49]

And really the point is clear. Conrad is out to show that slavery persists in everything but name and that, for all the banners of Holy War, the Congolese have done no better than suffer a change of masters. The passage looks forward to a central tenet among Leopold's critics after the formation of the Congo Reform Society in 1904 – and a commonplace of later colonial debate – to what

Dilke would term 'the general recrudescence of slave conditions in disguise'.[50] Perhaps the charge was most bluntly framed by Roger Casement when he refuted the claim that the Congo administration had abolished slavery with the retort:

> It has not suppressed the Slave Trade, it has merely substituted itself for the Arab who formerly exacted service from the native.[51]

The political pressures that sustained the supply of forced labour in the Congo were to be analysed by Morel in a series of books, one of which bears the title *The New African Slavery* (1904). Chief among these pressures were the appropriation of raw materials by the state; the imposition of taxes; and drastic restrictions on free trade. Though these measures were only partially in operation at the time of Conrad's visit to the Congo in 1890 (the situation there was to deteriorate rapidly in the early years of the decade) their implications are brought home, all the same, in *Heart of Darkness* (1899). The Manager's plan to remove the freelancing 'Harlequin' would later have received the sanction of law, but *that* he can do without:

> 'We will not be free from unfair competition till one of these fellows is hanged for an example,' he said. 'Certainly,' grunted the other; 'get him hanged! Why not? Anything – anything can be done in this country.'
>
> (p. 91)

No doubt the laws which Leopold introduced in the early nineties often articulated existing practices.[52] Kurtz's raids for ivory represent only a small deviation from the later, official uses of tax-collectors – which gives a dark twist to the question Marlow asks of the Manager: ' "Do *you*", said I . . . "call it 'unsound method'?" ' (pp. 128, 137, my italics).[53] The official raids were punitive: hands were sometimes brought back as a guarantee that the job had been properly done. And Conrad shows just how loose the concept of punishment at the stations was when the scapegoat for a burning shed is brutally flogged, a company man interjecting: 'Transgression – punishment – bang! Pitiless, pitiless. That's the only way' (pp. 76–7, 80). The true status of the chain-gang of 'criminals' described by Marlow would have been specially clear to a number of Conrad's readers. Under the title 'Cruelty in the Congo Free State', the *Century Magazine* had published the journals of Edward Glave, a young explorer who died at Matadi in 1895, and he tells how large groups of captives from the punitive raids were shipped, and then impressed as labour further down the river:

> In the fighting consequent upon this policy, owing to the inability or disinclination of natives to bring in rubber, slaves are taken – men, women, and children, called in state documents *libérés*! These slaves, or prisoners, are most of them sent down-stream, first to Leopoldville.[54]

To this damning testimony Glave adds the bitter comment:

> If the Arabs had been the masters, it would be styled iniquitous trafficking in human flesh and blood; but being under the administration of the Congo Free State, it is merely a part of their *philanthropic* system of *liberating* the natives.[55]

It is not surprising that Kurtz blindfolds the figure of Liberty in the painting that marks his disillusion, or that he presents her countenance as thrown into sinister relief by the light of her own torch (p. 79). The eyeless face recalls Marlow's verdict on the Roman conquest of Britain: 'It was just robbery with violence, aggravated murder on a great scale, and men going at it blind' (p. 50).

Conrad proceeds, in the course of a sentence, to turn the 'criminals' in the chain-gang into ordinary company workers, who despite the 'legality' of their contracts, are dying of despair in the grove of death: 'They were not enemies, they were not criminals, they were nothing earthly now', Marlow reports of the group of huddled figures emerging from the shade (p. 66). Throughout the episode attention is focused on the arbitrariness of the labels that are fixed to a reality which lies beyond immediate apprehension until hideously defaced. A recurring piece of symbolic action captures the sense of an imposition that is at once violent and futile. Marlow is made intermittently aware, as he makes his tour of the station, of blasting in progress on a cliff:

> A heavy and dull detonation shook the ground, a puff of smoke

came out of the cliff, and that was all. No change appeared on the face of the rock . . . The cliff was not in the way or anything; but this objectless blasting was all the work going on.

(p. 64)

The muffled explosions that leave the rockface unpuckered recall, from the previous page, the French frigate firing at 'enemies' or, in plainer words, shelling the continent. While gazing at the 'criminals' Marlow gathers these diverse strands to a single head:

Another report from the cliff made me think suddenly of that ship of war I had seen firing into a continent. It was the same kind of ominous voice; but these men could by no stretch of imagination be called enemies. They were called criminals, and the outraged law, like the bursting shells, had come to them, an insoluble mystery from the sea.

(p. 64)

The passage is a crucial one for it opens up a vista of cultural relativity against which the European presence stands out as an intrusion. Conrad boldly poses the question, so often shelved in colonial fiction, of what excuse there can be for such a 'fantastic invasion'. The phrase is repeated three times, and in a context on each occasion that reverberates the earlier 'objectless' blasting: the shadows of the Manager and his uncle, to quote one instance, trail 'behind them slowly over the tall grass without bending a single blade' (pp. 92, 76, 131). Marlow returns to the imagery of the cliff when he accounts for his feelings before that further manifestation of impenetrable innocence, the Intended, whose 'soul as translucently pure as a cliff of crystal' fends off the sepulchral voice that still runs in his head (pp. 151–2). On this important train of imagery the best possible gloss is supplied by Schopenhauer in a passage which probably contributed to Conrad's inspiration. In discussing the latent influence of Buddhism and other Oriental beliefs Schopenhauer remarks:

We, on the contrary, now send the Brahmans English clergymen and evangelical linen-weavers to set them right out of sympathy, and to show them that they are created out of nothing, and ought thankfully to rejoice in the fact. *But it is just the same as if we fired a bullet against a cliff.* In India our religions will never take root. The ancient wisdom of the human race will not be displaced by what happened in Galilee.[56]

His remark comes as part of a plea for self-transcendence (which implies cultural transcendence as well), without which there is no knowledge of justice.[57] In 'Autocracy and War' (1905) Conrad writes, in a similar vein, that it is 'our sympathetic imagination to which alone we can look for the ultimate triumph of concord and justice'; and the same essay reflects Schopenhauer's quietism in the well-known diagnosis it offers of empire building:

> The intellectual stage of mankind being as yet in its infancy, and States, like most individuals, having but a feeble and imperfect consciousness of the worth and force of the inner life, the need of making their existence manifest to themselves is determined in the direction of physical activity . . . Let us act lest we perish – is the cry. And the only form of action open to a State can be of no other than aggressive nature.[58]

An ability to see beyond the promptings of the appetitive and proselytizing will is the mark of maturity.

The characters in *Heart of Darkness* are distinguished, as has often been said, by the way they relate to their setting. On the one hand, there are the company agents who pass their time in a haze of self-absorption. Since nothing unconnected with personal gain is solid to them they lead a cut-throat existence unrelieved by either fellowship or compassion:

> The only real feeling was a desire to get appointed to a trading-post where . . . they could earn percentages. They intrigued and slandered and hated each other only on that account.
>
> (p. 78)

Their favoured form of contact with the aborigines takes the form of firing blindly into the bush. Marlow stands apart from these 'pilgrims' not only because of his ready sympathies but because he possesses from the first a sense of Africa as aggressively *real* – vested, indeed, with a stark immediacy that makes the pretences and daily business of the company, even memories of his own past, seem comparatively dream-like, surreal or farcical (pp. 61, 76, 78,

93). Because Marlow often draws attention to the opacity of the setting it is easy to lose sight of this important characteristic. And though he repeatedly stresses his failure to understand what he sees (in itself a token of his rapt attention) such negative capability confers, in any case, a proper freedom on the things he presents. He puzzles, for example, over the function of the charm or *keti* (a device commented on by Burton in *Central Africa*) worn around the neck of the dying man whom he tends in the grove; and the matter is left in doubt until clarified in the account of the stoker (pp. 67, 98).[59] Marlow, in short, learns to read the signs which he identifies as alien and this distinguishes him from the other company men who remain locked, like the Aunt, in a world of their making. Even the 'Harlequin', whose pure spirit of adventure is limited by narcissistic regard ('[he] enlarged my mind', p. 125), serves as a foil to those outgoing impulses which make Marlow in Conrad's judgement 'a most discreet, understanding man'.[60]

Like Melville's narrator in *Moby Dick*, Marlow is blessed with a gift for assimilation and, like Ishmael again, he is drawn to the idea of a mysteriously unified world. A vision of kinship is the outcome of his journey; and his chief epiphany, which comes midway in the text, is inspired by the beating of drums. Earlier still he has reflected on the possibility that the nightly tattoos have 'as profound a meaning as the sound of bells in a Christian country' (p. 71) and now he calls attention, again, to the apparent indeterminacy of tribal custom ('whether it meant war, peace, or prayer we could not tell', p. 95), even to an apparent discontinuity between Africa and the West ('we were cut off . . . we could not understand'), before confessing to his involvement in the Dionysian scene:

> if you were man enough you would admit to yourself that there was in you just the faintest trace of a response to the terrible frankness of that noise, a dim suspicion of there being a meaning in it which you – you so remote from the night of first ages – could comprehend.
>
> (p. 96)

It is then that Marlow reports his insight into the far-reaching sources of the individual life:

And why not? The mind of man is capable of anything – because everything is in it, all the past as well as all the future. What was there after all? Joy, fear, sorrow, devotion, valour, rage – who can tell? – but truth – truth stripped of its cloak of time. Let the fool gape and shudder – the man knows, and can look on without a wink.

(pp. 96–7)

The acuity of Marlow's intuitive response is illustrated later when he alone of the crew rightly interprets the cry that rises from Kurtz's disappointed followers – though seemingly from the mist – as an expression of grief rather than anger. His clairvoyance is virtually complete when he senses that the howl of pain fits his own feeling of loss for Kurtz, whom he supposes dead (pp. 106–7, 114). From time to time Marlow may cling (as Ishmael does) to a work-a-day ethic but he never confuses protective belief with the truth (p. 93); and his extended sympathies are shown in his deep intuition of kinship with the dying helmsman (p. 119) as well as in his progressive understanding of Kurtz.

If Marlow corresponds, then, to the man who in Schopenhauer's scheme has lifted the veil of illusion, Kurtz, until the very last stage of his life, represents the *principium individuationis*, the fully embodied will. Because he succeeds in *acting out* that collective mind of which Marlow speaks, Kurtz engrosses every primitive trait and appears as the epitome of his 'primeval' setting. 'There is all Africa and her prodigies in us', Sir Thomas Browne wrote in *Religio Medici* (1643), reviving an already outmoded myth of correspondence: in *Heart of Darkness* Marlow founds a similar notion on the evolutionary premise that every organism has grown out of, and so contains, antecedent forms of life. From an essentially biological idea of continuity Marlow extrapolates wildly, like most thinkers of the time, and his assumption that Africa mirrors a remote stage in the development of European civilization is in every way inadmissable. It is worth recognizing, however, that at a period when Africans were generally (and perhaps increasingly) seen as a race apart, the novella's stress on underlying kinship amounted to a restatement of the abolitionist's slogan, 'Am I not a man and a brother?'.[61] But the terms, of course, were different. In place of a myriad reflections of the Divine Image, Conrad proposes a brotherhood based on a nature red in tooth and claw. No one would mistake

Kurtz for the type of sociable man. He comes close, after all, to murdering his only confidant for a small supply of ivory, and voracity is the clue to every department of his life, as witnessed by his remark, 'My Intended, my station, my career' (p. 147). Where Marlow, true to Schopenhauer's contemplative man, abstracts from the particular in his search for a 'truth stripped of its cloak of time' (p. 97), Kurtz behaves like the prisoner of will who 'regards his person as absolutely different and separated by a wide gulf from all others'.[62] His internal struggles correspond, moreover, to the philosopher's picture of the 'inward horror' that overtakes the man who asserts himself 'to the absolute denial of the same will appearing in other individuals'.[63] What men have in common, however, is not necessarily what enables them to relate, and it is the rational virtue of restraint, enshrined in Marlow's cannibal crew, that Conrad in a most complex exposition (traced definitively by Watt) celebrates as the ground of civility.[64]

Marlow and Kurtz represent opposite nodes of experience and the worlds they inhabit are texturally distinct. Self-knowledge, in the classical sense, is Marlow's aim (p. 150) and he is associated throughout with the faculty of sight: 'do you see?', he demands of his listeners, and he conceives his relation to Kurtz as that of a man peering into a dark abyss (pp. 82–3, 149). More Judaic than Marlow, Kurtz is concerned to *be* rather than to *know*. His rage for expression is linked with the auditory and vocal ('He was . . . a voice', pp. 113–15); his life aptly summed up in the phrase, 'He said it' (p. 151). The polarity is complicated, however, by the fact that Marlow in the course of his self-exploration embraces those 'forgotten and brutal instincts' which are alive in Kurtz (p. 144). Indeed, Marlow encloses Kurtz and this sense is rendered texturally through the way he himself, in telling the story, becomes a voice speaking out of darkness (p. 83). Again, because Marlow's approach to Kurtz and his growing awareness of the wilderness are two faces of a single thing – his penetration of that hidden 'mind of man' – it is unsurprising that the same imagery attaches to each. Marlow when he first sees the coast catches 'an air of whispering' (p. 60), and this fancy, thrown back by the wilderness (p. 131), becomes at length a trait of Kurtz, who is all voice, or whisper (pp. 113, 151, 159). In much the same way the ambivalence that Marlow attributes to his surroundings ('smiling, frowning', 'grand, mean', p. 60) carries over into his intuitions of Kurtz who is 'an angel or a fiend', 'an appeal or . . . a menace' (pp. 81, 114). Kurtz might be said to *voice* his setting, if Marlow did not remind us at times that he is something of a ventriloquist. Holding beliefs about the unknown, he once suggests, is comparable to peopling Mars with creatures who walk on all-fours (pp. 81–2). Marlow is well on the way to creating Kurtz before they meet, and the truth of his projections is guaranteed by the 'mind of man', by an underlying uniformity in nature – a bald abstraction, true enough, but one brought to life in Conrad's treatment of the setting. And a single setting it is that envelops the action. The closing paragraph clinches a general awareness that *one* watercourse stretches from Gravesend to the heart of Africa, and, taking homogeneity still further, Marlow frequently compares the jungle, in its invasive and procrustean aspects, to the sea (pp. 86, 92, 156). Encoded in the solemn opening with its insistence on the illimitable ('an interminable waterway', 'vanishing flatness') and indifferentiable ('the sea and the sky were welded together without a joint') is the promise of a narrative in which boundaries will steadily dissolve.

Marlow's inner adventures are not conveyed analytically. Rather they are evoked through a symbolic mode appropriate to the inscrutable depths in which *Heart of Darkness* deals. One device which Conrad employs to link Marlow with Kurtz is that of the double. Much in the way that Scrooge in *A Christmas Carol* (1843) finds the face of his old partner Marley in his frontdoor knocker, Marlow on ringing the doorbell on his visit to the Intended, sees Kurtz staring at him out of the glassy panel; and the apparition, or reflection, immediately follows his attempt to suppress 'all that remained of him with me' (pp. 156, 155).[65] Earlier he has found himself so closely involved in Kurtz's illness that he narrowly escapes a similar fate: 'the pilgrims buried something in a muddy hole. And then they very nearly buried me' (p. 150). The tie between the two of them goes back to the fact that they are paired by the other company agents as alarmingly honest and influential men. Noting this, Marlow – despite his hatred of deceit – lies for Kurtz; and shortly afterwards Conrad sustains an ambiguity that leaves a momentary doubt as to which of them is to be the victim of the Manager's murderous schemes (p. 89).

It is formal pointers such as these that alert the reader to the common ground that is increasingly cleared between Marlow and Kurtz. Given the nature of his theme Conrad's dramatizations are often wonderfully light in touch. Cannibalism is among the uglier traits attaching to Kurtz, who opens his wide mouth 'as though he had wanted to swallow all the air, all the earth, all the men before him' (pp. 134 and 155) – the simile leads irresistibly to further dark thoughts about the 'unspeakable rites' (p. 118).[66] It is a comic moment, on the other hand, at which Marlow, wondering what can restrain the starving crew, first appraises the 'pilgrims' and then himself from a fresh angle:

> it occurred to me I might be eaten by them before very long, though I own to you that just then I perceived – in a new light, as it were – how unwholesome the pilgrims looked, and I hoped, yes, I positively hoped, that my aspect was not so – what shall I say? – so – unappetizing.
>
> (pp. 104–5)

How exactly right it is that Marlow should turn cannibal only in regard to his eyes.

Perhaps the most taxing problem posed by *Heart of Darkness* lies in the relation between Conrad's attitude to the Congo Free State and his attitude to Kurtz. We move from the exposure of a horrendous social evil to a figure who, though deeply implicated, is sufficiently magnetic to have convinced many readers that he is a hero. Part of Kurtz's function, of course, is to supply a moral index. His frank impiety serves to strip away the bogus pretences of a company whose motives and procedures are in the last analysis as brutal. But he emerges also, troublingly, as a fund of energy – as a 'devil', granted, but of a fiery rather than flabby variety (p. 65). Even if we allow that his glamour has sometimes been overdone – at his entrance on a stretcher he is 'appalling', 'atrocious', 'pitiful' – he does lend, the fact remains, a *natural* aspect to iniquity. That Conrad meant this to be so, and that he was aware of the sting in the tail of his story is pretty clear from a comment he made to Cunninghame Graham after the appearance of the first of the three instalments: 'So far the note struck chimes in with your convictions – mais après? There is an après.'[67] When the reality of Leopold's rule became public, there were those who sought to pass off the affair as a hideous accident – the result of a particular conjunction of laws in an unfortunate 'system of government'; for others, like Conrad, and later Keir Hardie, the Congo Free State yielded 'an image of the whole past of the human race'.[68]

Conrad dwells on the naturalness of evil, however, only to insist that nature is not enough. In common with many writers who absorbed the impact of evolutionary theory he sees that *physis* and *nomos* are essentially disjunct, and is determined to show that human ideals exist in defiance of what man, by instinct, is. His view matches that expressed by T. H. Huxley in the Romanes Lectures:

> Let us understand, once for all, that the ethical progress of society depends, not on imitating the cosmic process, still less in running away from it, but in combating it.[69]

It is no surprise, then, to find that although Marlow responds to a deep vitality in Kurtz, he honours him solely for the strenuousness of his struggle with himself, and for the judgement implied in his last words, 'The horror! The horror!' (pp. 145, 147, 149, 157). The Kurtz who finally comes in for celebration is the contemplative figure whose dying insight comprises a symbolic, if unavailing, 'moral victory' (p. 151).

To drive home the creative status of moral principle, Conrad resorts in the closing pages of *Heart of Darkness* to a ploy similar to that used by Wilde in his witty riposte to naturalism, 'The Decay of Lying' (1889), when he has Marlow lie to the Intended in order to save 'that great and saving illusion' which is her innocence (p. 159).[70] But although ignorance provides one way of transcending the material truth, it does not, as the easy collapse of Kurtz's original idealism shows, provide the best way of combating it. And so, even while Marlow acknowledges the value of cloistered belief ('lest [our world] gets worse', p. 115), he gently indicates that the Intended, like Kurtz before her, is the prisoner of an egocentric will:

> I pulled myself together and spoke slowly.
> 'The last word he pronounced was – your name.'
> I heard a light sigh and then my heart stood still, stopped dead short by an *exulting* and terrible cry, by the cry of *inconceivable triumph* and of unspeakable pain. '*I knew it – I was sure!*'
>
> (pp. 161–2, my italics)

It is a choice of nightmares that leads Marlow to stand by Kurtz, but the choice Conrad offers his readers is a less distressing one, for Marlow's contemplation is of a kind that sharpens understanding of the world, and he remains, despite his disillusionment, a man who can both act and know.

Of the great novelists Conrad was the last who could claim to be something of an explorer, and it is with a fair degree of truth that he presents himself, in an essay written towards the end of his life, as having outlived the era of exploration. The undiscovered places, he observes there with evident nostalgia, 'have vanished as utterly as the smoke of the travellers' camp fires in the icy night air of the Gobi Desert'.[71]

After Conrad, novelists dealing in the encounter with unknown places were mainly to rely on historical settings. Somerset Maugham in *The Explorer* (1907), a novel which hinges on a reworking of the last scene in *Heart of Darkness*, opts for the Africa known to Burton and Stanley.[72] There was otherwise a tendency to fall back on very vaguely located settings as Conan Doyle does, for example, in his ingeniously literal treatment of a return to the past in *The Lost World* (1910). Altogether apt but lucky is E. M. Forster's choice in *A Passage to India* (1924) of a specific setting which happens to qualify. If *Moby Dick* represents *terra incognita* on the move, the Barabar hills comprise a fossil form: rock so ancient as to suggest 'flesh of the sun's flesh' enfolds pockets of inner emptiness 'sealed up before the creation of pestilence or treasure'.[73] As the century advances, however, the remaining frontiers of earth and ocean become fewer as well as more specialized; while science fiction – at least in its more popular forms – steadily stales those belonging to the future. For the most part the explorer finds his base in the historical novel, and of this territory Patrick White has proved himself the genius.

These, then, on a straightforward view, are the chief directions taken in the twentieth century by the novel of exploration. It is worth noticing, all the same, that the kind has a separate issue in many of the masterpieces of modernism. The link is provided by a shared interest in *inner* exploration, in producing the hidden man. While it would be naïve to suggest that when the fund of exotic places ran low writers turned to the novel instead, it is the case, nonetheless, that the special concern of a work like *Heart of Darkness* – Marlow's search for the *mind of man* ('everything is in it,

all the past as well as all the future') – persists almost unchanged
into a fiction that is comparatively plotless and domestic.
Although Conrad's text was undoubtedly influential, the notion
of a collective mind gathered impetus, of course, quite
independently of it. D. H. Lawrence spoke for many when he
hailed Freud, in a resounding Homeric simile, as a 'supreme
explorer'.[74] Belief in the unconscious as something delimitable or
reclaimable like land, became standard, and its growth, as of
much else in the modern period, can be traced back to the seeds of
evolutionary theory. Though less thorough-going than Jung who
thought that his patients reproduced 'in every detail the myths,
cosmogonies and primitive conceptions of the early ages of man',
Freud raised elaborate theories of development – relating
narcissism to the 'animistic phase', and so forth – on the
assumption that each individual re-enacts the stages of cultural
life, or that 'ontogeny recapitulates phylogeny' as the biologists
had it.[75] While the competitive aspects of Darwin's theory,
deriving historically from Malthus, were taken up by Nietzsche
and by Marx (who once remarked that *The Origin of Species* (1859)
served him 'as a natural scientific basis for the class-struggle'), the
notion of an all-inclusive, unconscious mind seems to have been
precipitated by the idea of all creation sharing in a common
ancestry.[76]

Myths of correspondence have always appealed to the
imagination and writers in the early decades of the century were
only too eager to find terms and expressive means for the newly
sanctioned *Ineinsbildung*. So it is that Lawrence in his famous letter
to Garnett speaks of his desire to break away from the 'stable ego'
and deal instead with the elemental substrate that sustains the
various 'allotropes' of character;[77] that T. S. Eliot in *The Waste
Land* has Tiresias, the androgynous seer, 'unite' all the other
figures in the poem;[78] that Virginia Woolf in *To the Lighthouse*
relates the 'wedge-shaped core of darkness' that stands for Mrs
Ramsey's unrealized self to the 'triangular purple shape' which
Lily Briscoe, the artist, aims to portray;[79] or that James Joyce in
Ulysses develops the theme of 'all in all of us' with its corollary of
the self meeting the self in the other, and makes over *Finnegan's
Wake* to the dream of Here Comes Everybody.[80]

In the work of these writers there are many allusions to
Conrad's great novella, which more decisively, perhaps, than any
other single text, heralds the advent of modernism. Particularly

resonant, in this respect, is the imagery of tropical Africa which, while it provides a literal analogue to Marlow's inner nature in *Heart of Darkness*, later becomes a metaphor or sign for the instinctual life. The shift is already visible in Henry James's story *The Beast in the Jungle* (1903) where a hero who pictures some future achievement in terms of the title's heroic image and evades, on this excuse, sexual commitment to the woman he might love, learns too late that what the jungle truly denotes is the heart, from which he is never more estranged than on his travels in the tropics. From this it is a short step to the language of the rain-forest and nucleolating dark that Lawrence uses in *The Rainbow* (1915), after Skrebensky's return from Africa, to give substance to the regenerative forces of the blood. In the same novel he borrows an idea from *Heart of Darkness* to express his sense of the quicker man that lies buried in each citizen:

> He was out in the wilderness, alone with her. Having occasion to go to London, he marvelled, as he returned, thinking of naked, lurking savages on an island, how these had built up and created the great mass of Oxford Street or Piccadilly. How had helpless savages, running with their spears on the riverside, after fish, how had they come to rear up this great London, the ponderous, massive, ugly superstructure of a world of man upon a world of nature![81]

We have seen how a concern with man's underlying nature recurs in novels about exploration, and to this vibrant account of it Marlow, for all his wariness, had led the way.

8 The Country of the Mind:

Exploration as metaphor in *Voss*

Sidney Nolan, to whom Patrick White dedicated his künstler-roman *The Vivisector*, created in his series on Kelly a pictorial emblem that can readily be identified (alongside the documentary accounts of Leichhardt and other explorers) as a source of inspiration for *Voss*.[1] Ned Kelly, the plucky outlaw who played God to the colony of Victoria, figures, in Nolan's expressionist paintings, as a stark metallic centaur presiding over the outback. Through Kelly's grid-like head (which conveys the impression that he simultaneously faces inland and looks back) the spectator sees, in place of eyes, the desert or sky that lie beyond. In *Voss* (1957) White repeatedly presents his hero, like Ned Kelly, as a frame to the space through which he advances. Voss's eyes, 'light-coloured' or 'infinite blue', provide a disconcerting lack of resistance to the gazer.[2] To Mr Bonner who 'would never stray far beyond familiar objects' Voss remains unfathomed, 'lost to sight in his [eyes], as birds are in sky' (p. 20); while to Laura who 'might have sunk deeper than she had at first allowed herself into the peculiarly pale eyes' (p. 21), surrender to the unfathomable exists as a potential from the start. Even as narrator White succeeds in sustaining the pictorial emblem without any noticeable loss of realism. Voss is seen to hold the landscape in his eyes, either by reflection or through the fullness of his gaze:

> Seated on his horse and intent on inner matters, he would stare imperiously over the heads of men, possessing the whole country with his eyes. In those eyes the hills and valleys lay still, but expectant, or responded in ripples of leaf and grass, dutifully, to their bridegroom the sun, till all vision overflowed with the liquid gold of complete union.
>
> (p. 165)

Through this double exposure of mind and landscape, White points to that equation of spatial and psychological exploration which generates the form of *Voss* and finds a compressed statement towards the novel's close: knowledge comes of torture in the 'country of the mind' (p. 475).

That the narrative of Voss's exploration serves as an analogue to inner disclosure has been noted by several critics. In an early but perceptive monograph R. F. Brissenden observed that it was White's intention to 'cut through to the spiritual centre . . . just as . . . his hero struggles towards the geographical centre of the continent'.[3] More recently Brian Kiernan has commented on White's deployment of 'the romantic voyage of discovery as an exploration of the self', and called attention to the 'structural metaphor' of the novel by tracing the correspondences that develop between the experience of the expeditionary party, and of those who remain behind in Sydney, principally Laura but also Willie Pringle and Belle.[4] What I shall concentrate on are the meanings that White encodes on the concrete side of his extended and largely concealed metaphor – the meanings that he derives, in fact, from his treatment of landscape. The expressive values of the many plastic codes through which the central conflicts of the novel develop have not had, I believe, their proper share of attention.

Laura, we are told at the novel's start, has been suffocated by the 'fuzz of faith':

> She did believe, however, most palpably, in wood, with the reflections in it, and in clear daylight, and in water.
>
> (p. 11)

She provides a valuable guide to the text itself when in the closing pages she counsels the group of aspiring spirits gathered about her 'to interpret the ideas embodied in the less communicative forms of matter, such as rock, wood, metal, and water' (p. 475). We have only to recall a pervasive textural preoccupation of the novel – the metamorphosis of stone into flesh, and of living forms into vegetation – to see that the dreams and hallucinations which Voss experiences in the desert are given a significance that goes beyond his own, highly idiosyncratic, case. Around his central equation White builds up, by degrees, a language of sense that enables him (more fully perhaps than he realizes at times) to transmit the issues of psychological and ethical debate through the very landscape that his explorer perceives and half-creates. Because they unfold stage by stage, the procedures which generate the grammar of this language require gradual analysis.

At the start of *Voss* White establishes the co-ordinates of the exploratory metaphor through a series of muted comparisons relating inwardness to space. Hence Voss is reported 'happiest in silence, which is immeasurable, like distance, and the potentialities of self'; or again, coaxed into social response, he gestures 'out of that great distance to which he was so often withdrawn' (pp. 24, 34). The contrast between the silence that Voss shares with Laura (also 'happiest shut with her own thoughts', p. 9) and the stupor of self-satisfaction that prevails at the Bonners' meal is paralleled by the opposing attitudes towards the outback shown at the table, where indifference to Voss's quest is associated with a careless neglect of inner reality:

> 'Of course,' said Mrs Bonner, who loved all golden pastrywork, and especially when a scent of cloves was rising from it. 'Nor did we really have time to understand Mr Voss.'
> 'Laura did,' said Belle. 'Tell us about him, Lolly. What is he like?'
> 'I do not know,' said Laura Trevelyan.
> I do not know Laura, Mrs Bonner realised.
> The Palethorpes coughed, and rearranged the goblets out of which they had gratefully sipped their wine. Then a silence fell amongst the flakes of pastry.
>
> (p. 31)

True, it is at Laura's expense that the first equation of dreams with the interior is made:

> she was also afraid of the country . . . But this fear, like certain dreams, was something to which she would never have admitted.
>
> (p. 13)

But she is at least ready, after her first meeting with Voss, to admit to her fear of the inland and to generalize from it:

> 'Everyone is still afraid, or most of us, of this country, and will not say it. We are not yet possessed of understanding.'
>
> (p. 31)

In defending Voss, Laura affirms the value of introspection, and in doing so she offends the company gathered at the Bonners' table who retaliate with parochial complicity: 'she was of the same base metal as the German' (p. 32).[5]

Voss's commitment to the desert and Laura's equivalent commitment, her willed intimacy with Voss and, after his departure, with her emancipist servant Rose (each of whom holds up to her the challenge of a desert; pp. 94, 80–1), represent diverse if convergent quests, yet they provoke from Sydney society a similar reaction since both involve the realization of an uncovenanted self. At the Pringles' picnic where Laura and Voss are identified as 'sticks', there is little to choose, in the eyes of their mercenary host, between dreams and unprofitable land:

'There may, in fact, be a veritable paradise adorning the interior. Nobody can say. But I am inclined to believe, Mr Voss, that you will discover a few blackfellers, and a few flies, and something resembling the bottom of the sea. That is my humble opinion.'

Mr Pringle's stomach, which was less humble, rumbled.

'Have you walked upon the bottom of the sea, Mr Pringle?' the German asked.

'Eh?' said Mr Pringle. 'No.'

His eyes, however, had swum into unaccustomed depths.

'I have not,' said Voss. 'Except in dreams, of course. That is why I am fascinated by the prospect before me. Even if the future of great areas of sand is a purely metaphysical one.'

(p. 67)

Truth is not a valued commodity in the Bonners' world. It necessarily conflicts with Mr Bonner's determination to render himself 'safe . . . from attack by life' or with Mrs Bonner's self-protecting 'upholstery' which extends even to the euphemisms in which she swathes all reference to sex and death (pp. 372, 12). Although wonderfully acid, White's satiric treatment of prosperous Sydney seldom lacks good-humour. It spells out, all the same, a constrictive milieu in which cultural aspirations are ignored or reduced to a show and in which feelings are acknowledged only when they coincide with form. Alienation from such a society carries the possibility of grace.

Voss himself is never wholly exempt from the play of White's comedy and we intermittently view his self-confidence as a blank but unhonourable cheque – notably at the moment that Mr Bonner produces the scarcely charted map:

> 'The map?' said Voss.
> It was certainly a vast dream from which he had wakened.
>
> (p. 26)

But Voss's desire to 'attempt the infinite' holds the promise of a life richer than one 'choked by the trivialities of daily existence' (p. 38); and the social context delineated in the first part of the novel accordingly enforces an ambivalent estimate of his arrogance. We side with Laura's view that arrogance is the quality that 'just saves him, terrible though it is'(p. 78). The 'simplicity and sincerity' that underlie it (p. 26) are clearly evident in the reasons he gives Le Mesurier for joining him:

> Every man has a genius, though it is not always discoverable . . . But in this disturbing country, so far as I have become acquainted with it already, it is possible more easily to discard the inessential and to attempt the infinite . . . you will realise that genius of which you sometimes suspect you are possessed, and of which you will not tell me you are afraid.
>
> (pp. 38–9)

The expedition is founded on a faith in undisclosed resources of human potential; and the desert is the symbol of this dream before it proves its actual setting.

Among the visionary jottings in the notebook that represents his fulfilment Le Mesurier distils the most concentrated statement of the exploratory metaphor:

> We do not meet but in distances, and dreams are the distance brought close.
>
> (p. 315)

Patrick White may not uphold any systematic belief in the collective unconscious, but this statement does point to the way in which the movement through the desert is accompanied, on the part of the central characters at least, not only by a growing awareness of what has been hidden but also by a progressive disclosure of unanimity. The almost clairvoyant relationship that develops between Laura and Voss provides White with one means of dramatizing this 'meeting in distance', his application of a fairly homogeneous symbolic scheme another. The correspondence between geographic and psychic penetration accounts for the growing dominance of an expressionistic mode in which the 'world of dream' weighs equally with the 'world of semblance'. The image in which White expresses this oscillation between the internal and external – the opening and closing of a butterfly's wing (p. 277) – lends itself to the narrative switches which prevail in the later part of the novel, not only to the alternation of Sydney with the desert but, within each of these settings, to the parity bestowed by the narrator on the hallucinatory and the real. Voss's recreations of Laura's presence, for example, are given the same status as the events of the present:

> Voss, Palfreyman, and Laura continued to walk towards the cave. The selflessness of the other two was a terrible temptation to the German.
>
> (p. 308)

The novel becomes, to put it crudely, more modernist as the narrative proceeds; and White, if perhaps only unconsciously, reinforces this stylistic shift with a chronological succession of literary reminiscence. So the first chapter of the novel shares its situation with the first chapter of *The Europeans* (1878) – the young lady of the house while her family are at church offers a glass of wine to the young man who arrives unexpectedly from afar; and Rose Portion's story in the fourth chapter – she has been transported after conviction for the murder of her illegitimate child – echoes Hetty Sorel's history from *Adam Bede* (1859). Reminiscences of Henry James and George Eliot yield, however, to something closer to Tennessee Williams' *The Glass Menagerie* (1945) when we come to the account of Palfreyman's sister, the deformed girl who cherishes images of crystalline perfection, an account that leads to the heart of Voss's torment.

In accordance, then, with a trajectory that at once penetrates outer and inner space, the narrative increasingly transcends the historical distance of its setting. Before we trace Voss's discovery of 'the country of the mind' we need to return, however, to the novel's social matrix. For the two chief, and allied expressions of

Voss's development – the sequence of his presented dreams, and his creation of Laura – are given significance by the peculiar estrangement which he suffers prior to setting out. It proves, indeed, to be a psychologically as well as socially entrenched state that finds release in the ever more animated landscape that spells his change of heart.

The claustrophobia which repeatedly overwhelms Voss in the opening chapters testifies in part to the stuffiness of the Sydney ambience. Under bombardment in the Bonners' drawing-room, swaying on his legs and 'almost crazed by people', Voss experiences a desire to be at large which we are encouraged to respect:

> Deadly rocks through some perversity, inspired him with fresh life. He went on with the breath of life in his lungs. But words, even of benevolence and patronage, even when they fell wide, would leave him half-dead.
>
> (p. 21)

That asylum from unmentionable realities, the padded carriage from which he tears an exit on returning from the Pringles' picnic, again legitimizes his need for escape. We learn, however, that his fear of enclosure is more deep-seated – that it is often tantamount, in fact, to retreat. A revulsion from the 'palpitating bodies of men' determines, for example, his change from medicine to botany as a student in Germany (p. 16). It is, again, a suspect notion of freedom that prompts him to 'tread with his boot upon the trusting face of the old man, his father' (p. 16), and sever all ties with his family whose image continues to threaten across the world:

> He smelled the stovy air of old, winter houses, and flesh of human relationships, a dreadful, cloying tyranny, to which he was succumbing.
>
> (p. 120)

Voss's mission is inspired, in short, by a dread of intimacy, and the compensatory nature of his venture inland emerges in the telling phrase: 'I have every intention to know it with my heart' (p. 36). In common with Palfreyman who, it later turns out, has sought the desert to escape the recognition that he cannot save his sister, Voss seeks the oblivion as well as the challenge of the unknown. Propelled as much by his recoil from human need as by an ambition to realize his genius in the wilderness, Voss – like Nolan's Kelly – looks both forwards and back.[6] An urge to defuse all challenging relationships consigns him to a figurative waste long before the expedition sets out, and the splendours of 'solitary travel' continue to appeal even after the party has been settled (p. 133). His pride appears, too, in the way he retires into a private 'world of desert and dreams' the better to relish 'the illusion' of his own strength (pp. 29, 75).

The hint of pathological flight is concealed from Voss by the trappings of transcendental philosophy in which he clothes his quest. His utterances on the supremacy of the will have been ascribed (despite obvious anachronism, for the novel is set in 1848) to the influence of Friedrich Nietzsche but they belong rather, as their peculiarly ascetic bias shows, to a romantic strain of German idealism. Voss's belief that a gratuitous act of will can disclose a source of Divine Power (pp. 95-6), and his concomitant contempt for unbelief ('*Atheismus* is self-murder') are consonant with Fichte who in his *Vocation of Man* identified will as the key to the noumenal world, and celebrated its autonomy:

> the sensuous life of every finite being points toward a higher life, into which the will, by itself alone, may open the way . . . My will, directed by no foreign agency in the order of the supersensual world but by myself alone, is this source of true life, and of eternity . . . The will rejects absolutely all earthly purposes, all purposes lying outside itself, and recognizes itself, for its own sake, as its own ultimate end.[7]

The maxim, 'To make yourself, it is also necessary to destroy yourself' that Voss addresses to Le Mesurier – who excuses himself by disclaiming such heights ('I shall wallow a little in the gutter, I expect, look at the stars from a distance, then turn over', p. 38) – is in keeping with Fichte's pronouncements on dying into life through a sacrifice of 'the sensuous and all its objects', a sacrifice undertaken as a categorical act of will:

> By this renunciation of what is earthly, faith in the Eternal first arises in our soul, and is there enshrined apart, as the only support to which we can cling after we have given up all else, as

the only animating principle that can elevate our minds and inspire our lives. We must indeed, according to the figure of the sacred doctrine, first 'die unto the world and be born again, before we can enter the kingdom of God'.[8]

In this life-denying creed of aspiration, Voss masks his dread of human relationships. His ideal of self-sufficiency, his creation of an unassailable identity, that of the explorer attempting the infinite, derives from weakness as much as from intransigence. And though, given the limitations of the community in which he finds himself, his refusal to compromise takes on value, it never amounts to more than a preliminary condition of his development. Laura recognizes this when she sees, at different times, that if Voss is saved by his arrogance he is also damned by his pride (pp. 78, 96). Accordingly, in terms of the theological scheme stated towards the novel's close, Voss's self-exaltation comprises merely the starting point of 'the three stages': 'Of God into man. Man. And man returning into God' (p. 411). His idea of dying into life, appropriated from the *zeitgeist*, receives a broader and more traditional treatment at the hands of Patrick White, for it is through recognition of his frailty that Voss will ascend (p. 411), and through failing to achieve success as an explorer that he will experience 'the mystery of life' (p. 289).[9] The destiny and identity that Voss has chosen for himself are set, from the very first, on a collision course. To the petulant protest of the man who has deified himself – 'I detest humility . . . Is man so ignoble that he must lie in the dust, like worms?' (p. 161) – the desert has its answer, and what Voss the romantic *isolato* discovers there, even if that discovery takes place largely in solitude, is the self in relation. Unlike Kurtz who represents a starkly egotistical version of the natural man, Voss proves a social being at heart. It is through the erosion of the adamantine self that inspires, and continues to inspire his progress, that Voss finds grace.

Almost from the start he images his intransigence as crystalline and mineral, and the association is reinforced by his contrastive alignment of love with all that is 'soft and yielding', 'easily hurt' and thus to be evaded (p. 45). In his first recorded dream we see him seeking assurance that the identity he has elected for himself is proof against the claims of others:

It was not possible really, that anyone could damage the Idea, however much they scratched at it. Some vomited words. Some coughed up their dry souls in rebounding pea-pellets. To no earthly avail. Out of that sand, through which his own feet, with reverence for velvet, had begun to pay homage, rose the Idea, its granite monolith untouched. Except by Palfreyman – was it? He could not distinguish the face, but the presence was pervading the whole dream. And now Voss was stirring on his straight bed. It was a humid night. His hands were attempting to free his body from the sweat with which it had been fastened.

(p. 48)

To Voss who compares his strength to 'the power of rock or fire' (p. 67) the igneous monolith, combining homogeneity with the utmost recalcitrance, is the apt symbol of his willed identity. (The self-dependence of Laura and of Judd are by contrast those, respectively, of marble and oolitic stone, pp. 9, 145.) Palfreyman, whom Voss has identified as an apostle of humility, figures accordingly in his dream as an appropriate challenger to the supremacy of the Idea, to the extent that Voss is stirred from his sleep and, as the self-reflexive construction indicates, vainly attempts to free his body from self-induced bondage.

The debate between pride and humility is first fully joined when Voss, shrinking again from the 'soft and defenceless', fends off Laura's solicitude at the Bonners' party:

'Ah, the humility, the humility! This is what I find so particularly loathsome. My God, besides, is above humility.'

'Ah,' she said. 'Now I understand.'

It was clear. She saw him standing in the glare of his own brilliant desert. Of course, He was Himself indestructible.

And she did then begin to pity him. She no longer pitied herself, as she had for many weeks in the house of her uncle, whose unfailingly benevolent materialism encouraged the practice of self-pity. Love seemed to return to her with humility.

(p. 96)

Hectic in isolated quotation, this statement evolves out of the sensuous details of a minutely realized scene in which shifting states of mind are dramatized through the perceived textural contrasts between the crystalline and the yielding, between stone and flesh. A dish of jellied quinces hardens under Voss's gaze into a group of garnets and pale jade lozenges (p. 89), while the reverse transformation is effected through the eyes of Laura: 'Miss

Hollier's garnet brooch [seemed] edible, like the quinces' (pp. 88–9). Mrs Bonner's concern to preside over her guests rather than liberate them provides a parody of Voss's obsession with fixity:

> Mrs Bonner, however, was creating groups of statuary. This was her strength, to coax out of flesh the marble that is hidden in it. So her guests became transfixed upon the furniture. Then Mrs Bonner, having control, was almost happy.
>
> (p. 90)

Her daughter Belle is released from her statuesque pose when Tom Radclyffe sings to her with such intensity that the glass ornaments begin to rattle, and Belle is then seen as an embodiment of that capacity for merging which enables love:

> Now [she] was neither flesh nor marble. She was enveloped in, and had herself become, a cloud of the most assiduous tenderness. To have remained in such a trance, of cloud wrapping cloud, would have been perpetual bliss.
>
> (p. 91)

It is Belle's presence that causes Voss to suffer a pang for what he has put behind him, but he swiftly translates his sexual desire into a nostalgia for the German summer with its flowing rivers and brilliant trees (p. 87); and to just such a landscape he finds himself transported when he arrives at the Sandersons' farm, appropriately named Rhine Towers. What first impress him there are the mineral-like aspects of the scene ('veins of silver loomed in the gullies, knobs of amethyst and sapphire glowed on the hills', p. 137) but it is ultimately the flowing movements of the light that overwhelm him until alarm at his access of feeling causes him to rein back:

> He had been wrong to surrender to sensuous delights, and must now suffer accordingly.
>
> (p. 138)

With a sweeping gesture of self-punishment he attempts to sabotage the Sandersons' hospitality by insisting that his men sleep out of doors.

The dream of which Voss remains largely unconscious on

waking to his first morning at Rhine Towers (he is grateful for the bed) provides the only transition between his perfunctory leave-taking of Laura on the Sydney quay and the letter, written before he leaves for Jildra, in which he proposes marriage. Since it reveals his condition before setting off, and marks out the decisive forces in the conflict that lies ahead, this, the first of Voss's dreams to be presented in any detail, asks for close attention.

Going to bed in the best room the Sandersons could offer, between exquisitely clean sheets and a lingering scent of verbena, Voss was not long with his body, and those thoughts which had been buzzing like blowflies in his head. At once the hills were enfolding him. All that he had observed, now survived by touch. So he was touching those same hills and was not surprised at their suave flesh. That which would have been reprehensible, nauseating, frightening in life, was permissible, even desirable, in sleep. And could solve, as well as dis-solve. He took the hand to read it out aloud, whatever might be printed on it. Here there were hills, too. They would not be gone around. This is the hill of love, his voice said, as if it had been most natural. That, she pointed, was burnt in the fire of the kiln as I pushed the clay in, and, insignificant though it is, will show for life. Then, roughly, he threw away the hand, which broke into pieces. Even in dreams he was deceived by the appearance of things, and had taken the wrong hand. Here it is, she said without grudge, and brought him another, which had not been baked. It was of white grain. It still had, most terribly, most poignantly, its semblance of flesh. So he shut it up in his bosom. He was afraid to look at it again. Till she bent down from her horse. The woman with the thumping breasts, who had almost got trampled, and whose teeth had been currying black horsehair, began to shout: Laura, Laura. For assistance. All that happens, happens in spite of the horsehair woman, who is, in fact, stuffed. Laura is smiling. They are sharing this knowledge. Then, how are names lost, which the hands have known by touch, and faces, like laborious, raw jugs? Laura is the name. But the name, all is lost, the veil is blowing, the wind. Is it not the same stuff with which the hills are shrouded, and of which the white word is, *ach, Musselin, natürlich,* but what else?

(p. 149)

In a study of the motives of fictive adventurers Paul Zweig comments on the frequency with which an initial flight from women leads to a rediscovery and reassertion of feminine values in the wilderness.[10] True to this pattern Voss who has austerely deflected his desires into the landscape now unravels this process in his dream, turning stone back into flesh, as Laura materializes – however disjointedly – from the desert. The suave flesh of the hills manifests the capacity for love that Voss has suppressed, and shows up the element of compensation in his trek. His sudden surrender to sleep recalls the earlier occasion on which he 'fell, straight, deeply into himself' to find comfort in his dream of the Idea as an *untouchable* monolith, but the sense of secure possession imaged there is now held at risk by a switch of agency, for it is the landscape that is now doing the touching ('At once the hills were enfolding him'), and yet his confidence survives the change into flesh ('So he was touching those same hills and was not surprised at their suave flesh'). Voss in his sleep is relieved by the expression of a desire which remains threatening to him in life, but protected too by the censorship that is available to him even in his dream, and in this sense the images of his unconscious can 'solve, as well as dis-solve'. He accepts the offered hand only conditionally, 'to read it out aloud, whatever might be printed on it', and on the palm finds evidence of an independent destiny. Not liking this, he distances himself by returning the hand to the realm of the natural – the language of palmistry offers a latent pun (on 'mons') that assists the transformation: 'Here there were hills, too. They would not be gone around.' But the restatement only stresses that love, as Laura has already said, is more demanding than landscape. Voss appears reluctant, however, to avoid the hill of love for he allows Laura to offer him two further hands.[11] Made of fired clay, the first of these is in keeping with the texture of the landscape and Voss's taste for the vitreous, but like the pottery of the Sandersons – 'distorted by the intense heat in which [it] had been tried' (p. 140) – the hand disturbs Voss with the poignancy of its imperfection and suffering, and so he shatters it. Though this hand is supposed to be of clay the syntax, suggesting some doubleness in the image of the dream, registers the real scars caused by Voss's preoccupation with the mineral. But deep down it is the hand of grain that he wants – the image recalls the bread which he has hungered after and rejected (pp. 30, 39) – and so he snatches it up although in such a way as to pretend that it is not there:

> It still had, most terribly, most poignantly, its semblance of flesh. So he shut it up in his bosom. He was afraid to look at it again.

The hand shut in his bosom accusingly recalls the actual scene of leave-taking in which a distracted Voss holds Laura's extended hand without passing a word while he watches a woman brushed on the mouth by a horse's tail in the turmoil (p. 125). This woman, stuffed with horse-hair in the dream, stands in for the hollow-men of Sydney society against whom Laura and himself are united in complicity. The contrast between their closeness and vast separation in space challenges the limits of memory. Words and names, the vanishing points of identity, are set against the unfinished stuff of experience ('raw jugs') until Laura, retiring behind a mist of white muslin, turns back into the landscape out of which she came.

Voss's conflict is brought into the open by the letter from Laura in which she accepts his proposal on condition that they both struggle to subdue the arrogance that blinds them to their frailty. With the word 'together' from Laura's parting injunction still resonating, Voss questions Palfreyman about his latest botanical acquisition, a lily with seeds 'like testes, attached to the rather virginal flower', before he drifts into the most revealing of his dreams:

> Then Voss began to float, and those words last received. But *together*. Written words take some time to thaw, but the words of lilies were now flowing in full summer water, whether it was the water or the leaves of water, and dark hairs of roots plastered on the mouth as water blew across. Now they were swimming so close they were joined together at the waist, and were the same flesh of lilies, their mouths, together, were drowning in the same love-stream. I do not wish this yet, or *nie nie nie, niemals. Nein.* You will, she said, if you will cut and examine the word. *Together* is filled with little cells. And cuts open with a knife. It is a see seed. But I do not. All human obligations are painful, Mr Johann Ulrich, until they are learnt, variety by variety. But

gold is painful, crushing, and cold on the forehead, while wholly desirable, because immaculate. Only resist the Christ-thorn. Tear out the black thing by the roots before it has taken hold. She was humbly grateful for it, however. In her kneeling position, she continued to bathe her hair in all flesh, whether of imperial lilies, or the black, putrefying, human kind.

(pp. 200–1)

This dream which vividly embodies Voss's desire for merging opens appropriately with a sequence of associations, the zeugma in the first sentence providing a lexical equivalent to the conjoined images ('words of lilies', 'leaves of water') and apposed sensations (floating, thawing, flowing, swimming, drowning, blowing) that occupy Voss. Whereas in the previous dream Laura moves between stone and flesh, Voss now envisages his surrender in images that are half-way between the plant-like and fleshly. Joined at the waist Laura and he become one entity, the 'same flesh' of a single flower. Through the visual presentation of the word 'together' as a lily pod 'filled with little cells', Voss who has formerly rejected 'the voluptuous transports' of selflessness as feminine is now brought to recognize that merging and fertility are also the preserve of the male. The intimation is sufficiently disturbing to be instantly suppressed: he refuses to see – although, in the word 'seed', the imperative continues to stare him in the face. So the dream proceeds to resolve itself into an internal colloquy between the self dedicated to Laura and the old obdurate Voss, who attempts to fend Laura off by opposing, against her insistence on human obligation, mortality and sacrifice, his emblem of the golden crown. The old Voss signally fails, however, to maintain the upper hand and the dream stubbornly returns to the seed-pod which he has refused to see:

I do accept the terms. It was the sweat that prevented me from seeing them.
You are in no position to accept. It is the woman who un-makes men, to make saints.
Mutual. It is all mutual.
It was his tongue that would not come unstuck.
You have gained that point, the mouth was laughing.
Two *zusammen* should gain by numbers, but lose in fact. Numbers weaken.

The weaker is stronger, O Voooos.

(p. 201)

Through a typographical device typical of James Joyce (compare Stephen's trailing ashplant in *Ulysses* – 'my familiar, after me, calling Steeeeeeeeeephen'),[12] given particular force here by the visual vehicle of the dream, Patrick White signals a decisive turning-point in the development of his hero. Voss who has savoured his own name as 'a crystal in his mouth' (p. 45) now finds it turned into a seed-pod which serves as an emblem of strength through humility.

The image of the woman choked with horse-hair, though only latent in the dream – 'dark hairs of roots plastered on the mouth' – reasserts itself in protean forms that testify to Voss's continuing fear of entanglement. So he reflects bitterly on his dependence after delaying his departure from Jildra to await Laura's letter: 'he could blame no one else for his own human weakness. He had delivered up his throat to the long, cold, glistening braids of her hair, and was truly strangling in them' (p. 191). It is Judd's paradoxical weakness that later provokes the essential formulation of his conflict:

> But when the fellow had gone away, he continued to suspect him of exercising great power, though within human limits. For compassion, a feminine virtue, or even grace, of some sensual origin, was undoubtedly human, and did limit will.
>
> So the German was despising what he most desired: to peel the whale-bone off the lily stem and bruise the mouth of flesh ... He lay thinking of the wife from whose hands he would accept salvation, if he were intended to renounce the crown of fire for the ring of gentle gold. That was the perpetual question which grappled him as coldly as iron.

(p. 227)

Like the lion and the unicorn in D. H. Lawrence's doctrinal essay who support the crown by each fighting for its possession, the values represented in *Voss* by the crown of fire and the ring of gold exist in a necessary tension.[13] Though he initially enshrines an extreme, even pathological ideal of independence, Voss humbles himself sufficiently to realize his capacity for love, and accordingly epitomizes two passions that are at war in every individual – the itch for self-exaltation and the thirst for self-transcendence. In place of a stable resolution the novel offers the prospect only of perpetual struggle. Voss who will both kill and have, and kiss as well as kill (pp. 285–6), is torn between the crown and the ring, and suspended between those symbolic presences that extend them, the 'X-ray'-like spirits of the dead and the warmly pigmented figures of the living, painted on the surfaces of the cave in which the explorers winter. A skeletal Voss shoots Gyp and callously scrutinizes Palfreyman on the way to his death while a being who 'had taken human form, at least temporarily' (p. 277) submits to the ministrations of Judd and nurses Le Mesurier through his illness. The supernatural powers that preside over the action of the novel are at once creative and destructive.[14] God crucifies his son; and the Rainbow Serpent of Aboriginal mythology, manifest in the comet, descends through the heavens intent on swallowing what it has created (p. 403).[15] The Great Snake comes to rest in the Southern Cross shortly before Voss is betrayed by Jackie; but both snake and cross symbolize the idea that suffering leads to renewal, a motif that recurs constantly throughout the novel in compressed images (such as 'green lightning') or in extended episodes of symbolic action. 'Dying is creation', Le Mesurier notes on the last leg of the journey (p. 385), and his own delirious struggle with the Rainbow Serpent recalls Jacob wrestling with the angel but, more crucially, the initiation of a medicine man:

> Towards morning, Le Mesurier was wrestling with the great snake, his King, the divine powers of which were not disguised by the earth-colours of its scales. Friction of days had worn its fangs to a yellow-grey, but it could arch itself like a rainbow out of the mud of tribulation. At one point during his struggles, the sick man, or visionary, kissed the slime of the beast's mouth, and at once spat out a shower of diamonds.
>
> (pp. 299–300)

Humility quickens his engagement in the stark realities of strife – a far cry from Fichte's notion of dying into life – leaving him in possession of the crystalline.[16]

Voss ends his last letter to Laura with the words: 'This is the true marriage, I know. We have wrestled with the gristle and the bones before daring to assume the flesh' (p. 232). One of White's triumphs in *Voss* is to make us aware of relationships as acts of creation. The dreams in which Voss discovers the extent of his desire for Laura yield to a series of hallucinatory scenes and images through which he expands his conception of her. (Some sixteen such episodes are presented, in the last three of which Laura is given her own point of view.) A maxim of Nietzsche's applies with particular force:

> What we do in dreams we also do when we are awake: we invent and fabricate the person with whom we associate – and immediately forget we have done so.[17]

Laura's physical absence isolates that unconscious work of the imagination that underlies all relationships, allowing us to observe the stages by which she assumes predominance in Voss's mind. Out of stone, at first a hooded figure, masked by her hair, by the collar of her coat, or with her back turned, Laura in the desert is slow to gain distinct human form. Her growth in Voss's mind is dependent on his relationships to the other members of the expedition, and controlled by the success of his struggle against pride. It is after Voss has allowed Judd to dress his head that Laura smiles; after nursing Le Mesurier that he first imagines Laura bearing a child. Finally, shortly before he is tended by her in the cave and they make a sacramental meal of lily plant together, he sees her – all fears of entanglement exorcised – 'Quite naked. And beautiful', shorn of her hair. It is Mrs Bonner who is turned to stone by the 'medusa-head' of her daughter (p. 410). To Voss the leeches are merely the knives that incessantly stab the elliptical soul, visible to him, at last, in the desert (p. 418).

Voss, 'truly humbled' at the end, dies in a chrysalis-like initiation hut (pp. 401, 414). Here, as throughout, White uses imagery connected with rites of passage to flesh out his persistent concern with sacrifice as a prelude to regeneration.[18] It is Voss's after-life that the novel goes on to trace in the subtle but palpable impact of his legend on Sydney society; so that the idea of creative dying is ultimately written into the plot itself.[19] One of the most vivid realizations of this motif comes earlier in the text when Voss, moving to the mouth of his cave at dawn, witnesses a nature that seems in the throes of creation. The landscape that has previously mimed his awakened desire now responds to his feeling that 'each morning is, like the creative act, the first'. While the gradual emergence of form through the mist parallels his discovery of Laura, the stress laid on death and suffering again sounds the notion that fresh life is always rooted in anguish:

> The rain was withdrawn temporarily into the great shapelessness, but a tingling of moisture suggested the presence of an earth that might absorb further punishment. First, an animal somewhere in the darkness was forced to part with its life. Then the grey was let loose to creep on subtle pads, from branch to branch, over rocks, slithering in native coils upon the surface of the waters.
>
> (pp. 300–1)

The scene owes a good deal, as the last detail shows, to the Aboriginal belief that the founding Gods (foremost among them the Great Snake) formed the world out of pre-existent but amorphous matter – the 'protoplast' or 'gelatinous, half-created' mass mentioned later in the same passage.[20] At a time when the anthropologist Mircea Eliade was developing his view that the initiation rites of a culture recapitulate its cosmogony, White extends a psychological emblem of *continuous* death and rebirth into a myth of creation, a myth which serves to underline the always *un*finished state of nature – a myth more consistent, in this respect, with evolution than is Genesis.[21]

Although largely overlooked by commentators on *Voss*, White's annexations of indigenous lore are as many-sided as they are crucial. In addition to the Rainbow Serpent and related ritual there is the notion of dual fatherhood that underlies the parenthood of Rose Portion's daughter, Mercy. White goes out of his way, also, to associate the celebrated 'X-ray' style of rock-painting with his own technique of presenting the unseen at face value (p. 299), and Voss's apparent clairvoyance begs comparison, too, with Aboriginal belief in a 'dream time'. So extensive an assimilation is without precedent. Never before in fiction had an explorer been transparent to the culture of the land through which he travelled.

9 The Sacramental Wild:

A Fringe of Leaves

'There was somebody murdered here in the beginning': when White, at the climax of *The Eye of the Storm* (1973), has the Warming children weave a private myth of creation round the story of Eliza Fraser, a famous castaway off the Queensland coast in 1836, he anticipates his own fictional working of this material in his next novel, *A Fringe of Leaves* (1976).[1] The island on which White's heroine comes ashore, holds in its sunlit stretches the promise of 'paradise itself', but it is here that Ellen Roxburgh first confronts the darkly perplexed sources of passion, a theme articulated later in the remark she makes to her rescuer Jack Chance – 'many have murdered those they love'; and it is here, too, after her capture by a tribe, that she exults in a meal of human flesh.[2] In the earlier novel, the same island witnesses the still centre of the typhoon during which the rapacious Mrs Hunter, after seducing away her daughter's would-be lover, finds peace in the clear-eyed recognition of her predatory nature. That the object of the rivalry between the two women is a marine biologist whose special interest, the sea-bed, is repeatedly linked with the unfathomed mind (while his testicles more plainly recall cuttlefish) hints that it is evolution that lies at the heart of nature's turbulent mandala.[3] Aetiology, however, plays little part in *A Fringe of Leaves* which from its 'prologue' to its last sentence goes straight to the question of *what* human nature is. But though White pursues the limits of 'people's frightfulness' much further here than in *Voss*, where the theme of betrayal is only partly developed, his affirmations are seldom more firmly based than they are in this moving and astringent piece.[4]

'GOD IS LOVE': the legend dribbled in ochre across the whitewashed wall of the unconsecrated chapel built by Ellen's fellow survivor, Pilcher, is as bald as it is simple. What gives instant sense to it is Ellen's perception of the way the humble building generously accommodates the natural – the sky, sun, nesting birds and, with them, the thoughts that pass through her head. There she can accordingly relive the 'betrayal of her earthly loves', concentrating experience that ranges from tenderness to lust and reaches a consummation in the 'sensual joy' of her relationship with the escaped convict, Jack Chance (pp. 390, 302).

Pilcher's chapel closely corresponds to that ideal place of worship sketched, after a visit to Lincoln cathedral, by Will Brangwen in *The Rainbow* (1915) – 'a temple . . . ruined and mixed up with the winds and the sky and the herbs'.[5] Lawrence and White share a distrust of systems and habits of mind that shut out, and they both celebrate freedom by enshrining the wild. It is no surprise then to find a suitable frame for White's treatment of the Australian landscape in Lawrence's fiercely polemical novel *Kangaroo* (1923) which, in pitting the dark gods against received Christian belief, conscripts even the terrain. While the glib creed of brotherly love, upheld by Kangaroo, is associated with the soft pastoral of the coastal fringe, his sceptical disciple Jaz looks to the interior (his eyes are of the same grey as the bush) and Somers, the author's spokesman, not only welcomes the 'uncreatedness' of the new country but repeatedly pictures human nature as volcanic since energy issues, he explains, from a source beyond the will.[6] In a chapter headed 'Volcanic Evidence' Lawrence translates this idea – which includes the sense that 'destruction is part of creation' – into the bedrock of the continent, identifying Fraser island, curiously enough, as the centre of a hidden fault that will yet rain fire on the land.[7] '*Some* men', Somers observes of himself, 'have to be bombs, to explode and make breaches in the walls that shut life in'.[8] What underlies his half-entertained revolutionary schemes is a psychological conviction that integrity can only be won at the risk of including forces that threaten secure existence.

White's primitivism is more muted, his finely grained realism a far cry from the tendentious mode of Lawrence's essay-novel, but there is, all the same, much common ground. Although Ellen's attitudes to civility and the wilderness are so delicately balanced that she is brought, by turns, to the brink of escaping on her own from each, her growth is nevertheless charted against an ever outward movement into nature. She begins, in terms of the novel's action, as Mrs Austin Roxburgh cabined with her invalid husband aboard the *Bristol Maid* on their return to England from

Van Diemen's Land, and the voyage, before it ends in shipwreck, unfolds her past in a series of layered settings. While still at Sydney, waiting for the boat to sail, she escapes from the 'narrow saloon' to glimpse something of the 'forbidding landscape' that lies beyond the harbour town, and immediately conjures up two other contrastive landscapes – the recent lush fields of Dulcet, the estate belonging to her brother-in-law Garnet whom the Roxburghs have travelled across the world to see, and the relatively pinched farm of her Cornish childhood (pp. 32–3). As the stages of her history surface successively over the ocean, we learn of her painful transformation from country girl to Cheltenham lady after her marriage (shortly following her father's death) to Austin, a paying convalescent. For the bejewelled and gloved Mrs Roxburgh the refinements of Birdlip House with its polished surfaces, caged linnets and netted pears entail some distance from reality, a distance realized earlier in the tension between Austin's pastoral expectations of a Cornish farm and the pig pegged down for slaughter across which he stumbles. And while it is true that Ellen retains a vision broader than her social roles would seem to permit, and that her love of Austin is restricted, chiefly, by his intolerance of passion, a deeply repressed urge in her for further experience becomes apparent on her first excursion into the wild.

About to drift asleep in an indigenous forest on the mountainside of Garnet's farm, she feels herself 'only remotely related to Ellen Roxburgh, or even Ellen Gluyas', and reflects, 'she was probably closer to the being her glass could not reveal, nor her powers of perception grasp' (p. 92). In the compression of her dream, Garnet – his presence signalled by ripe plums – coalesces with the figure of her chosen lover who in a visual idiom revived from her adolescent fantasy, sails into Tintagel cove. Although the dream is instantly forgotten, it is not long before an un-Roxburghian self stage-manages her seduction by Garnet in exactly the same part of the wood. Her feelings towards her brother-in-law which have up to this point been mixed – revulsion masking the depth of her desire – now rapidly shift to self-disgust as her loyalty to Austin combines with growing insight into the real brutality that underlies Garnet's sensual charm. Both her awakened sensuality and guilt leave a lasting impression. She dreams that she has been 'GARNurd'; or, on another occasion, watches a stake pass through Austin's heart, transferring to him the fate that Garnet has spitefully arranged for her mare (pp. 182, 157–8). Paradoxical though it may seem, Ellen's first encounter with the wilderness, because it opens an anguished consciousness of her capacity for betrayal, contributes as much to her moral growth as to her gain in experience. Ellen, in exacting knowledge of her flawed nature, remains true to the maxim quoted among the epigraphs – 'If there is some true good in a man, it can only be unknown to himself'.[9] Simone Weil's precept reaches, too, into the second and more crucial stage of her development which is once again initiated, after her meeting on the mainland with Jack Chance, by 'a passion discovered only in a country of thorns, whips, murderers, thieves, shipwreck, and adulteresses' (pp. 311–12).

That the narrator retails the experiences of Dulcet while Ellen lies huddled in the empty form left by Austin in the lower bunk of their cabin, gently points to the psychological nature of the frontiers which face Ellen as Mrs Roxburgh (pp. 70, 78). A 'theory of prevention by suffocation' (p. 66) is her unwanted legacy from her mother-in-law and she often has cause to regret Austin's attempts to protect her in return. Throughout the novel we are alerted to the inner barriers dictated not only by the pressures of intimacy but by social convention and, ultimately, by class. In this respect Ellen's progress closely resembles that undergone in *Voss* by Laura Trevelyan, for whom exploration takes the form of befriending her emancipist servant Rose Portion and adopting her child. Ellen goes further, however, in her violation of social taboo. Indeed, where Voss is impelled towards growth by deeds which patently fall under the heading of Christian service, Ellen's path of deliverance leads through the underworld. A ready sympathy disables the middle-class stereotypes which threaten to enclose her, and it is precisely to the development of this gift that she owes her almost visionary, final stature. When she recalls, after her return, Garnet's sneering dismissal of 'these miscreants, the sweepings of the London streets', she realizes that 'unrestricted association with the convict made her his accomplice' and that, in society's eyes, she herself stands effectively condemned not only of cannibalism but of murder (p. 316). But from the first, her Cornish roots quicken insight into the arbitrariness of social definition. On learning, for example, that the housemaid has suffered transportation for the same offence that has caused her master to emigrate, she asks herself how much of the miscreant there is in Garnet; and is swift to add, 'Or in *myself*?', so calling attention to a kinship, felt the moment she sets eyes on a convict gang, that goes back to the hardship of her childhood (pp. 89, 84). In retrospect it becomes clear, as I hope to show, that a structure of social relations forms the core of Ellen's discoveries in the wild. Landscape, which represents for Voss both the driving force and minutely rendered record of an inward journey, serves in *A Fringe of Leaves* rather as a series of pointers.

Although the intense and varied processes of bonding that increasingly absorb the text after the wreck of the *Bristol Maid* develop the novel's concern with *sympathy*, the word itself proves too broad for analysis, and a distinction drawn by Jung between two ways of approaching the new, turns out to be a help. While 'assimilation', in his terms, involves approximating fresh things to old experience, 'identification' amounts to its opposite – the formation of a 'secondary character' to accommodate the fresh.[10] Ellen then *assimilates* Holly when she sees that 'the girl's fate might have been her own, that of a scullery-maid becoming a drudge-wife' (p. 91), and her aroused sense of affinity is sealed by the gift of the garnet ear-rings that make her look 'trumpery' – though they point also to a further tie, their sharing of Garnet, which she is less keen to acknowledge. Further examples of assimilation occur when she repeatedly brings Captain Purdew into focus as an image of her father, or slots Oswald into the role of her lost son. These approaches by 'proxy', as White calls them, crop up throughout and play a part in almost all the relationships, but most strikingly perhaps in Austin's life with Ellen, who happily unites those 'opposite poles of his existence', his mother and his brother (pp. 310, 149).

The opening chapter introduces us to a quite different sort of social participation in the brief account given of Austin's childhood illness:

'And the strange part was, it seemed to draw him closer to his very unlikely brother. As though he hoped to borrow some of Garnet's health and strength.'

(pp. 14–15)

Mr Merrivale's remark is later filled out by Austin's dream of Garnet as a type of the full-blooded person he would have had himself be (his brother stands aflame on the far side of the nursery fender after a bath), and by the statement that their forced separation affected him 'as though he had suffered the amputation of a limb' (pp. 148–9). This source of energy remains untapped, however, for once the brothers are reunited Austin withdraws, making no more than the odd gesture towards their shared past. Only after shipwreck and privation have stripped him of his props and accustomed roles does he begin to grapple with those 'substantial shadows' which his readings of Virgil have grimly underlined (pp. 34, 68).[11] And only on the longboat does he taste the first fruit of his belated growth, an ecstatic sense of union with his wife:

> Plastered together in their drenched condition, they were truly 'one flesh', an expression he had been inclined to reject as in bad taste, until the senseless caprices of nature invested it with a reality which had become his mainstay.
>
> (p. 198)

His joy on this occasion is preceded by a further image of Garnet freshly bathed by the nurse, and a related memory fuels the episode that follows – an episode crucial not only to his development but to the novel's symbolic scheme. Applying a remedy once applied to Garnet by Nurse Hayes, Austin tends to a boil on the neck of the dying second mate. The sense of fellowship released by this act leads Austin to dream, shortly after Spurgeon's death, of a rite which begins as a displaced version of the Christian sacrament:

> Yet his thoughts were only cut to a traditional pattern, as Captain Purdew must have recognized, who now came stepping between the heads of the sleepers, to bend and whisper, *This is the body of Spurgeon which I have reserved for thee, take eat, and give thanks for a boil which was spiritual matter* . . . Austin Roxburgh was not only ravenous for the living flesh, but found himself anxiously licking the corners of his mouth to prevent any overflow of precious blood.
>
> (p. 231)

Though the dream provides its own gory transubstantiation of the Host, the usual implications of Eucharist apply, even if their textual enactment, thus far, is largely notional. The sacrament raises, in the first place, the idea of identification – of an enlargement undergone by the self in taking on the qualities of another being, in this case Garnet's distant proxy. Secondly, it demonstrates a common bond among the celebrants; a sense introduced by the pannikin of rum which, sent round the longboat at the sight of land, recalls a chalice (p. 203).

Austin's dream provides a prelude to that pregnant phase of existence that Ellen enters after her capture by an Aboriginal tribe. The moment of her stripping, and separation from the other survivors, comes at the end of a series of losses so severe as to leave her clinging to the last outward sign of public identity, the ring given her by Austin. So complete is her bereavement – Austin's death following her miscarriage and the drowning of Oswald – that she is withheld, for some time, from the people who make up a fresh life about her. The tribal society which the novel portrays here is free, for once, of that symbolic freight which commonly distinguishes the role of primitives in texts dealing with exploration. By articulating the features of a distinct culture White dispels the concept of race, and with it goes the myth of a *Naturvolk*. Life among the Aborigines is shown to consist in an intricate balance between ritual and need, instinct and code; and Ellen in learning the ways of her community is alternately reminded of her Cornish background and of her time at Cheltenham. Such approaches fall into the category of assimilation, but they take Ellen only part of the distance towards feeling at home in her new context, and it is telling that the sick baby girl whom she is obliged to suckle, conspicuously fails to replace the children she has lost. It is rather her shocked understanding of the child's state that sparks the first intimations of kinship between her and the group. In a vibrant scene White shows an old – possibly infirm – medicine man extracting, first, a crystal from the baby's mouth and then, after the child's death, doing his utmost to persuade the crowd that Ellen is to blame. The family seem almost convinced, but all is changed when, giving vent to emotions she has long checked back, Ellen bursts into tears: 'For the first time since the meeting on the beach', the narrator comments, 'the captive and her masters, especially the women, were united in a common humanity' (p. 261). In a seminal study of cross-cultural perception Edward Said has pertinently questioned whether 'ethnic origins and religion are the best, or at least the most useful, basic, and clear, definitions of human experience'.[12] White supplies a valuable corrective to ethnographic determinism when he focuses on the gap between daily living and the official creeds.

What precipitates Ellen's identification with the Aboriginal tribe is a bizarre ritual that follows on a number of her encounters with a beautiful girl whom she first sees diving for water-lilies. The sight is memorable for it provides a brilliant relief from the stale task of collecting food, and Ellen is quick to recognize the lily-diver when she finds herself drawn later into a compromising tangle by the girl's powerful lover. In making an advance to Ellen, this man, already flanked by two mistresses, puts her in a position towards the young girl similar to that she has entertained towards Holly in her liaison with Garnet, or will occupy towards the Irish girl in her relationship with Jack Chance. She sees the lily-gatherer killed in a fight with her rival, and the next day stumbles on, and devours, a cooked thigh-bone which is all that remains of the girl after a secretly held feast. Although bewildered by the violence of her act Ellen instantly recognizes her fulfilment of 'some darker need of the hungry spirit' (pp. 272–4). She realizes, in sum, that the rite holds a significance for her that goes beyond the fact of her having broken a taboo of her own culture.

Each of the sacramental principles suggested earlier in the text now comes into play. In the first place, a sense of unanimity steals over Ellen who begins to regard herself as a member of the tribe. At the grand corroboree she accordingly joins the swaying figures in the dance until all are 'melted together'; and her new role soon proves sufficiently secure to allow her to pass judgement on the life she led at Cheltenham (pp. 283, 286). She keeps her old identity to the extent, it is true, of continuing to look out for means of escape, but the contrary urge to belong is already clear from her response to the children she mothers on her way to the festival – 'she could have eaten them' (p. 276). White's treatment of the other principle is more extensive.

A wish to acquire the qualities of the creature consumed underlies, it seems, not only the Eucharist but many cannibal rites. The point is made by Janet Lewis in her novel *The Invasion* (1932), a vivid account of cultural assimilation on the early American frontier:

On another evening they talked of the Christian mystery.

'I understand you,' said the Indian, 'when you say that your god becomes bread and that you eat of the bread, not to eat your god but his godliness. We too when we eat of the heart of a brave man eat not the heart but the courage. There is no Ojibway who would taste of the blood of a coward.'[13]

White bases the cannibal feast in *A Fringe of Leaves* on a mortuary custom reported among the Aborigines – particularly in the South Queensland region, which fits the setting.[14] 'Acquisition of the dead person's qualities' forms the underlying tenet of this rite;[15] and round it White constructs an elaborate symbolic fable.[16] One afternoon at the height of her relationship with Jack Chance, Ellen busies herself in his absence by practising a skill she has learnt from her time with the tribe, so that on his return with a slaughtered emu, a bird so human that it immediately recalls her feast of flesh, he is met by a woman in the image of the lily-gatherer – 'hair plastered, shoulders gleaming and rustling with water' – and greets Ellen as his *lubra* (pp. 316–17). In the sheet of lilies they tumble and embrace, but the scene is important not only for showing their 'sensual joy' (in the lily imagery White carries over a motif of sexual merging from *Voss*) but for illustrating Ellen's capacity for extending her repertoire of selves. Ellen, who shifts by turns between Gluyas and Roxburgh, speaker of dialect and standard English, figurine and wench, slave and demi-goddess, *lubra* and nun, prude and miscreant, who sees herself in the shoes of Holly, Pilcher and Garnet's dead wife; and who later actually takes herself to be both Jack and his mistress Mab, proves the most protean of heroines. Nothing could characterize her better than what amounts to a myth of continuous incarnation.

But Ellen's sacrament, which she herself regards as unredeemably pagan, reveals other, and darker, depths. It stands as far from the eucharist imagery of *Voss* with its attendant celebrations of 'togetherness' as it does from Austin's selfless care of Spurgeon, more closely resembling, indeed, that black mass which Brendan Boyle envisages in the outback.[17] The severest of White's concerns in *Voss*, the paradox of growth-in-destruction is taken up with renewed energy in *A Fringe of Leaves*, where it is imaged by the very nature of Ellen's rite which distils life from the dead. Over Ellen's meeting with Chance there presides the Rainbow Serpent embodied by the dancers at the corroboree, and it prefigures a pattern of falling and rising fortune in which the lovers will lose as they have gained. It is at the moment that Ellen, already absorbed in the dance, pictures herself consuming the burnt remains of her husband, that the mysterious 'Ulappi' detaches himself from the tail of the serpent to enter her life (pp. 283–4). The idea of loss as a prerequisite to creation finds an emblem later in the torn lilies at the place of their passionate encounter,

> it was sad they should destroy such a sheet of lilies, but so it must be if they were to become re-united
>
> (p. 317)

and in a variety of guises this notion is to haunt each emotional climax of the novel's most potent relationship.

The cannibal imagery that White applies to erotic love takes its place in a series of comparisons relating sex to eating; and the flamboyant nature of many of these – Ellen locked in Garnet's embrace sees herself as a 'partially disabled, obscene bird, on whose breast he was feeding' (p. 116) – makes the plain, almost idiomatic statement of her feeling for Jack start into relief:

> She would have swallowed him had she been capable of it.
>
> (p. 299)

White engineers a context in which this remark, along with the earlier aside – 'she could have eaten them', tempts us to question just how figurative the everyday endearment is. While the lovers feast on a couple of pigeons (birds foreshadow human destinies throughout) Jack, going back to his days as a bird-catcher, dwells on the force of necessity, and brings home to Ellen the fecklessness of ordinary drives:

> 'Most birds and animals – plants too – is neglected – once the whim to own 'em dies in the owner.'
> 'Then why did you carry on, Jack, at what amounts to an immoral trade?'
> 'If we considered only what's moral we'd go 'ungry, wouldn't we? an' curl up an' die. There's too much thinkin' – an' not enough. Would men go with women, or women with men, if they started thinkin' of the trouble – the deceit and treachery they might run into?'
>
> (p. 294)

That the sources of human energy are tainted appears both in Ellen's fruitful disloyalty to Austin and in the urge for preservation that prompts her, at length, to sacrifice Chance. But even before the plot unfolds its appalling symmetries of betrayal, White alerts us bit by bit to the callous conduct that triumphs, as if irresistibly, over the most tenderly nurtured intentions. Here casual words and gestures play their part. We see Ellen blasting Oswald's trust when she accuses him of 'ferreting' out her thoughts (a ferret being the subject of their first confidence); and Austin shows himself ready to mock his wife in order to win the approval of the crew (pp. 197, 203). The lie to selfless merging is given, again, by a comic succession of buffetings and tramplings – accidental, unconscious, or even intended – that attach impartially to all love relations in turn. It is while demonstrating her sympathy and altruism, for example, that Ellen knocks Austin with an outflung arm, or, on a later occasion, rams Jack with her knee (pp. 218, 319); and though deeply put out to find herself standing on the hand of her husband's corpse she later quite deliberately brings down a foot into her rescuer's face in order to prevent him climbing up to her in the tree (pp. 244, 318, 319).

In so far as Ellen discovers a source of grace in the wilderness, it is through her pained but ever increasing recognition of human ruthlessness, and she is faced with a crowning disclosure when Jack, shortly before they reach the outskirts of settlement, confesses to the murder of his mistress, Mab. In this act Ellen feels herself to be doubly implicated – like Mab she has been unfaithful, and her violence to Austin, whom she has imaged with a stake through his heart, aligns her also with Jack. That Jack should kill Mab's other man, the sword-swallower, with his own weapon, calls up the well-known lines from *The Ballad of Reading Gaol*, echoed in Ellen's self-inculpating response, 'many have murdered those they love' (p. 324):

> Yet each man kills the thing he loves,
> By each let this be heard,
> Some do it with a bitter look,
> Some with a flattering word.
> The coward does it with a kiss,
> The brave man with a sword![18]

As a foil to Jack's passionate brutality, White includes the account of Pilcher's wife who dies of a loveless marriage, and makes it clear that the accident suffered by the wealthy Mrs (Dormer) Roxburgh was carefully premeditated by Garnet who remains unconvicted (pp. 378, 90, 101). Though only notional, Ellen's involvement in Jack's crime is further intensified by the guilt she feels over the drowning of her beloved Oswald, and even over Austin's killing for she cannot forget that in drawing the spear from his neck she supplied the immediate cause of death (pp. 218, 240). The imaginative resources which she brings to bear on the events following Mab's murder are profound, and her almost hallucinatory reconstructions of Jack's refuge in the London sewers and his return to the cottage at Putney full of dead birds, represent a correspondingly rich expression of her power to empathize (pp. 325–7). Nor is her exploration of these events limited to her lover's point of view. Having already taken on the experience of Mab to the extent of weeping at her supposed separation from Jack, and with a complicity strengthened, too, by their common adultery, Ellen now casts a nervous glance at Jack's axe. The passages in which she recreates the unseen (rendered by White in the X-ray style of *Voss*) prepare the reader for the confused identity which she reveals in her delirium on reaching the colony. 'I am Mab', she tells Mrs Oakes, but she is as much Jack for she pleads to be spared flogging at the triangle (p. 337). The answer to the question she frames at Dulcet before her journey has really begun – how much is she a miscreant – comes partly in her formal statement to the Commandant at the settlement, 'most of us are guilty of brutal acts, if not actual murder', less soberly in her retrospective agony over her desertion of the man she loves: 'Even if Jack is not – destroyed – if he simply lies down and dies – I must give myself up as his murderess' (pp. 367, 344).

We see, nonetheless, that whenever Ellen believes her survival is at stake – the tree-climbing incident provides a good example – compassion counts for little or nothing. Chief, indeed, among many paradoxes focused by the cannibalism of the novel's central rite is the implication that Ellen's sympathies and betrayals are not easily disentangled. It is, in truth, a relentless urge for experience ('a matter of choice', as Miss Scrimshaw notes, p. 23) that leads to her wide-ranging insight into the plight of others. The 'continued immanence' of her victims and loves (p. 255) represents the more positive aspect of her tragic life, as it does of her dark sacrament; and this aspect appears in the breadth and readiness of her emotional response to society on her return to the penal settlement of Moreton Bay. Here, when the long-expected convict gang comes into view, she finds herself without any of the defensive screens available to her earlier at Van Diemen's Land: with the familiarly roughened men she is instantly 'united in one terrible spasm', a union the more cruel for being wholly one-sided (p. 370). Still more poignant, however, is her meeting with the Irish convict responsible for Jack's getaway – a woman who has entered her fantasy as deeply as Mab (pp. 310–12) – for the rapport established between them only highlights the barrier that keeps them apart (pp. 372–3). Ellen has cause to brood over the effects of a divided society, each side of which she has come to contain in the course of her wandering:

> It saddened her to think she might never become acceptable to either of the two incompatible worlds even as they might never accept to merge.
>
> (p. 371)

The priest who drops in and blithely continues his prayer oblivious to the rending cries of a man at the triangle, typifies the 'moral classes' referred to by Spurgeon (p. 210), from which she has made her escape. Ellen's journey translates at last into a penetration of the community about her, and her progress is mapped in these terms by a narrator who applies the metaphor of space. Conversing with the crew aboard the *Bristol Maid*, Ellen has yet 'to bridge the gulf separating life from their own lives'; but when she approaches the party of female convicts in search of the Irish girl it is to discover that she has in effect eaten through 'the distance separating her from the women' (pp. 154, 372).

The penal colony that stands in for the larger society at the close of *A Fringe of Leaves* is in many ways uglier than anything Ellen experiences in the wild. Very much as Garnet's murder of his wife surpasses in its cold calculation the evil of Jack's impulsive violence, the exacted labour and controlled exploitation of Moreton Bay prove more deeply invasive than Ellen's informal enslavement by the tribe. And although White varies the stress in his final chapter – we see Ellen drawing comfort from frequent kindness, and specially from the candour of the Lovells' children – he sets out to warn his readers of the way in which a society can conceal the blood-thirstiness which it has institutionalized. His view comes close, here, to that boldly advanced by Nietzsche in *Beyond Good and Evil*:

> Almost everything we call 'higher culture' is based on the spiritualization and intensification of *cruelty* – this is my proposition; the 'wild beast' had not been laid to rest at all, it lives, it flourishes, it has merely become – deified.[19]

It often appears that Ellen in escaping from the wilderness has merely leapt, so to speak, from the frying pan into the fire. But this particular irony, bitter though it is, is one widely found among contemporary treatments of the explorer theme.

A vivid instance is supplied by the ending of Golding's *Lord of the Flies* (1954) where there suddenly opens up, beyond the catastrophic present, a vista of cruelty on a greatly extended, if more distant scale: a warship waits for the fleeing boys, and the uniform of its Captain chimes disturbingly with the masks devised by Jack for his warmongering party. By way of corollary, flight from society is rewarded in *An Imaginary Life* (1978) – David Malouf's brilliant fusion of atavism and metamorphosis – for here Ovid, accompanied by an adopted wild boy, escapes from the community where he has passed his exile, to push ever further into the wilderness until he meets with an ecstatic death. In *Dusklands* (1974) J. M. Coetzee achieves a comparable emphasis by reversing the chiaroscuro traditional to much of the genre and challenging, with limpid irony its implication. An explorer accordingly demonstrates his 'true savagery' when he turns his back on the broad daylight of the interior, descends into familiar twilit terrain, and finally celebrates his home-coming with a bout of slaughter that he blames on Bushmen; the only dark streak in the desert is the shadow cast by his presence.[20] André Brink in *An Instant in the Wind* (1976), a quite independent working of the Fraser-Bracefell legend adapted to the Cape Colony of the eighteenth century, takes the contrast between the ethos of settlement and wilderness even further. His heroine, the wife of an explorer widowed far beyond the frontier, is initiated into paradise by Adam Mantoor, the escaped slave who rescues her. The rapid stages by which the values of a wilfully repressive society erode their relationship, after their return to the Colony, are compellingly observed until, advancing on her original, the rescued widow has her lover condemned to death.[21] While making use of a documentary apparatus, both Coetzee and Brink create historical fictions which embody an image of the present in the past.[22]

Though less glowing than Adam's paradise, Ellen's experience of the wilderness has no less value, for what she discovers there provides, again, a yardstick for the appraisal of society. Indeed, the metaphors of imprisonment which White freely draws from the penal settlement point not only at particular, restrictive codes but also – as when we are told that Ellen 'had been sentenced, a lifer from birth' (p. 359) – at the condition of civility itself. So, too, the sudden cry of pain that breaks from Ellen once aboard the boat that will bear her back to the thoroughfares of urban life, expresses the passion she has lost in rejecting Chance but voices also the unspoken grief felt by civilization's every discontent. While the shades of the prison-house begin to close round White's Wordsworthian woman, who has learnt from her truancy in the wild just how much she 'desired to love without reserve' (p. 302), it becomes clear, however, that her story is meant as a moral viaticum as much as an antidote to repression.[23] In acquiring the self-knowledge that she recognizes as 'a source of embarrassment, even danger' in her society (p. 341), in despairing at times of finding any good in herself, Ellen grows quick at least to penetrate evil. Her insight into the difference between 'instinctive brutality' and the malevolence of a 'calculating mind' increasingly irradiates her response, informing finally her determined fulfilment of the promise to procure Jack's pardon as well as the words on justice that she passes to the Commandant (pp. 138, 342). Her development illustrates, overall, a remark made by Simone Weil that supplements the saying quoted by White as an epigraph: 'sin is nothing else but the failure to recognize human misery'.[24]

Weil writes elsewhere of the 'monstrous discrepancy between man's body, man's mind and the things which at the present time constitute the elements of human existence'.[25] An appeal to human nature underwrites every bid to show that society is not the measure of man – it is difficult to see how any comparative judgement of social life could be possible without it – and ever since Defoe novelists have turned to explorers and castaways to found such appeals on the presentation of experience in the wild. That these pictures are all to some extent a reflection of the contexts in which they arose hardly saps the impulse to search for extrinsic standards on distant ground. And for this reason the explorer theme is likely to persist in fiction, even if predominantly in historical guise. The hero of Faulkner's novella, *The Bear* (1942), who returns annually to a forest which shrinks until it eventually disappears, speaks for the genre when he tells himself that he can 'never lose it'. What he feels, after all, is 'the old life of the heart, as pristine as ever, as on the first day'.[26]

Notes and References

1. THE EXPLORER, AND VIEWS OF CREATION

1. From 'The Letter on his Third Voyage, October 1498', in *Select Documents Illustrating the Four Voyages of Columbus*, translated and edited by Cecil Jane (London, 1933) II, 16–18.
2. Although he would not have read Mandeville in English the *Travels* were available to Columbus in any one of 'several Italian, French, or Latin editions, or in manuscript in Spanish', as Josephine Bennett observes in *The Rediscovery of Sir John Mandeville* (New York, 1954) p. 235. M. C. Seymour in the preface to his edition of the *Travels* (Oxford, 1967, xx) remarks: 'When the *Santa Cruz* sighted land on 12 October 1492, a copy of *Mandeville's Travels* lay beside Marco Polo's book in the admiral's day-cabin'. Frequent and often detailed references throughout Columbus's writings leave no doubt as to the truth of this claim.
3. *Mandeville's Travels*, edited by M. C. Seymour (Oxford, 1967) pp. 221–2.
4. *Select Documents*, II, 36.
5. See J. S. Collis, *Christopher Columbus* (London, 1976) pp. 32–4; and for a discussion of his Messianic intuitions Cecil Jane's introduction to *Select Documents*, I, lii.
6. *Select Documents*, II, 26.
7. In *Aids to Reflection* (1825): see *OED* under 'Projective. 5'. The two inset examples are also from the *OED*. Coleridge's concern with projection is central to 'Dejection: An Ode', and to 'Constancy to an Ideal Object'; but important also in most of the earlier 'conversation poems'.
8. *À la recherche du temps perdu*, translated by C. K. Scott Moncrieff, *Swann's Way: Part One* (London, 1941) pp. 9–11. For an earlier (and wonderfully controlled) use of the optical metaphor see Pope's *Epistle to Cobham*, lines 23–8:

> the diff'rence is as great between
> The optics seeing, as the objects seen.
> All Manners take a tincture from our own,
> Or come discolour'd thro' our Passions shown.
> Or Fancy's beam enlarges, multiplies,
> Contracts, inverts, and gives ten thousand dyes.

In the one-volume edition of the Twickenham text, edited by John Butt (London, 1963) p. 550.

9. *Select Documents*, I, 4–6.

10. *Paradise Lost*, IV, lines 600–4. The phrase is a close translation of the Spanish 'por allí donde yo andava'.

11. On the *mappa-mundi* and its developments see Erwin Raisz, *Mapping the World* (London, 1956) pp. 35–7; and J. H. Parry, *The Age of Reconnaissance* (Berkeley, 1981) pp. 107–9.

12. From 'Arthur Barlowe's Narrative of the 1584 Voyage' in *Virginian Voyages from Hakluyt*, edited by David and Alison Quinn (London, 1973) p. 8.

13. 'A Briefe Relation of the New Founde Land' (1583) in Richard Hakluyt's *The Principall Navigations . . . of the English Nation*, first published in 1589 and enlarged 1598–1600 (Glasgow, 1903–5) VIII, 60.

14. For example, John Smith who knew the American coastline from Florida to Maine remarked, 'Could I haue but means to transport a Colony, I would rather liue here than any where'. *Works, 1608–31*, edited by Edward Arber (London, 1895) II, 708.

15. Collected in Perry Miller's anthology, *The American Puritans* (New York, 1956) p. 17.

16. In an open letter addressed by Hakluyt to Sir Walter Raleigh. *Principall Navigations*, VIII, 443.

17. *The Tempest*, II. i. 45–53. See the New Arden text, edited by Frank Kermode (London, 1958) p. 45. For a fuller account of this theme in *The Tempest* see my article ' "The Man in the Island": Shakespeare's concern with projection in *The Tempest*', *Theoria*, LXI (1983) pp. 23–36.

18. 'An Outpost of Progress' in *Tales of Unrest*, Dent's Uniform Edition (London, 1923–8) p. 92.

19. See J. G. Frazer, 'Some Primitive Theories of the Origin of Man', in A. C. Seward, *Darwin and Modern Science* (Cambridge, 1909) p. 159; and I. Petrov, *Report on the Population, Industries, and Resources of Alaska* (Washington, 1884).

20. R. R. Cawley cites eleven instances, all of them independent of mine. *The Voyagers and Elizabethan Drama* (Boston, 1938) pp. 290–1.

21. From 'The True and Last Discouerie of Florida made by Captain John Ribault in the yeere 1562' in *Divers Voyages Touching the Discovery of America* (1582), translated and edited by Richard Hakluyt. Edited by J. W. Jones (New York, 1850, reprinted [1971]) pp. 101–2.

22. *The Essayes of Montaigne*, translated by John Florio (London, 1891) p. 94.

23. Genesis 2:15.

24. *The Metamorphoses of Ovid*, translated by Mary M. Innes (Harmondsworth, 1955) pp. 31–2.

25. 'To the Virginian Voyage'. *Poems of Michael Drayton*, edited by John Buxton (London, 1953) I, 124.

26. *The Tempest*, II. i. 147–53.

27. Sir Henry Morton Stanley, *In Darkest Africa* (London, 1890) II, 73.

28. *In Darkest Africa*, II, 70–1.

29. *In Darkest Africa*, II, 78–9.

30. *In Darkest Africa*, II, 79–80.

31. Genesis 1:28.

32. I Samuel 15:22. The context would certainly have been known to Stanley who read the Bible twice over on this expedition. See *In Darkest Africa*, I, 291.

33. *In Darkest Africa*, II, 80.

34. Robert I. Rotberg comments on Stanley's lack of patience with Livingstone's lenience towards stragglers, and goes on to quote from Stanley: 'My blood is up . . . It is a murderous world, and I have begun to hate the filthy, vulturous shoals who inhabit it.' *Africa and its Explorers* (Cambridge, Mass., 1970) p. 243.
35. See the introduction to *Divers Voyages* by J. W. Jones, ciii–civ.
36. See David B. Davis, *The Problem of Slavery in Western Culture* (New York, 1966) p. 8.
37. 'The discoverie of Guiana' in Hakluyt's *Principall Navigations*, x, 428.
38. *The Exploration Diaries of H. M. Stanley*, edited by Richard Stanley and Alan Neame (London, 1961) p. 105.
39. Herodotus, *The Histories*, translated by Aubrey de Selincourt (London, 1954) p. 219.
40. *Mandeville's Travels*, p. 228.
41. Quoted by George Seaver in *Edward Wilson of the Antarctic* (London, 1933) p. 119.
42. William Burchell, *Travels in the Interior of Southern Africa* (London, 1822–4, reprinted 1953) I, 5.
43. François Le Vaillant, *Travels into the Interior Parts of Africa, 1780–5*, translated from the French, second edition (London, 1796) I, 145.
44. *Travels*, I, 132–3.
45. *Travels*, I, 127.
46. *Travels*, II, 13.
47. *Travels*, II, 14. My italics.
48. *Travels*, II, 125.
49. Humboldt comments on Columbus's location of Paradise in *Aspects of Nature*. See Mrs Sabine's translation (London, 1849) I, 210–11.
50. *Aspects of Nature*, I, 268–9.
51. *Aspects of Nature*, I, 221.
52. *Cosmos*, [translated by Mrs Sabine] (London, 1846–58) II, 61.
53. *Aspects of Nature*, I, 208.
54. *The Voyage of the 'Beagle'*, Everyman text (London, 1906) p. 396. For a discussion of the eighteenth-century myth of the South Seas Paradise see Hoxie Neal Fairchild, *The Noble Savage* (New York, 1928) pp. 107–12. On the pictorial tradition see 'William Hodges' Paintings of the South Pacific' by Jane Roundell in the *Connoisseur*, CC, 804 (February 1979) 85–9.
55. See *Captain Cook's Journal during his First Voyage round the World . . . 1768–71*, edited by W. Wharton (London, 1893) p. 305.
56. *The Voyage of the 'Beagle'*, pp. 269–71.
57. *The Voyage of the 'Beagle'*, pp. 243, 318–19.
58. *The Voyage of the 'Beagle'*, p. 363.
59. *The Voyage of the 'Beagle'*, pp. 485–6.
60. *The Voyage of the 'Beagle'*, p. 485.
61. See Loren Eiseley, *Darwin's Century* (London, 1959) p. 95.
62. In *Christianity, Islam and the Negro Race* (Edinburgh, 1887) the penetrating West Indian sociologist Edward W. Blyden protests against this harmful orthodoxy: 'The two races are not moving in the same groove with an immeasurable distance between them, but on parallel lines . . . they are *distinct* but equal' (p. 277).

63. 'The Method of Nature' in *Nature, Addresses, and Lectures*, Riverside Edition (London, 1886) p. 187.
64. Ludwig Leichhardt, *Journal of an Overland Expedition in Australia, 1844–5* (London, 1847) p. 266.
65. Indeed the idea became so popular as to attract literary parody. 'Do you mean', a character enquires in William Mallock's *The Veil of the Temple* (1904), 'that we are now asked to regard ourselves not only as the children of monkeys, but as the grandchildren of beans and potatoes?' (London, 1906) p. 236.
66. Hence the words of the Offertory: 'Deus, qui humanae substantiae dignitatem mirabiliter condidisti'.
67. Charles Rycroft, *A Critical Dictionary of Psychoanalysis* (London, 1968) p. 126.
68. 'Man lives according to his own idea of himself', Lawrence observes in *Kangaroo* (London, 1923) p. 295; and in the case of an individual with a deep-seated belief in the innate goodness of man it is reasonable to suppose that projection would reflect the tokens of an unfallen world as well as educe the marks of personal depravity.
69. *The Prelude* (1850) I, lines 357–400. See the text edited by Ernest de Selincourt, revised by Helen Darbishire (Oxford, 1959) pp. 23–6.
70. Ludwig Feuerbach, *The Essence of Christianity*, translated by George Eliot (New York, 1957) p. 5.

2. CRUSOE, DESERT ISLE VENTRILOQUIST

1. In the preface to *Familiar Letters*, his first substantial publication, Samuel Richardson appointed himself the task of describing 'the social, and relative duties'. See *Familiar Letters*, edited by Brian W. Downs (London, 1928) xxvii.
2. The account given by Ian Watt in *The Rise of the Novel* (London, 1957) remains the most influential. For a critical survey of more recent contributions in this field see Pat Rogers, *The Augustan Vision* (London, 1974) pp. 245–54.
3. All references to *Robinson Crusoe* are to the text edited by J. Donald Crowley (London, 1972), which has the same pagination as the later World's Classics text (Oxford, 1981).
4. See Pat Rogers, *Robinson Crusoe* (London, 1979) pp. 96–101.
5. See *Robinson Crusoe*, pp. 109, 112, 119, 180–1, as well as pp. 142–4.
6. See W. B. Carnochan, *Confinement and Flight* (Berkeley, 1977) pp. 29–45. Though indebted to this reading I disagree with the view that Crusoe's despair is largely a matter of pretence.
7. 'The Garden', lines 61–4.
8. Collected in Perry Miller's anthology *The American Puritans* (New York, 1956) p. 17, my italics.
9. Psalm 78:19.
10. *A Midsummer Night's Dream*, v. i. 2–22.
11. George A. Starr, *Defoe and Spiritual Autobiography* (Princeton, 1965); pp. 74–125 are on *Robinson Crusoe*.

12. From *The Life and Strange Surprizing Adventures of Mr D . . . De F . . . , of London, Hosier,* collected in *Defoe: The Critical Heritage,* edited by Pat Rogers (London, 1972) p. 41.
13. *The Pilgrim's Progress* (1678), edited by James Wharey (Oxford, 1928) pp. 36–7.
14. *The Pilgrim's Progress,* p. 263.
15. Chapters Five and Twelve of Bryan Little's biography of Woodes Rogers, *Crusoe's Captain* (London, 1960), provide a valuable supplement to the discussion of *Robinson Crusoe* in the standard work on Defoe's sources, A. W. Secord's *Studies in the Narrative Method of Defoe* (Urbana, 1924). See also Pat Rogers, *Robinson Crusoe,* pp. 16–34.
16. Woodes Rogers, *A Cruising Voyage Round the World* (London, 1712) p. 126.
17. *A Cruising Voyage,* p. 126.
18. *A Cruising Voyage,* p. 128.
19. *The Englishman: A Political Journal by Richard Steele,* edited by Rae Blanchard (Oxford, 1955); No. 26 (3 December 1713) pp. 107–8.
20. *The Englishman,* p. 108.
21. *An Essay on Man,* Epistle I, lines 5–8. In the one-volume edition of the Twickenham text, edited by John Butt (London, 1963) pp. 503–4.
22. See, for example, J. W. Jones's edition of *Divers Voyages Touching the Discovery of America,* translated and edited by Richard Hakluyt (New York, 1850, reprinted [1971]) p. 102.
23. *The Pilgrim's Progress,* p. 59.
24. *The Pilgrim's Progress,* p. 126.
25. Defoe's acquaintance with Locke's works is widely assumed. The section on human identity in *An Essay Concerning Human Understanding* (Book II, Chapter XXVII, paragraphs 5–10) contains the account (which Locke surprisingly found credible) of a 'very intelligent rational' parrot observed by a traveller in Brazil. Many supposed this bird possessed by the devil. See the text edited by A. C. Fraser (Oxford, 1894) I, 446–8. Poll shows no sign of special gifts. It is striking, however, that Crusoe should remark that any visitor to the island would, on hearing Poll, 'certainly believe it was the Devil' (p. 180).
26. *A General History of Discoveries and Improvements* (London, 1726–7). In this treatise Defoe argues that exploratory navigation is the 'parent of trade' (p. 32), and supplies an elaborate history of technological development ever since the Flood.
27. In his essay 'Of the Caniballes' Montaigne asks whether it is any worse to eat the body of a dead enemy than to torture the living in the name of religion.

3. DEFOE'S WILDERNESS

1. See John J. Richetti, *Defoe's Narratives* (Oxford, 1975) p. 83.
2. All quotations from *The Life, Adventures and Piracies of the Famous Captain Singleton* are from the Everyman text, edited by James Sutherland (London, 1963).
3. 'On Poetry: A Rapsody', *The Poems of Jonathan Swift,* edited by Harold

Williams (Oxford, 1937) II, 645. Gary J. Scrimgeour, 'The Problem of Realism in Defoe's *Captain Singleton*', *Huntington Library Quarterly*, XXVII (1963) 21–38 (p. 23).

4. See particularly *The Principall Navigations* (Glasgow, 1903–5) IX, 287; also VIII, 376, 453.
5. John R. Moore, *Daniel Defoe: Citizen of the Modern World* (Chicago, 1958) p. 252.
6. '*Captain Avery* and *Captain Singleton*: Revisions of Popular Legend': *Defoe's Narratives*, Chapter III; for the quotation see p. 78.
7. *Jure Divino* (London, 1706) p. 1.
8. *Leviathan*, Chapter XIII. In *The English Works of Thomas Hobbes*, edited by Sir William Molesworth (London, 1839–45), III, 113–14.
9. From 'Human Nature', *The English Works of Thomas Hobbes*, IV, 72.
10. M. van Wyk Smith, 'The Origins of Some Victorian Images of Africa', *English in Africa*, VI, 1 (1979) 12–32. The quotation from the *Atlas Geographus* is given on p. 15; the italics are mine.
11. *Atlas Maritimus et Commercialis* (London, 1728); for Defoe's account of Africa see pp. 236–76; for the quotation p. 237.
12. Defoe refers to African agriculture in *Captain Singleton* (p. 87) and indeed in the *Atlas* itself (p. 238). *Leviathan* in *The English Works*, III, 113.
13. For an excellent summary of Defoe's relation to Hobbes see Maximillian E. Novak, *Defoe and the Nature of Man* (Oxford, 1963) pp. 14–19.
14. Novak prefaces a quotation from Defoe's *The Political History of the Devil* (1726) with the remark: 'the picture which Defoe draws of the condition of the human race after the Flood is similar to Hobbes's state of nature'. *Defoe and the Nature of Man*, p. 16.
15. *Robinson Crusoe*, edited by J. D. Crowley (Oxford, 1972); see particularly pp. 92, 99.
16. See, for example, a passage on the Peruvians in *A New Voyage Round the World* (London, 1725) I, 202. Such instances are, however, the exception rather than the rule. Later in the same text Defoe retracts his generous primitivism (II, 78); and, as Novak remarks: 'in the majority of his writings he pictured the savage as an inferior being, condemned to a bestial life on earth and to eternal torment after death' (*Defoe and the Nature of Man*, p. 42).
17. *A Review*, III, 431a. Quoted by Novak, *Defoe and the Nature of Man*, p. 15.
18. See *Leviathan* in *The English Works*, III, 117–18; *Captain Singleton*, pp. 66, 85, 92; and for references to other 'Natural Laws', pp. 191, 228, 266.
19. *Leviathan* in *The English Works*, III, 126–7.
20. *Leviathan* in *The English Works*, III, 144.
21. Defoe began work on his Atlas in 1723–4. See Peter Earle, *The World of Defoe* (London, 1976) p. 296. *Atlas Maritimus*, p. 252.
22. John R. Moore traces the tale of the Portuguese explorers to the pages of the *London Gazette* (see *Citizen*, pp. 252, 379), and he is followed here by Scrimgeour (p. 36); in each case the reference is wrongly given. Although many critics have noted Defoe's reference to 'Mr Freeman' in the *Atlas Maritimus* the historical identity of Mr John Freeman, Manager of the Royal African Company at Sherbro, has not till now been established.
23. K. G. Davies, *The Royal African Company* (London, 1957) p. 256.

24. On Defoe's connections with the Royal African Company see Peter Earle (pp. 131–3) and John R. Moore (p. 289).

25. Novak comments on the tale of Valentine and Orson in his essay 'The Wild Man Comes to Tea', collected in *The Wild Man Within*, edited by Edward Dudley and himself (Pittsburgh, 1972) p. 186.

26. The archives of the Royal African Company are kept among the records of the Treasury in the Public Record Office. References for the last paragraph are as follows: T. 70/5, ff. 19a, 23b, 31b, 31a, 19a, 19b, 56a, 31b, 45b, 54b, 76b, 69a, 72a, 86b, 107a.

27. T. 70/51 ff. 265–76.

28. T. 70/14 ff. 596, 65b; *Atlas Maritimus* pp. 238, 252; *Captain Singleton*, pp. 106–7.

29. Swift's violent subversion of Sir William Petty's mercantilist tracts in *A Modest Proposal* provides perhaps the finest of many examples of the Augustan protest. The exactitude of Swift's reference is seldom appreciated. See *The Economic Writings of Sir William Petty*, edited by C. H. Hull (Cambridge, 1899) I, 244, 267, 308, 335–7, 346.

30. *A New Voyage Round the World* (London, 1725) I, 200.

31. *A New Voyage*, I, 115.

32. *The World of Defoe*, p. 54.

33. *The Commentator*, XL (20.5.1720), quoted in *The World of Defoe*, p. 205.

34. *A General History of Discoveries and Improvements* (London, 1726–7) pp. 80, 92.

35. *A Review*, III, ii (3.1.1706) collected in *Daniel Defoe*, edited by James Boulton (London, 1965) pp. 120–1.

36. *A General History*, p. 1.

37. *Mere Nature Delineated* (London, 1726) p. 61. See Novak in *The Wild Man Within*, p. 197.

38. *The Reformation of Manners* (London, 1702) p. 17. For an account of Defoe's attitudes to slavery see Peter Earle, pp. 67–70.

39. *A Review*, VII (6. 3. 1711) p. 591; quoted by Scrimgeour, p. 35.

40. 'The Life and Strange Surprizing Adventures of Mr D . . . De F . . .' (1719), collected in Ioan Williams, *The Novel and Romance* (London, 1970), see pp. 62–3.

41. *An Essay upon Projects* (London, 1702) p. 104. *An Essay upon the Trade to Africa* (London, 1711) p. 37.

4. MELVILLE'S HAPPY VALLEY

1. All references to *Typee* are to the Penguin edition, edited by George Woodcock (Harmondsworth, 1972). The text is substantially based on the Northwestern-Newberry edition of 1968.

2. In the introduction to his edition of *Typee*, George Woodcock remarks on Melville's debt to Defoe and Swift. He acutely observes: 'The literary convention within which Melville worked was that of the eighteenth-century imaginary voyage modified by a romantic conception of primitive man derived from Rousseau', pp. 17–18.

3. For a succinct account of Melville's experiences in the Marquesas see Leon Howard, *Herman Melville: A Biography* (Berkeley, 1951) pp. 50–4.
4. See *The Journals of Captain James Cook*, edited by J. C. Beaglehole, II, *The Voyage of the 'Resolution' and 'Adventure' 1772–1775* (Cambridge, 1969) pp. 372–5.
5. See, for example, the passage in which Crusoe explicitly relates his divergent responses to the island to his conversion: *Robinson Crusoe*, edited by J. Donald Crowley (Oxford, 1981) pp. 112–13.
6. Compare, for example, the description of Crusoe shattering the silence that has reigned since 'the Creation of the World' when he fires his gun. *Robinson Crusoe*, pp. 52–3.
7. Edgar A. Dryden makes this point in the course of an interesting discussion of Tommo's psychosomatic injury in *Melville's Thematics of Form* (Baltimore, 1968) pp. 40–3.
8. The allusion would not have been lost on Melville's readers. One reviewer commented: 'the Happy Valley of the gentle cannibals compares very well with the best contrivances of the learned Dr Johnson to produce similar impressions' (*New York Daily Tribune*, 4 April 1846). See Jay Leyda, *The Melville Log: A Documentary Life of Herman Melville 1819–1891* (New York, 1969) I, 209.
9. References to *Rasselas* are to the text edited by Geoffrey Tillotson and Brian Jenkins (Oxford, 1977). See p. 4 and elsewhere.
10. See *Moby Dick* Chapter XII: in the text edited by Charles Feidelson, Jr. (Indianapolis, 1964) pp. 88–90.
11. *The Dunciad*, Book IV, lines 293–4. In the one-volume edition of the Twickenham text, edited by John Butt (London, 1963) p. 782.
12. *Windsor-Forest*, line 406. In the one-volume Twickenham text, p. 210.
13. See *Gulliver's Travels*, edited by Peter Dixon (Harmondsworth, 1973) p. 343.
14. *A Sentimental Journey through France and Italy* in *The Works of Sterne* (New York, 1900) II, 236.
15. Johnson had translated *A Voyage to Abyssinia by Father Jerome Lobo, A Portuguese Jesuit* from the French of Le Grand in 1735. See Donald Lockhart's article ' "The Fourth Son of the Mighty Emperor": The Ethiopian Background of Johnson's *Rasselas*', *PMLA*, LXXVIII (1963) 516–28.
16. See James Boswell, *The Life of Samuel Johnson*, edited by Roger Ingpen (Bath, 1925) I, 512.
17. James Bruce, *Travels to Discover the Source of the Nile in the Years 1768–73* (Edinburgh, 1790) III, 598.
18. Compare Johnson's remark, made in the course of a discussion of David Hume, 'The human mind is so limited, that it cannot take in all the parts of a subject'. Boswell, I, 270.
19. Boswell, II, 774.
20. Amhara is numbered among the inferior paradises in *Paradise Lost* – see Book IV, lines 280–4. In *Kubla Khan* the relation between Mount Abora and the damsel's song parallels that between the creations of Kubla Khan and the poet.
21. In his *Discours sur l'origine et les fondements de l'inégalité* Rousseau writes, 'the greater part of our ills are of our own making, and . . . we might have avoided them all by adhering to that simple, uniform and solitary manner of life

which nature originally prescribed'. See *A Dissertation on the Origin and Foundation of the Inequality of Mankind*, collected in *The Miscellaneous Works of Mr J. J. Rousseau*, translated from the French in 1767 (London, 1767) I, 174.

22. *The Miscellaneous Works*, I, 154, 156, 160.
23. *The Miscellaneous Works*, I, 197–8.
24. *The Miscellaneous Works*, I, 154, 174.
25. *The Miscellaneous Works*, I, 205.
26. On this point see Geoffrey Symcox's essay 'The Wild Man's Return', collected in *The Wild Man Within*, edited by Edward Dudley and Maximillian E. Novak (Pittsburgh, 1972) p. 227.
27. This convention is called 'the negative formula' by Harry Levin in *The Myth of the Golden Age in the Renaissance* (New York, 1969) p. 20.
28. *Typee*, p. 295; cf. pp. 195, 204. *The Miscellaneous Works of Mr J. J. Rousseau*, I, 205.
29. So much so, indeed, that it is questionable whether the massive restoration of essay passages from the original manuscript in the Northwestern-Newberry edition of 1968 (on which the current Penguin edition is largely based) is altogether an advantage to the text.
30. James Fenimore Cooper, *The Prairie* (San Francisco, 1950) p. 210.
31. *The Prairie*, p. 212.
32. Luis Vaz De Camoens, *The Lusiads* (1572), Canto IX: translated and edited by C. Atkinson in the Penguin text (Harmondsworth, 1952) pp. 209–17.
33. Charles Darwin, *The Voyage of the 'Beagle'*, Everyman text, (London, 1906) p. 398.
34. See *Typee*, p. 200, where the statement of the paradox is particularly explicit in the text.
35. From *The Marriage of Heaven and Hell*; see *The Complete Writings of William Blake*, edited by Geoffrey Keynes (London, 1966) p. 158.
36. *The Miscellaneous Works*, I, 229–31.
37. *The Miscellaneous Works*, I, 167.
38. *The Confessions of Jean-Jacques Rousseau*, Book Two. In the Penguin text, translated by J. M. Cohen (Harmondsworth, 1953) pp. 63–4.

5.   CAPTAIN AHAB AND THE ALBATROSS

1. Charles Olson, *Call me Ishmael* (San Francisco, 1947) p. 13.
2. In a letter to Amy Lowell written on 23 August 1916. See *The Letters of D. H. Lawrence*, II, edited by G. J. Zytaruk and J. T. Boulton (Cambridge, 1981) p. 645.
3. All references to *Moby Dick* are to the text edited and annotated by Charles Feidelson, Jr. (Indianapolis, 1964).
   For *Euroclydon* see Acts 27:14.
4. Leon Howard comments on Melville's debts to Carlyle and Byron in his excellent account of the evolution of *Moby Dick*, see *Herman Melville: A Biography* (Berkeley, 1951) pp. 162–79. He is more concerned, however, with specific matters of literary influence than with a context of ideas. In *Melville's Quarrel With God* (Princeton, 1952) Lawrance Thompson is concerned with questions of belief but the treatment is largely internal.

5. See *The Letters of Herman Melville*, edited by M. R. Davis and W. H. Gilman (New Haven, 1960) p. 130.

6. *Mardi* began the same way too, but the voyage through the South Seas became increasingly the vehicle of allegory. See Leon Howard, *Herman Melville*, pp. 113–15.

7. Ian Cameron, *To the Farthest Ends of the Earth: The History of the Royal Geographical Society 1830–1980* (London, 1980) p. 16.

8. In Mrs Sabine's English translation Humboldt's full title runs 'Aspects of Nature in Different Lands and Different Climates; with *Scientific Elucidations*'.

9. Alexander von Humboldt, *Cosmos*, [translated by Mrs Sabine] (London, 1846–58) ii, 68.

10. Alexander von Humboldt, *Aspects of Nature* (London, 1849) i, 211; quoted by Douglas Botting in *Humboldt and the Cosmos* (London, 1973) p. 40.

11. Quoted by Botting, p. 40.

12. *Cosmos*, i, xviii.

13. Lytton Strachey, *Book and Characters* (London, 1922) p. 41.

14. See Charles Rycroft, *A Critical Dictionary of Psychoanalysis* (London, 1968) p. 105.

15. Addressed to Nathaniel Hawthorne from Pittsfield on 1 June 1851. *The Letters*, pp. 130–1. Davis and Gilman remark that Melville's exact source for the quotation from Goethe remains to be discovered, but suggest a likely passage from Carlyle.

16. 'Hawthorne and his Mosses' (1850) collected in *Hawthorne: The Critical Heritage*, edited by J. Donald Crowley (London, 1970) p. 116.

17. For a valuable account of the history of this idea see Lilian R. Furst on 'The "Esemplastic" Power' in her *Romanticism in Perspective* (New York, 1969) pp. 136–47.

18. Alan Sandison, *The Wheel of Empire* (London, 1967) p. 58. His quotations are from René Wellek's 'Romanticism Re-examined' in *Romanticism Reconsidered*, edited by Northrop Frye (1963) p. 130; and from Albert Guerard's 'The Logic of Romanticism' in *Essays and Criticism*, vii (1957).

19. Keats advances this distinction in his letter to Bailey (22 November 1817). *The Letters of John Keats*, edited by H. E. Rollins (Cambridge, 1958) i, 184; see also i, 193, 387.

   Davis and Gilman in their edition of Melville's letters trace the quotation from Goethe to his 'Generalbeichte'. J. G. Fichte proposes this view in *The Vocation of Man*. For a brief but lucid account see Sandison's *The Wheel of Empire*, pp. 49–51.

20. *Biographia Literaria*, Chapter xii. In the Everyman text, edited by George Watson (London, 1965) see pp. 137–8.

21. The idea is basic to the structure of Browning's 'A Grammarian's Funeral'; to Ibsen's *Brand*, *John Gabriel Borkman* and *When We Dead Awaken*; and to Olive Schreiner's allegory of the search for truth in *The Story of an African Farm*, separately published as 'The Hunter' in *Dreams* (London, 1890). The metaphor is in wide use in Nietzsche's writing but for a particularly explicit passage see *Ecce Homo*, translated by A. M. Ludovici (London, 1911), Preface (Section 3) pp. 2–3. Sir Leslie Stephen avails himself of the analogy in an essay entitled 'Heredity', see *Social Rights and Duties* (London, 1896) ii, 34.

22. See Jay Leyda, *The Melville Log* (New York, 1969) I, 271.
23. See 'Dejection: an Ode', stanza VI. *Coleridge: Poems*, edited by John Beer (London, 1974) p. 282.
24. All quotations from *The Rime of the Ancient Mariner* are from the text edited by John Beer, pp. 173–89.
25. R. Penn Warren, 'A Poem of Pure Imagination' (1946) collected in *Selected Essays* (London, 1964) pp. 199–305.
26. See J. L. Lowes, *The Road to Xanadu*, Sentry edition (Boston, 1955) p. 276.
27. For some interesting conjecture on the context of Melville's remark see *Melville's Quarrel With God*, pp. 140–1.
28. After witnessing the might of Leviathan Job declares: 'I know that thou canst do every thing, and that no thought can be withholden from thee'. Job 42:2.
29. See Charles Darwin, *The Voyage of the 'Beagle'*, Everyman text (London, 1906) pp. 364–70. Melville visited the Galapagos Islands in 1841, six years after Darwin, and bought a copy of *The Voyage* in 1847 – though he may have read it earlier: see *The Melville Log*, I, 180, 240.
30. *The Encantadas*, in *The Complete Stories of Herman Melville*, edited by Jay Leyda (New York, 1949) p. 58.

6. CONRAD DISMANTLES PROVIDENCE

1. All references to Conrad are to Dent's Uniform Edition (London, 1923–8) the pagination of which is identical to all later Dent editions and also to the Doubleday edition (1924).
2. *Falk*, in *Typhoon and Other Stories*, p. 211.
3. In a letter to W. Blackwood, Conrad wrote, 'I never did set up as an authority on Malaysia. I looked for a medium in which to express myself'. *Joseph Conrad: Letters to William Blackwood and David S. Meldrum*, edited by W. Blackburn (North Carolina, 1958) p. 34.
4. Ian Watt, *Conrad in the Nineteenth Century* (London, 1980) p. 154.
5. *A Personal Record*, p. 92.
6. *Joseph Conrad's Letters to R. B. Cunninghame Graham*, edited by C. T. Watts (Cambridge, 1969) p. 56.
7. 14 January 1898. *Letters to Cunninghame Graham*, p. 65.
8. Although *An Outcast* is among Conrad's relatively neglected works there is some valuable commentary on it. In his definitive account of the novel's sources in *Conrad's Eastern World* (Cambridge, 1966), Norman Sherry calls attention to the recurrent concern with patronage (p. 112). R. Roussel in *The Metaphysics of Darkness* (Baltimore, 1971) speaks of the subjective imprisonment undergone by the novel's major figures (pp. 52–5); and Bruce Johnson in *Conrad's Models of Mind* (Minneapolis, 1971), while examining Conrad's probing of the atrophied will, touches on the theme of projection, though he does not himself use the term (pp. 20–3).
9. *Almayer's Folly*, p. 192.
10. *Almayer's Folly*, p. 179. Norman Sherry mentions the fact that William

Lingard (on whom Conrad's Tom Lingard is based) owned a boat named *Nina: Conrad's Eastern World*, p. 90. Conrad would certainly have been aware of the reference to Columbus.

11. *Lord Jim*, p. 323.
12. Willems eventually begs Lingard to give him asylum on a 'deserted island' (p. 274).
13. Unsigned review: *Daily Chronicle*, 16 March 1896. See *Conrad: The Critical Heritage*, edited by Norman Sherry (London, 1973) p. 63.
14. In a letter to Humphrey Milford, 15 January 1907. See *Moby Dick As Doubloon*, edited by H. Parker and H. Hayford (New York, 1970) p. 123.
15. See *Spectator*, 30 May 1896, in *Critical Heritage*, p. 79.
16. By Omar, Abdullah, Lakamba, Almayer and Lingard.
17. 8 February 1899. *Letters to Cunninghame Graham*, p. 117.
18. See Barbara Hardy, *The Appropriate Form: An Essay on the Novel* (London, 1964, revised 1971) p. 53.
19. References to R. M. Ballantyne's *Coral Island* are to the Everyman text (London, 1907, reprinted 1954).
20. Author's Note to *An Outcast*, ix.
21. In *Speaker*, 12 November 1904. See *Critical Heritage*, p. 177.
22. *Almayer's Folly*, p. 165.
23. 'Praise, my soul, the King of Heaven', written by H. F. Lyte in 1834. *Hymns Ancient and Modern* (London, 1922) No 298, p. 326.
24. Author's Note, ix.
25. Royal Roussel, p. 32.
26. Bruce Johnson cites Schopenhauer in discussing *An Outcast* but in a quite different connection: see *Conrad's Models of Mind*, pp. 9, 11, 23. Johnson takes the view that Willems finds a refuge in the wilderness from competition and the exercise of will (p. 16). The narrator makes it clear, however, that Willems is no shirker and that he particularly regrets his lost chances: 'He gnashed his teeth when he thought of the wasted days, of the life thrown away. . . . He heard the reproach of his idleness in the murmurs of the river. . . .' (p. 65).
27. Arthur Schopenhauer, *The World as Will and Idea*, translated from the German by R. B. Haldane and J. Kemp, (London, 1896) I, 256.
28. Bruce Johnson, p. 15.
29. 'Naboth' from Rudyard Kipling's *Life's Handicap* (London, 1896) p. 340.
30. The '*Man-bap*' theme is especially to the fore in the exposition of Barbie's faith and of Teddie's death [see, particularly, *The Towers of Silence* (London, 1971) p. 364 and *The Day of the Scorpion* (London, 1968) p. 404] it inheres also, of course, in the central icon of the jewel in the crown.
31. *Under Western Eyes*, p. 8.
32. See *Under Western Eyes*, pp. 103, 263, 245, 281–2.
33. *Under Western Eyes*, p. 350.
34. See *Under Western Eyes*, pp. 289, 296, 301.
35. *Almayer's Folly*, p. 66.
36. In *Almayer's Folly* we see Lingard drinking in 'the approbative shouts of his half-intoxicated auditors' (p. 23).
37. Alfred Russel Wallace, *The Malay Archipelago*, (London, 1869) I, 146. My italics.

38. *The Malay Archipelago*, I, 397. Chapters VII and XVII have a particular bearing on this theme.

39. *The Malay Archipelago*, I, 397–8.

40. *The Malay Archipelago*, I, 402.

41. *The Malay Archipelago*, I, 144, 131.

42. *The Malay Archipelago*, I, 402.

43. Thomas Hardy, *Tess of the D'Urbervilles* (1891; London, 1974) p. 66.

44. Sigmund Freud, 'The Justification for Detaching from Neurasthenia a Particular Syndrome: The Anxiety-Neurosis' (1894) in *Collected Papers: Volume One*, translated by Joan Riviere (New York, 1924) pp. 76–106. See particularly pp. 101–2.

45. Sigmund Freud, 'Psycho-Analytic Notes upon an Autobiographical Account of a Case of Paranoia' (1911) in *Collected Papers: Volume Three*, translated by Alix and James Strachey (London, 1925). Freud writes: 'The intensity of the emotion is projected outwards in the shape of external power, while its quality is changed into the opposite. The person who is now hated and feared as a persecutor was at one time loved and honoured' (p. 424).

46. Sigmund Freud, 'A Difficulty in the Path of Psycho-Analysis' (1917) in *Complete Psychological Works: Volume Seventeen*, translated and edited by James Strachey (London, 1955) p. 140.

47. See Albert J. Guerard, *Conrad: The Novelist* (Cambridge, Mass., 1978) p. 80.

48. Georges Bataille, *Death and Sensuality: A Study of Eroticism and the Taboo*, translated from the French (New York, 1962) p. 17.

49. *The Malay Archipelago*, I, 120. For a good instance of the providential reading of nature see Livingstone's celebrated account of lion attack: he sees the release of the victim's adrenalin as 'a merciful provision by our benevolent Creator for lessening the pain of death'. *Missionary Travels and Researches in South Africa* (London, 1857) p. 12.

50. Richard Curle's testimony is quoted by Norman Sherry in *Conrad's Eastern World*, pp. 141–2.

7. THE HIDDEN MAN

1. *Joseph Conrad: Life and Letters*, edited by G. Jean-Aubry (London, 1927) II, 338. In a letter to F. N. Doubleday Conrad stresses the aesthetic unity of the volume.

    All references to Conrad are to Dent's Uniform Edition (London, 1923–8) which has the same pagination as later Dent editions.

2. Arthur Schopenhauer, *The World as Will and Idea* (1819, first English translation 1883) translated by R. B. Haldane and J. Kemp, fourth edition (London, 1896). Of particular relevance here is the Fourth Book, 'The Assertion and Denial of the Will'.

    In a short memoir on Conrad written in 1924 John Galsworthy recalls: 'Of philosophy he had read a good deal . . . Schopenhauer used to give him satisfaction twenty years and more ago'. *Castles in Spain* (London, 1927) p. 91. See also C. T. Watt's introduction to *Joseph Conrad's Letters to R. B. Cunninghame Graham*, p. 25.

3. *Joseph Conrad's Letters to R. B. Cunninghame Graham*, edited by C. T. Watts (Cambridge, 1969) p. 70. For a comparable passage in *The World as Will and Idea* see I, 400–1.

4. Edward Garnett, *Letters from Conrad, 1895–1924* (London, 1928) xii.

5. *Youth*, pp. 26, 30.

6. *The World as Will and Idea*, pp. 456, 454.

7. See Author's Note, xi.

8. *Youth*, pp. 37, 41.

9. *Youth*, p. 33.
    In 'Geography and Some Explorers' (1924) Conrad recalls that Sir Leopold McClintock's account of the recovery expedition, *The Voyage of the Fox* (1859), was among the favourite books of his childhood. The expedition was funded by Franklin's widow and Sir Leopold breathes no word of cannibalism, referring only to the depredations of 'large and powerful animals', (London, 1908) p. 223. Conrad refers in his essay, however, to the gradual revelations of the crew's fate in this 'darkest' of dramas, *Last Essays*, pp. 10–11. The revelations actually predate McClintock, see John Rae, *The Melancholy Fate of Sir John Franklin and his Party* (London, 1854).

10. *Youth*, p. 37.

11. H. M. Stanley, *Through the Dark Continent* (1878; London, 1907) p. 449.

12. 'Geography and Some Explorers', *Last Essays*, p. 17.

13. Quoted by Neal Ascherson in *The King Incorporated: Leopold II in the Age of Trusts* (London, 1963) p. 248.

14. See Norman Sherry, *Conrad's Western World* (Cambridge, 1971) pp. 12, 14.

15. Conrad refers, in the course of his essay, to Park, Barth, Burton, Speke, Livingstone and Stanley.

16. Schweinfurth, *The Heart of Africa*, translated by Ellen Frewer (London, 1873) I, 13–15. Appalled by his first view of colonial exploitation on a gypsum mine at Gimsah, the explorer compares the workers to 'beasts . . . caged in hopeless imprisonment' and equates fumes of sulphur rising from the site with the fires of hell. The passage is comparable in many respects to Marlow's description of the company station with its grove of death.

17. H. M. Stanley, *In Darkest Africa* (London, 1890). Barttelot, a possible model for Kurtz (see Ian Watt, *Conrad in the Nineteenth Century*, pp. 142–3) seems not to have heeded the lecture on forbearance (I, 124–6), if it was ever given, for his death was caused by a fit of pique (I, 490), and rumours of his excesses were rife at the rear camp (I, 483).
    Some of Stanley's descriptive passages are remarkably close to Conrad's: see, for example, *In Darkest Africa*, II, 80–1, 75–6; I, 195, 268. For sea and beast similes in *Heart of Darkness* see pp. 86, 92, 156; 96, 105. Compare also the passages from *Almayer's Folly* (1895) and *In Darkest Africa* (1890) already quoted on pp. 122, 14.

18. Schweinfurth quotes the proverb, 'When fame paints a serpent, she attaches feet to its body'. His purpose, in his own metaphor, is to remove the tail that mythology has appended to all things African: see *Heart of Africa*, II, 176; I, 68. For Stanley's remarks see *In Darkest Africa*, II, 147, 150, 137.

19. Philip D. Curtin, *The Image of Africa* (London, 1965) p. 207.

20. For an interesting discussion of this topic see H. Alan Cairns, *Prelude to*

Imperialism: British Reactions to Central African Society 1840–1890 (London, 1965) Chapter 3, 'Contemporary Ancestors'.

21. *The Heart of Africa*, II, 2, 17, 127.
22. See Richard Burton, *The Lake Regions of Central Africa* (1860; London, 1961) II, 324; and *Livingstone's Private Journals 1851–53*, edited by I. Schapera (London, 1960) p. 156.
23. *In Darkest Africa*, II, 40–2, 44; I, 327; I, 131; I, 151.
24. For an account of this theme see Leo J. Henkin, *Darwinism in the English Novel 1860–1910* (New York, 1940, reprinted 1963) Chapter 9, 'The Anthropological Romance'.
25. Ian Watt, *Conrad in the Nineteenth Century* (London, 1980) p. 166.
26. Richard Burton, *First Footsteps in East Africa*, Memorial Edition (London, 1894) I, 4.
27. *First Footsteps*, I, 5, 27. The line from Almanzor's first important speech in *The Conquest of Granada* reads, 'I am as free as nature e'er made man'.
28. Richard Burton, *Zanzibar: City, Island, and Coast* (London, 1872) I, 17.
29. *The Matabele Journals of Robert Moffat 1829–1860*, edited by J. P. R. Wallis (London, 1945) pp. 118–19.
30. *The Heart of Africa*, I, 331.
31. Richard Burton, *A Mission to Gelele King of Dahome*, edited by C. W. Newbury (London, 1966) pp. 221, 285.
32. *A Mission to Gelele*, p. 230.
33. *A Mission to Gelele*, pp. 221, 233, 223n.
34. See Christopher Hibbert, *Africa Explored: Europeans in the Dark Continent 1769–1889* (London, 1982) pp. 279, 203; and Burton's *First Footsteps*, I, 28.
35. See Fawn Brodie, *The Devil Drives: A Life of Sir Richard Burton* (New York, 1967) pp. 15–20, 290–9.
36. Swinburne quoted by Alan Moorehead in *The White Nile* (London, 1960) p. 20; Speke by Hibbert in *Africa Explored*, p. 209.
37. In the preface to one of his own poems. See *The Devil Drives*, pp. 276, 278.
38. See *The White Nile*, p. 20.
39. Arthur Symons quoted by Hibbert in *Africa Explored*, p. 203; Frank Harris, *Contemporary Portraits* (London, 1915) pp. 166–7.
40. For an account of this trend see Bernard Porter, *Critics of Empire* (London, 1968).
41. See *In Darkest Africa*, I, 390; II, 227. Stanley also spells out the suffering entailed by the 'trade' in ivory: 'for every five pounds a hut has been burned; for every two tusks a whole village has been destroyed . . . It is simply incredible that, because ivory is required for ornaments or billiard games, the rich heart of Africa should be laid waste' (I, 230).
42. See *The King Incorporated*, particularly Chapters 9 and 10.
43. See Jack Simmons, *Livingstone and Africa* (London, 1955) p. 152 and *The King Incorporated*, p. 92. Livingstone was buried in 1874; Leopold made his speech to an international audience in Brussels two years later.
44. See *The King Incorporated*, pp. 94, 88, 113.
45. See Edward Glave, 'Cruelty in the Congo Free State' in *The Century Magazine*, LIV, 5 (September 1897) p. 709.
46. Descriptions are legion: for plates see, for example, John Speke, *Journal of the*

Discovery of the Source of the Nile (Edinburgh, 1863) p. 102; Verney Cameron, *Across Africa* (London, 1877) i, 166; ii, 147; Livingstone, *Last Journals* (London, 1874) i, 56.

47. Mungo Park, *Travels in the Interior of Africa* (1799) edited by Ronald Miller (London, 1954) pp. 249, 18, 265.

48. *The Last Journals of David Livingstone*, edited by Horace Waller (London, 1874) ii, 92. The passage concerned is pieced together from the testimony of Chuma and Susi.

49. See *Conrad's Western World*, pp. 30–4.

50. Quoted in *Critics of Empire*, p. 304. For an account of the Congo Reform Society see Bernard Porter also.

51. Quoted by S. J. S. Cookey in *Britain and the Congo Question 1885–1913* (London, 1968) p. 76. Casement made this comment in 1903.

52. By a decree of 1892, for example, Leopold excluded all private companies and traders from a large area of the Congo known as the *Domaine Privé*.

53. S. J. S. Cookey notes that 'company agents were free to levy what taxes they liked, to collect them by whatever means they chose, and to impose any punishment they fancied in case of a default'. *Britain and the Congo Question*, p. 16. The agents were entitled to a percentage of the total takings as Conrad indicates, see *Heart of Darkness*, p. 78.

54. See *The Century Magazine*, liv, pp. 699–715. Glave's stark reports are an invaluable background to *Heart of Darkness*. The quotation is from a letter, printed separately in the same magazine, p. 796.

55. 'Glave's Last Letter', *The Century Magazine*, p. 797.

56. *The World as Will and Idea*, pp. 460–1. My italics.

57. Schopenhauer opens his preceding paragraph with the remark that 'knowledge of eternal justice . . . demands the complete transcending of individuality', p. 458.

58. 'Autocracy and War' in *Notes on Life and Letters*, pp. 84, 108–9.

59. *The Lake Regions of Central Africa*, ii, 352–3.

60. 'Author's Note', x.

61. C. W. Newbury in his introduction to Burton's *Mission to Gelele* remarks that a 'major question posed by the age was whether Africa could be considered as part of the human race' (p. 38). The question was raised by Burton himself in a chapter entitled 'Of The Negro's Place in Nature' (left out of the new edition) where he suggests that the theory of 'a great structural gulf between the black and white races' was gaining rather than losing ground in his own period. See Memorial Edition (London, 1893) ii, 121, 122, 126. For some interesting discussion of this topic and of related issues such as *polygenesis* see Bernard Porter, *Critics of Empire*, Chapter 5; and P. D. Curtin, *The Image of Africa*, Chapters 9 and 15.

62. *The World as Will and Idea*, p. 471.

63. *The World as Will and Idea*, p. 472.

64. See *Conrad in the Nineteenth Century*, pp. 225–30.

65. Charles Dickens, *A Christmas Carol* in *Christmas Books*, Oxford India Paper Dickens (London, n.d.) pp. 23–4. Marley's ghost images Scrooge's inner state, see p. 30.

66. In a Frazer-like reconstruction of these rites, Stephen Reid argues that Kurtz should be supposed to make a ritual meal of his sacrificial victims. See

'The "Unspeakable Rites" in *Heart of Darkness*' in *Conrad: A Collection of Critical Essays*, edited by Marvin Mudrick (Englewood Cliffs, N.J., 1966) p. 48.

67. *Letters to R. B. Cunninghame Graham*, p. 116.
68. The view that the atrocities were the 'natural outcome' of the system of government was taken by Pickersgill, see *Britain and the Congo Question*, p. 49; for Keir Hardie's more pessimistic view, summarized by Neal Ascherson in the quotation, see *The King Incorporated*, p. 260.
69. T. H. Huxley, 'Evolution and Ethics', *Collected Essays* (London, 1892–5) IX, 83.
70. For a finely argued defence of Marlow's lie see Jacques Berthoud, *Joseph Conrad: The Major Phase* (Cambridge, 1978) pp. 60–3.
71. See 'Travel' in *Last Essays*, p. 90.
72. The climactic scene in which Alan McKenzie makes his honourable lie reverberates with Conradian echoes. See Somerset Maugham, *The Explorer*, Collected Edition (London, 1967) pp. 152–6.
73. E. M. Forster, *A Passage to India* (Harmondsworth, 1957) pp. 123, 125; but see the whole of Chapter 12. In *Moby Dick* Melville describes the sea as 'an everlasting terra incognita' (p. 362).
74. D. H. Lawrence, *Psychoanalysis and the Unconscious* (1921), Adelphi Library (London, 1931) pp. 13–16, 14.
75. For the reference to Jung see Fritz Wittels, *Sigmund Freud: his Personality, his Teaching and his School*, translated by Eden and Cedar Paul (New York, 1924) p. 182. For Freud's theory see, for example, *Totem and Taboo*, translated by James Strachey (London, 1950) pp. 88–90.
76. For the quotation from Marx and a discussion of his relation to Darwin see Gillian Beer, *Darwin's Plots* (London, 1983) pp. 57–8.
77. To Edward Garnett, 5 June 1914. *The Letters of D. H. Lawrence*, II, edited by G. J. Zytaruk and J. T. Boulton (Cambridge, 1981) pp. 182–4. In the preface to *Miss Julia* Strindberg relates a very similar notion of fluid identity to evolutionary theory. See August Strindberg, *Eight Famous Plays*, translated by Edwin Björkman (London, 1968) pp. 106–7.
78. See T. S. Eliot's note to line 218.
79. Virginia Woolf, *To the Lighthouse* (London, 1977) pp. 99, 84.
80. James Joyce, *Ulysses* (London, 1960) pp. 272–4.
81. D. H. Lawrence, *The Rainbow* (London, 1926) pp. 445–50, and p. 190. I am indebted to Sue McClintock for pointing out this last quotation.

8. THE COUNTRY OF THE MIND

1. In *A Fringe of Leaves* White draws again on the Kelly paintings when he describes Jack Chance: 'He had withdrawn inside his leather mask, through the slits in which, eyes of a pale, drained blue were looking at her suspiciously . . . The mask in wrinkled leather immediately set into a rusted-iron visor' (London, 1976) p. 281. Nolan's series on the Fraser legend undoubtedly contributed to this novel as well.

There are several details in *Voss* that correspond to Leichhardt's account of his first expedition to Port Essington: Leichhardt himself was badly kicked by a horse, and Gilbert, the botanist of the party, was killed by a spear. White would certainly have noticed the German's interest in the mineral and crystalline, which seems far in excess of strictly scientific ends. See *Journal of an Overland Expedition in Australia* (London, 1847) pp. 308–10, 435, 221. Also mentioned by White are the journals of Eyre, and here too there are points of resemblance, particularly Baxter's wish – half-way through the journey – to abandon his leader and return. White may equally well have remembered, however, the split between Burke and his second-in-command at Menindee. See *Flaws in the Glass* (London, 1981) p. 103; and Edward Eyre, *Journals of Expeditions of Discovery into Central Australia and Overland* (London, 1845) I, 378, 384.

2. All references to *Voss* are to the edition published by Jonathan Cape (London, 1980). For the eye motif see pp. 29, 31, 101, 122, 224, 419, apart from those cited below.

3. R. F. Brissenden, *Patrick White* (London, 1966, revised 1969) p. 25.

4. Brian Kiernan, *Patrick White* (London, 1980) p. 51. A striking precedent for this alternation of literal and figurative journeying exists in the third section of *To the Lighthouse*. Virginia Woolf is one of the many twentieth-century writers whose influence White has potently assimilated.

5. The reference to 'base metal' represents the first of a train of alchemical images applied to Voss's development. White's interests in this field seem to derive from his reading of Jung's *Psychology and Alchemy*: see *Flaws in the Glass*, p. 146.

6. Though this holds of many paintings in the series, I am thinking particularly of the one entitled *Kelly* (1954).

7. J. G. Fichte, *The Vocation of Man*, translated by William Smith, revised and edited by R. M. Chisholm (New York, 1956) pp. 124–6.

8. *The Vocation of Man*, p. 128.

9. Patricia Morley refers to the 'New Testament theme of dying to sin in order to live unto God' in her discussion of *Voss*: see *The Mystery of Unity* (Montreal, 1972) p. 124.

10. See the chapter entitled 'The Flight from Women' in Paul Zweig's *The Adventurer* (London, 1974) particularly p. 71.

11. Central to the dream, this image – the offered and rejected hand – also recurs through the text, notably in the scene of Palfreyman's death (p. 365), and in the description of the first meeting with the Aborigines:

> At first the blackfellow was reluctant, but then took the hand as if it had been some inanimate object of barter, and was turning it over, examining its grain, the pattern of veins, and, on its palm, the lines of fate.
>
> (p. 219)

'It would seem that all human relationships hung in the balance', the narrator observes on this occasion, indicating also the generic significance that attaches to the relationship of Voss and Laura.

12. James Joyce, *Ulysses* (London, 1960) p. 24.

13. D. H. Lawrence, 'The Crown', collected in *Phoenix II*, edited by Warren Roberts and Harry T. Moore (London, 1968) pp. 365–415.

14. A. R. Radcliffe-Brown in his pioneering essay, 'The Rainbow-Serpent Myth in South-East Australia', advances the view that the Great Snake is the Aborigines' 'most important representation of the creative and destructive power of nature'. *Oceania*, I (1930) p. 342–7; see p. 347. Principally through the character of Jackie, White gives a colourful exposition of this view: the Rainbow Serpent is *'gut'* and 'Father my father, all blackfeller' (pp. 292–3), but also death-bringer – ' "Snake eat, eat," cried the black boy, snapping at the darkness with his white teeth' (p. 403). Voss, as befits his transition from God to man, is pictured both as the swallower and the swallowed, as Rainbow Serpent and victim, in his closing scene (pp. 400, 402).

15. L. R. Hiatt's article, 'Swallowing and Regurgitation in Australian Myth and Rite', collected in *Australian Aboriginal Mythology*, edited by himself (Canberra, 1975), is full of interest for the student of Patrick White. Like a postulant who emerges as an initiate from the belly of the Rainbow Serpent Voss is 'swallowed' (p. 400) by the cleft (with its 'folds of grey earth') in which he completes his process of self-recognition (p. 414).

16. Elkin notes that the initiation of medicine men takes the form of a ritualized death followed by 'a rebirth and endowment with new life'. For the postulant the transitional phase is often associated (as in Le Mesurier's case) with illness and madness; while the final possession of crystals (Le Mesurier has to be prevented from raking up the live embers in the cave) symbolizes the immanence of the Rainbow Serpent with which, because of their prismatic qualities, the crystals are linked. See A. P. Elkin, *Aboriginal Men of High Degree* (Sydney, 1945) p. 123; and *The Australian Aborigines* (Sydney, 1943) p. 226.

17. Friedrich Nietzsche, 'Maxims and Interludes, 138' from *Beyond Good and Evil*, translated by R. J. Hollingdale (Harmondsworth, 1973) p. 83.

18. Peter Beatson calls attention to the ritual detail of the knocked-out tooth in *Voss*. See 'The Three Stages: Mysticism in Patrick White's *Voss*', *Southerly*, 30 (1970) p. 121. Other such details include Laura's metaphoric emergence from an initiation hut at the moment of her deepening intimacy with Voss (p. 64); and the imagery of metamorphosis that White applies to Belle's marriage, and to the farewell party (pp. 351, 86–7).

19. Of the portrayal of Sydney in the last phase of the novel G. A. Wilkes remarks, 'the whole *Zeitgeist* has been changed by the experience [of Voss]'. See 'A Reading of Patrick White's *Voss*' in *Southerly*, 27 (1967) 159–73 (p. 173).

20. See, for example, Mircea Eliade's summary of the Aranda myths of origin in *Australian Religions* (Ithaca, 1973) pp. 44–50.

21. Sketched under the heading 'Repetition of the Cosmogony' in *The Myth of the Eternal Return* (translated by Willard R. Trask, Princeton, N.J., 1954) pp. 17–21, this theory repeatedly returns in Eliade's writings. See, for example, *Myths, Dreams and Mysteries*, translated by Philip Mairet (London, 1960) pp. 218–23.

9. THE SACRAMENTAL WILD

1. *The Eye of the Storm* (London, 1973) p. 378. The Warmer children base their cult on a supposed burial ground under the floor of their holiday house on Brumby – which exactly corresponds to Fraser Island of the atlas.

   For a full exposition and criticism of the many versions of Eliza Fraser's story see Michael Alexander, *Mrs Fraser on the Fatal Shore* (London, 1971). White's novel is loosely based on the unlikely tale told by Bracefell, sympathetically recorded by Henry Stuart Russell in *The Genesis of Queensland* (Sydney, 1888) and summarized by Alexander, pp. 108–23.

2. All references to *A Fringe of Leaves* are to the edition published by Jonathan Cape (London, 1976). See pp. 233, 324.

3. *The Eye of the Storm*, Chapter 8; pp. 403, 382.

4. 'Most of us have committed murders', Voss remarks; and adds later – 'we shall be eaten by somebody eventually. By a friend, perhaps'. See *Voss* (London, 1980) pp. 25, 403.

5. D. H. Lawrence, *The Rainbow* (London, 1926) p. 203.

6. D. H. Lawrence, *Kangaroo* (London, 1923) pp. 228–9, 213.

7. *Kangaroo*, Chapter 8; and see pp. 165, 183–5, 294–5.

8. *Kangaroo*, p. 183.

9. For a discussion of White's (self-acknowledged) debt to Simone Weil see Veronica Brady 'The Novelist and the Reign of Necessity: Patrick White and Simone Weil', in *Patrick White: A Critical Symposium*, edited by R. Shepherd and K. Singh (Adelaide, 1978) pp. 108–16.

10. See C. G. Jung, *Psychological Types*, translated by H. Godwin Baynes (London, 1923) pp. 525–6, 551–2.

11. For an excellent account of the Virgilian and other levels of allusion in the novel see Manly Johnson, '*A Fringe of Leaves*: White's Genethlicon' in *Texas Studies in Language and Literature*, 21 (1979) 226–39. There are several valuable articles in this volume which is wholly given over to White.

12. Edward W. Said, *Orientalism* (London, 1978) p. 305.

13. Janet Lewis, *The Invasion* (Chicago, 1960) p. 76.

14. See, for example, Baldwin Spencer, *Wanderings in Wild Australia* (London, 1928) I, 203; and his *The Arunta* (London, 1927) p. 495; N. W. Thomas, *Natives of Australia* (London, 1906) p. 109. In *The Man-Eating Myth* (New York, 1979), W. Arens challenges the reliability of all evidence relating to ritual cannibalism but repeatedly overlooks testimony of considerable weight in favour of his men-of-straw. He quotes with approval Livingstone's comments on alleged cannibalism among the Manyuema, 'A Scotch jury would say, "Not proven," ' and goes on to generalize from it – 'his experienced testimony should be of some value' (p. 85). Livingstone did, however, believe in the existence of cannibalism in Africa, and in a late entry of his Journal, not many pages on, accepts and records a graphic report of the practice among the Manyuema who 'seem to eat their foes to inspire courage'. See *The Last Journals of David Livingstone* (London, 1874) II, 98, 148; also II, 48–9, 117–18. First-hand evidence though uncommon is not as rare as Arens makes out; the Fraser material provides an instance in the testimony of John Baxter, see Michael Alexander's book, pp. 57–8.

15. B. A. L. Cranstone, *The Australian Aborigines* (London, 1973) p. 28.
16. For a different interpretation of Ellen's cannibal rite see 'A Severed Leg: Anthropophagy and Communion in Patrick White's Fiction' in *Southerly*, 40 (1980) 399–417, where Don Anderson takes the austerely psychoanalytic view that Ellen in 'eating the phallus, in partaking of the insistent thigh . . . "kills" the father-totem within her' (p. 415). For Anderson it is the leg rather than the act of ingestion which seems important. One recorder of South Queensland rites notes, though, that 'most parts of the body are eaten, the thighs being the *bonne bouche*'. *Natives of Australia*, p. 109.
17. *Voss*, p. 180.
18. *The Ballad of Reading Gaol*, stanza 7. See *The Works of Oscar Wilde*, edited by G. F. Maine (London, 1948) p. 823.
19. Friedrich Nietzsche, *Beyond Good and Evil*, translated by R. J. Hollingdale (Harmondsworth, 1973) Section 229, p. 140.
20. *Dusklands* (Johannesburg, 1974) pp. 104, 106.
21. According to Bracefell, Mrs Fraser withdrew her promise on approaching the colony – threatening, indeed, to complain of him instead – and so he returned to the tribe. *Mrs Fraser on the Fatal Shore*, pp. 113–14.
22. For an account of J. M. Coetzee's strategy in this regard see my article '*Dusklands*: A Metaphysics of Violence' in *Contrast 53*, xiv, 1 (1982) 26–38.
23. White quotes 'A perfect Woman, nobly planned, / To warn, to comfort, and command' from 'She was a Phantom of Delight' among the novel's epigraphs.
24. *The Notebooks of Simone Weil*, translated by Arthur Wills (London, 1956) i, 235.
25. Simone Weil, *Oppression and Liberty*, translated by Arthur Wills and John Petrie (London, 1958) p. 108.
26. William Faulkner, *The Bear*, collected in *Go Down Moses* (Harmondsworth, 1960) p. 177.

Bibliography

Unless otherwise stated, place of publication is London.

I. EXPLORATION AND RELATED WORKS

Alexander, Michael, *Mrs Fraser on the Fatal Shore* (1971).

Axelson, Eric, *Congo to Cape: Early Portuguese Explorers* (1973).

Bagrow, Leo, *History of Cartography*, rev. R. A. Skelton (1964).

Baker, Sir Samuel W., *The Albert N'yanza, Great Basin of the Nile*, 2 vols (1886).

Barrow, Sir John, *An Account of Travels into the Interior of Southern Africa in the years 1797 and 1798*, 2 vols (1801–4).

Beaglehole, J. C., *The Exploration of the Pacific* (1934).

Bennett, Josephine, *The Rediscovery of Sir John Mandeville* (New York, 1954).

Botting, Douglas, *Humboldt and the Cosmos* (1973).

Brodie, Fawn, *The Devil Drives: A Life of Sir Richard Burton* (New York, 1967).

Bruce, James, *Travels to Discover the Source of the Nile in the years 1768–73*, 5 vols (Edinburgh, 1790).

Burchell, William, *Travels in the Interior of Southern Africa*, 2 vols (1822–4, repr. 1953).

Burton, Isabel, *Life of Captain Sir Richd. F. Burton*, 2 vols (1893).

Burton, Richard F., *First Footsteps in East Africa or, An Exploration of Harar*, Memorial Edition, 2 vols (1894).

——, *The Lake Regions of Central Africa*, 2 vols (1860, repr. 1961).

——, *Mission to Gelele King of Dahome*, Memorial Edition, 2 vols (1893).

——, *Mission to Gelele King of Dahome*, ed. C. W. Newbury (1966).

——, *Zanzibar: City, Island, and Coast* (1872).

Cameron, Ian, *To the Furthest Ends of the Earth: The History of the Royal Geographical Society 1830–1980* (1980).

Cameron, Verney, *Across Africa*, 2 vols (1877).

Collis, J. S., *Christopher Columbus* (1976).

Columbus, Christopher, *Select Documents Illustrating the Four Voyages of Columbus*, trans. and ed. Cecil Jane, 2 vols (1933).

Cook, James, *Captain Cook's Journal during his First Voyage round the World* . . . *1768–71*, ed. W. Wharton (1893).
——, *The Journals of Captain James Cook*, ed. J. C. Beaglehole, 4 vols (Cambridge, 1955–74).
——, *A Voyage to the Pacific Ocean* . . . *1776–80*, 3 vols (1784).
Dampier, William, *A New Voyage round the World*, 2nd edn (1697–1703).
Darwin, Charles, *The Voyage of the 'Beagle'* (Everyman, 1906).
Debenham, Frank, *Discovery and Exploration* (1960).
Encyclopaedia of Discovery and Exploration, 18 vols (1971).
Eyre, Edward J., *Journals of Expeditions of Discovery into Central Australia and Overland in the years 1840–1*, 2 vols (1845).
Forster, Georg, *A Voyage round the World* . . . *1772–5*, 2 vols (1777).
Forster, John Reinold, *Observations made during a Voyage round the World* (1778).
Hakluyt, Richard, *Divers Voyages touching the Discovery of America*, ed. J. W. Jones (New York 1850, repr. [1971]).
——, *The Principall Navigations*, 12 vols (Glasgow, 1903–5).
——, *Virginian Voyages from Hakluyt*, ed. David and Alison Quinn (1973).
Hall, Richard, *Stanley: An Adventurer Explored* (1974).
Haresnape, G. L. (ed.), *The Great Hunters* (Cape Town, 1974).
Hibbert, Christopher, *Africa Explored: Europeans in the Dark Continent, 1769–1889* (1982).
Humboldt, Alexander von, *Aspects of Nature*, trans. Mrs Sabine, 2 vols (1849).
Jameson, James Sligo, *Story of the Rear Column of the Emin Pasha Relief Expedition* (1890).
Jones, Howard Mumford, *O Strange New World: American Culture: The Formative Years* (New York, 1964).
Leichhardt, Ludwig, *Journal of an Overland Expedition in Australia 1844–5* (1847).
——, *The Letters of F. W. Ludwig Leichhardt*, coll. and trans. M. Aurousseau, 3 vols (Cambridge, 1968).
Lichtenstein, Martin H. K., *Travels in Southern Africa in the years 1803–6*, trans. Anne Plumptre, 2 vols (1812–15).
Little, Bryan, *Crusoe's Captain: Being the Life of Woodes Rogers, Seaman, Trader, Colonial Governor* (1960).
Livingstone, David, *The Last Journals of David Livingstone*, ed. Horace Waller, 2 vols (1874).
——, *Livingstone's Private Journals, 1851–3*, ed. I. Schapera (1960).
——, *Missionary Travels and Researches in South Africa* (1857).
McClintock, Sir Leopold, *The Voyage of the Fox in Arctic Seas* (1859, repr. 1908).
Moffat, Robert, *The Matabele Journals of Robert Moffat, 1829–60*, ed. J. P. R. Wallis (1945).
Moorehead, Alan, *The Blue Nile* (1962).
——, *Darwin and the Beagle* (1969).
——, *The White Nile* (1960).
Newby, Eric, *The World Atlas of Exploration* (1975).
Park, Mungo, *Mungo Park's Travels in Africa*, ed. Ronald Miller (1954).
Parry, J. H., *The Age of Reconnaissance* (Berkeley, 1981).
——, *The Discovery of the Sea* (Berkeley, 1981).
Polo, Marco, *The Book of Ser Marco Polo*, trans. and ed. Sir Henry Yule, 3rd edn, 3 vols (1903).

Purchas, Samuel, *Hakluytus Posthumus; or Purchas his Pilgrimes*, 20 vols (Glasgow, 1905–7).
Rae, John, *The Melancholy Fate of Sir J. Franklin and his Party* (1854).
Raisz, Erwin, *Mapping the World* (1956).
Rogers, Woodes, *A Cruising Voyage round the World . . . 1708–11* (1712).
Rotberg, Robert, *Africa and its Explorers* (Cambridge, Mass., 1970).
Russell, Henry Stuart, *The Genesis of Queensland* (Sydney, 1888).
Schweinfurth, Georg, *The Heart of Africa*, trans. Ellen E. Frewer, 2 vols (1873).
Seaver, George, *Edward Wilson of the Antarctic* (1933).
Simmons, Jack, *Livingstone and Africa* (1955).
Simpson, Donald, *Dark Companions: The African Contribution to the European Exploration of East Africa* (1975).
Smith, Bernard, *European Vision and the South Pacific* (1960).
Smith, Captain John, *Works 1608–31*, ed. Edward Arber, 2 vols (1895).
Speke, John, *Journal of the Discovery of the Source of the Nile*, Edinburgh (1863).
Stanley, Henry Morton, *The Exploration Diaries of H. M. Stanley*, ed. Richard Stanley and Alan Neame (1961).
——, *How I Found Livingstone*, 2nd edn (1872).
——, *In Darkest Africa*, 2 vols (1890).
——, *Through the Dark Continent* (1878, repr. 1907).
Symons, A. J. A., *H. M. Stanley* (1933).
Thomson, Joseph, *Through Masai Land . . . 1883–4*, 4th edn (1885).
Thwaites, R. G. (ed.), *The Jesuit Relations and Allied Documents: Travels and Explorations of the Jesuit Missionaries in New France, 1610–1791*, 73 vols (Cleveland, 1896–1901).
Vaillant, François Le, *Travels into the Interior Parts of Africa 1780–5*, trans. from the French, 2nd edn, 2 vols (1796).
Wallace, Alfred Russel, *The Malay Archipelago*, 2 vols (1869).
Wilkinson, Clennell, *William Dampier* (1929).

II. SOCIAL AND ANTHROPOLOGICAL BACKGROUND

Arens, W., *The Man-Eating Myth: Anthropology and Anthropophagy* (New York, 1979).
Ascherson, Neal, *The King Incorporated: Leopold II in the Age of Trusts* (1963).
Blyden, Edward W., *Christianity, Islam and the Negro Race* (1887, repr. Edinburgh, 1967).
Burrow, John W., *Evolution in Society: A Study in Victorian Social Theory* (Cambridge, 1966).
Cairns, H. Alan, *Prelude to Imperialism: British Reactions to Central African Society 1840–90* (1965).
Cookey, S. J. S., *Britain and the Congo Question 1885–1913* (1968).
Cranstone, B. A. L., *The Australian Aborigines* (1973).
Curtin, Philip D., *The Image of Africa: British Ideas and Action, 1780–1850* (1965).
Davidson, Basil, *Black Mother: The Years of Trial* (1961).

Davies, K. G., *The Royal African Company* (1957).
Davis, David B., *The Problem of Slavery in Western Culture* (New York, 1966).
Durand, Gilbert, *Les structures anthropologiques de l'imaginaire* (Paris, 1969).
Earle, Peter, *The World of Defoe* (1976).
Eliade, Mircea, *Australian Religions: An Introduction* (Ithaca, 1973).
——, *The Myth of the Eternal Return*, trans. Willard R. Trask (Princeton, 1954, repr. 1965).
——, *Myths, Dreams and Mysteries: The Encounter between Contemporary Faiths and Archaic Realities*, trans. Philip Mairet [1960].
Elkin, A. P., *Aboriginal Men of High Degree* (Sydney, 1945).
——, *The Australian Aborigines: How to Understand Them*, 2nd edn (1943).
Faber, Richard, *The Vision and the Need: Late Victorian Imperialist Aims* (1966).
Frazer, Sir James G., *The Golden Bough*, 3rd edn, 12 vols (1907–15).
Glave, Edward, 'Cruelty in the Congo Free State', *Century Magazine*, LIV, 5 (1897) 699–715.
Hair, P. E. H., *The Atlantic Slave Trade and Black Africa* (1978).
Hallett, Robin, *Africa Since 1875* (Ann Arbor, 1974).
——, *Africa to 1875: A Modern History* (Ann Arbor, 1970).
Harris, Marvin, *The Rise of Anthropological Theory* (New York, 1968).
Hiatt, L. R. (ed.), *Australian Aboriginal Mythology* (Canberra, 1975).
Hofstadter, Richard and Lipset, S. M., *Turner and the Sociology of the Frontier* (New York, 1968).
Jordan, Winthrop D., *White over Black: American Attitudes towards the Negro, 1550–1812* (Chapel Hill, 1968).
Koebner, Richard and Schmidt, H., *Imperialism: The Story and Significance of a Political Word, 1840–1960* (Cambridge, 1964).
Lévi-Strauss, Claude, *Elementary Structures of Kinship*, rev. edn, trans. J. H. Bell and J. R. von Sturmer, ed. R. Needham (1969).
——, *The Savage Mind* (1966).
——, *Tristres tropiques*, trans. John and Doreen Weightman (1973).
Mannix, Daniel P. and Cowley, M., *Black Cargoes: A History of the Atlantic Slave Trade, 1518–1865* (1963).
Memmi, Albert, *The Colonizer and the Colonized* (New York, 1965).
Middleton, John (ed.), *Myth and Cosmos* (New York, 1967).
Miller, Perry (ed.), *The American Puritans* (New York, 1956).
——, *The New England Mind*, 2 vols (Boston 1961, repr. 1968–70).
Nadel, G. H. and Curtis, P., *Imperialism and Colonialism* (New York, 1964).
Neill, Stephen, *A History of Christian Missions* (Harmondsworth, 1964).
Northrop, F. S. C. and Livingston, H. H. (eds), *Cross-Cultural Understanding: Epistemology in Anthropology* (New York, 1964).
Porter, Bernard, *Critics of Empire: British Radical Attitudes to Colonialism in Africa, 1895–1914* (1968).
Public Record Office, Treasury Records, Royal African Company Archives, T.70.
Radcliffe-Brown, A. R., 'The Rainbow-Serpent Myth in South-East Australia', *Oceania*, I (1930) 342–7.
Reece, R. H. W., *Aborigines and Colonists* (Sydney, 1974).
Spencer, Sir Baldwin, *The Arunta* (1927).
——, *Wanderings in Wild Australia*, 2 vols (1928).

Stevenson, R. L., *In the South Seas* (1900).

Sypher, Wylie, *Guinea's Captive Kings: British Anti-Slavery Literature of the Eighteenth Century* (Chapel Hill, 1942).

Turner, F. J., *The Frontier in American History* (New York, 1920).

Williams, Neville, *Captains Outrageous: Seven Centuries of Piracy* (1961).

III. PHILOSOPHICAL AND PSYCHOLOGICAL BACKGROUND

Batailles, Georges, *Death and Sensuality: A Study of Eroticism and the Taboo* (New York, 1962).

Copleston, Frederick, *Arthur Schopenhauer: Philosopher of Pessimism* (1946).

Darwin, Charles, *The Origin of Species* (1859).

Eiseley, Loren, *Darwin's Century* (1959).

Feuerbach, Ludwig, *The Essence of Christianity*, trans. George Eliot (New York, 1957).

Fichte, J. G., *The Vocation of Man*, trans. William Smith, rev. and ed. R. M. Chisholm (New York, 1956).

Foucault, Michel, *Madness and Civilization*, trans. R. Howard (1967).

——, *The Order of Things*, trans. from the French (1970).

Freud, Sigmund, *Civilization and its Discontents*, trans. J. Riviere (1939).

——, *Collected Papers*, trans. under supervision of J. Riviere, 5 vols (1924–50).

——, *The Standard Edition of the Complete Psychological Works*, trans. under gen. ed. James Strachey, 24 vols (1953–74).

——, *Totem and Taboo*, trans. James Strachey (1950).

Gauthier, David P., *The Logic of Leviathan: The Moral and Political Theory of Thomas Hobbes* (Oxford, 1969).

Hobbes, Thomas, *The English Works*, ed. Sir W. Molesworth, 11 vols (1839–45).

Humboldt, Alexander von, *Cosmos*, [trans. Mrs Sabine], 4 vols (1846–58).

Huxley, T. H., 'Evolution and Ethics', *Collected Essays*, 9 vols (1892–5) ix.

Irvine, William, *Apes, Angels and Victorians: A Joint Biography of Darwin and Huxley* (1955).

Jung, C. G., *Psychological Types*, trans. H. Godwin Baynes (1923).

——, *Psychology and Alchemy*, trans. R. G. C. Hull (1953).

Locke, John, *An Essay Concerning Human Understanding*, ed. A. C. Fraser, 2 vols (Oxford, 1894).

Lovejoy, A. O., *Essays in the History of Ideas* (Baltimore, 1948).

——, *The Great Chain of Being* (1933, reprint. Cambridge, Mass., 1942).

——, and Boas, G., *Primitivism and Related Ideas in Antiquity* (New York, 1965).

Nietzsche, Friedrich, *Beyond Good and Evil*, trans. R. J. Hollingdale (Harmondsworth, 1973).

——, *Ecce Homo*, trans. A. M. Ludovici (1911).

——, *The Gay Science*, trans. Walter Kaufmann (New York, 1974).

——, *Philosophy and Truth: Selections from Nietzsche's Notebooks of the Early Seventies*, trans. and ed. D. Breazeale (Brighton, 1979).

——, *Twilight of the Idols and The Anti-Christ*, trans. R. J. Hollingdale (Harmondsworth, 1968).

Petty, Sir William, *The Economic Writings*, ed. C. H. Hull, 2 vols (Cambridge, 1899).

Rousseau, Jean Jacques, *The Miscellaneous Works*, 5 vols (1767).

Rycroft, Charles, *A Critical Dictionary of Psychoanalysis* (1968).

Schopenhauer, Arthur, *The World as Will and Idea*, trans. R. B. Haldane and J. Kemp, 4th edn, 3 vols (1896).

Seward, A. C. (ed.), *Darwin and Modern Science* (Cambridge, 1909).

Stephen, Leslie, *Social Rights and Duties*, 2 vols (1896).

Weil, Simone, *The Notebooks of Simone Weil*, trans. A. Wills, 2 vols (1956).

——, *Oppression and Liberty*, trans. A. Wills and J. Petrie (1958).

Wells, H. G., 'Human Evolution, an Artificial Process', *Fortnightly Review*, LXVI (1898) 590–5.

Wittels, Fritz, *Sigmund Freud, his Personality, his Teaching and his School*, trans. E. and C. Paul (New York, 1924).

IV. CRITICAL WORKS

Adams, Percy G., *Travel Literature and the Evolution of the Novel* (Lexington, Ky, 1983).

Anderson, Don, 'A Severed Leg: Anthropophagy and Communion in Patrick White's Fiction', *Southerly*, 40 (1980) 399–417.

Argyle, Barry, *Patrick White* (1967).

Atkinson, Geoffroy, *The Extraordinary Voyage in French Literature before 1700* (New York, 1920).

——, *The Extraordinary Voyage . . . from 1700 to 1720* (Paris, 1922).

Auerbach, Erich, *Mimesis: The Representation of Reality in Western Literature*, trans. Willard R. Trask (New York, 1957).

Beatson, Peter, 'The Three Stages: Mysticism in Patrick White's *Voss*', *Southerly*, 30 (1970) 111–21.

Beer, Gillian, *Darwin's Plots: Evolutionary Narrative in Darwin, George Eliot and Nineteenth-Century Fiction* (1983).

Bell, Michael, *Primitivism* (1972).

Berthoud, Jacques, *Joseph Conrad: The Major Phase* (Cambridge, 1978).

Bradbrook, M. C., *Joseph Conrad: Poland's English Genius* (Cambridge, 1942).

——, *Literature in Action: Studies in Continental and Commonwealth Society* (1972).

Brissenden, R. F., *Patrick White* (rev. edn. 1969).

Butler, Marilyn, *Romantics, Rebels and Reactionaries: English Literature and its Background, 1760–1830* (Oxford, 1981).

Carnochan, W. B., *Confinement and Flight* (Berkeley, 1977).

Cawley, R. R., *The Voyagers and Elizabethan Drama* (Boston, 1938).

Chase, Richard, *Herman Melville: A Critical Study* (New York, 1949).

——, (ed.), *Melville: A Collection of Critical Essays* (Englewood Cliffs, N. J., 1962).

Conrad, Peter, *Imagining America* (1980).

Darras, Jacques, *Joseph Conrad and the West: Signs of Empire*, trans. A. Luyat and J. Darras (1982).

Dryden, Edgar A., *Melville's Thematics of Form* (Baltimore, 1968).

Dudley, Edward and Novak, Maximillian E. (eds), *The Wild Man Within* (Pittsburgh, 1972).

Dutton, Geoffrey (ed.), *The Literature of Australia* (Harmondsworth, 1964).

——, *Patrick White*, 4th edn (Melbourne, 1971).

Fairchild, Hoxie Neal, *The Noble Savage: A Study in Romantic Naturalism* (New York, 1928).

FitzGerald, Margaret M., *First Follow Nature: Primitivism in English Poetry, 1725–50* (New York, 1976).

Furst, Lilian R., *The Contours of European Romanticism* (1979).

——, *Romanticism in Perspective* (New York, 1969).

Fussell, Paul, *Abroad: British Literary Traveling Between the Wars* (New York, 1980).

Green, Martin, *Dreams of Adventure, Deeds of Empire* (New York, 1979).

Guerard, Albert J., *Conrad: The Novelist* (Cambridge, Mass., 1958, 1979).

Hardy, Barbara, *The Appropriate Form: An Essay on the Novel* (1971).

Heller, Erich, *The Disinherited Mind: Essays in Modern German Literature and Thought* (Cambridge, 1952).

Henkin, Leo J., *Darwinism in the English Novel* (New York 1940, 1964).

Howard, Leon, *Herman Melville: A Biography* (Berkeley, 1951).

Hunter, Allan, *Joseph Conrad and the Ethics of Darwinism* (Beckenham, 1983).

Johnson, Bruce, *Conrad's Models of Mind* (Minneapolis, 1971).

Johnson, Manly, 'A Fringe of Leaves: White's Genethlicon', *Texas Studies in Language and Literature*, 21 (1979) 226–39.

Jones, Howard Mumford, *The Frontier in American Fiction* (1956).

Karl, Frederick R. (ed.), *Joseph Conrad: A Collection of Criticism* (New York, 1975).

Kermode, Frank, 'Introduction' to *The Tempest*, Arden Shakespeare, 6th edn (1958).

Kiernan, Brian, *Patrick White* (1980).

Levin, Harry, *The Myth of the Golden Age in the Renaissance* (New York, 1969).

Lewis, R. W. B., *The American Adam: Innocence, Tragedy and Tradition in the Nineteenth Century* (Chicago, 1955, 1971).

Leyda, Jay, *The Melville Log: A Documentary Life of Herman Melville, 1819–91*, 2 vols (New York, 1969).

Lockhardt, Donald, ' "The Fourth Son of the Mighty Emperor": The Ethiopian Background of Johnson's *Rasselas*', *PMLA*, LXXVIII (1963) 516–28.

Lowes, J. L., *The Road to Xanadu*, Sentry Edition (Boston, 1955).

Mahood, Molly M., *The Colonial Encounter: A Reading of Six Novels* (1977).

Mannoni, Otave, *Prospero and Caliban: The Psychology of Colonization*, trans. P. Powesland (New York, 1956).

Miller, J. Hillis, *The Disappearance of God: Five Nineteenth Century Writers* (Cambridge, Mass., 1975).

Monk, Samuel H., *The Sublime: A Study of Critical Theories in Eighteenth-Century England* (Ann Arbor, 1935, 1960).

Moore, John R., *Daniel Defoe: Citizen of the Modern World* (Chicago, 1958).

Morley, Patricia A., *The Mystery of Unity: Theme and Technique in the Novels of Patrick White* (Montreal, 1972).

Mudrick, Marvin (ed.), *Conrad: A Collection of Critical Essays* (Englewood Cliffs, N.J., 1966).

Novak, Maximillian E., *Defoe and the Nature of Man* (Oxford, 1963).

Olson, Charles, *Call Me Ishmael* (San Francisco, 1947).

Parker, H. and Hayford, H. (eds), *Moby Dick as Doubloon* (New York, 1970).

Richetti, John J., *Defoe's Narratives* (Oxford, 1975).

Ridley Hugh, *Images of Imperial Rule* (1983).

Rogers, Pat, *The Augustan Vision* (1974).

——, (ed.). *Defoe: The Critical Heritage* (1972).

——, *Robinson Crusoe* (1979).

Roussel, Royal, *The Metaphysics of Darkness: A Study in the Unity and Development of Conrad's Fiction* (Baltimore, 1971).

Said, Edward W., *Orientalism* (1978).

Sandison, Alan, *The Wheel of Empire* (1967).

Scrimgeour, Gary J., 'The Problem of Realism in Defoe's *Captain Singleton*', *Huntingdon Library Quarterly*, xxvii (1963) 21–38.

Secord, A. W., *Studies in the Narrative Method of Defoe* (Urbana, 1924).

Shepherd, R. and Singh, K. (eds), *Patrick White: A Critical Symposium* (Adelaide, 1978).

Sherry, Norman, *Conrad's Eastern World* (Cambridge, 1966).

——, *Conrad's Western World* (Cambridge, 1971).

——, (ed.), *Conrad: The Critical Heritage* (1973).

——, (ed.), *Joseph Conrad: A Commemoration* (1976).

Smith, M. van Wyk, 'The Origins of Some Victorian Images of Africa', *English in Africa*, vi, 1 (1979) 12–32.

Spears, Monroe K., *Dionysus and the City: Modernism in Twentieth-Century Poetry* (New York, 1970).

Starr, George A., *Defoe and Spiritual Autobiography* (Princeton, 1965).

Street, Brian V., *The Savage in Literature: Representatives of 'Primitive' Society in English Fiction, 1858–1920* (1975).

Sutherland, James R., *Daniel Defoe: A Critical Study* (Cambridge, Mass., 1954).

Tanner, Tony, *City of Words: American Fiction 1950–70* (1971).

Thompson, Lawrance, *Melville's Quarrel with God* (Princeton, 1952).

Trilling, Lionel, *Beyond Culture: Essays on Literature and Learning* (1966).

Turner, James G., *The Politics of Landscape: Rural Scenery and Society in English Poetry, 1630–60* (Oxford, 1979).

Walsh, William, *Patrick White's Fiction* (Sydney, 1977).

Warren, Robert Penn, *Selected Essays* (1964).

Watt, Ian, *Conrad in the Nineteenth Century* (1980).

——, *The Rise of the Novel* (1957).

Watts, Cedric, *A Preface to Conrad* (New York, 1982).

Way, Brian, *Herman Melville: Moby Dick* (1978).

Wilkes, G. A., 'A Reading of Patrick White's *Voss*', *Southerly*, 27 (1967) 159–73.

——, *The Stockyard and the Croquet Lawn: Literary Evidence for Australian Cultural Development* (1981).

Williams, Ioan, *The Novel and Romance* (1970).

Williams, Raymond, *The Country and the City* (1973).

Zweig, Paul, *The Adventurer* (1974).

V. LITERARY TEXTS

Ballantyne, R. M., *Coral Island* (Everyman, 1907).

Brink, André, *An Instant in the Wind* (1976).

Buchan, John, *Prester John* (1910).

Bunyan, John, *The Pilgrim's Progress*, ed. James Wharey (Oxford, 1928).

Camoens, Luis Vaz De, *The Lusiads*, trans. and ed. C. Atkinson (Harmondsworth, 1952).

Coetzee, John M., *Dusklands* (Johannesburg, 1974).

Coleridge, Samuel Taylor, *Biographia Literaria*, ed. George Watson (1965).

——, *Coleridge: Poems*, ed. John Beer (1974).

Conrad, Joseph, *Joseph Conrad: Letters to William Blackwood and David S. Meldrum*, ed. W. Blackburn (Durham, N.C., 1958).

——, *Joseph Conrad's Letters to R. B. Cunninghame Graham*, ed. C. T. Watts (Cambridge, 1969).

——, *Joseph Conrad: Life and Letters*, ed. G. Jean-Aubry, 2 vols (1927).

——, *The Works of Joseph Conrad*, Uniform Edition, 22 vols (1923–8).

Cooper, James Fenimore, *The Prairie* (San Francisco, 1950).

Defoe, Daniel, *Atlas Maritimus et Commercialis* (1728).

——, *An Essay upon Projects* (1702).

——, *An Essay upon the Trade to Africa* (1711).

——, *A General History of Discoveries and Improvements* (1726–7).

——, *General History . . . of the Pyrates* (1724).

——, *Jure Divino* (1706).

——, *The Life, Adventures and Piracies of the Famous Captain Singleton*, ed. James Sutherland (Everyman, 1963).

——, *The Life and Strange Surprising Adventures of Robinson Crusoe of York, Mariner*, ed. J. Donald Crowley, Oxford English Novels (1972).

——, *Mere Nature Delineated* (1726).

——, *A New Voyage Around the World*, 2 vols (1725).

——, *Political History of the Devil* (1726).

——, *The Reformation of Manners* (1702).

——, *A Review*, 9 vols (1704–13).

Doyle, Arthur Conan, *The Lost World* (1912).

Faulkner, William, *The Bear*, collected in *Go Down Moses* (Harmondsworth, 1960).

Forster, E. M., *A Passage to India* (Harmondsworth, 1957).

Garnett, Edward, *Letters from Conrad, 1895–1924* (1928).

Golding, William, *Lord of the Flies* (1954).

Haggard, H. Rider, *King Solomon's Mines* (1886).

Hemingway, Ernest, 'Big Two-Hearted River' in *The Short Stories of Ernest Hemingway* (New York, 1938).

Hope, A. D., *Collected Poems, 1930–65* (Sydney, 1965).

Johnson, Samuel, *Rasselas*, ed. Geoffrey Tillotson and Brian Jenkins (Oxford, 1977).

Kipling, Rudyard, *Life's Handicap* (1896).

Lawrence, D. H., *Kangaroo* (1923).

——, *Letters of D. H. Lawrence*, ed. J. T. Boulton *et al.*, 7 vols (Cambridge, 1979–).

Zweig, Paul, *Phoenix II*, ed. Warren Roberts and Harry T. Moore (1968).

——, *Psychoanalysis and the Unconscious*, Adelphi Library (1931).

——, *The Rainbow* (1915, repr. 1923).

Lewis, Janet, *The Invasion* (Chicago, 1932, repr. 1960).

Malouf, David, *An Imaginary Life* (1978).

Mandeville's Travels, ed. M. C. Seymour (Oxford, 1967).

Maugham, W. Somerset, *The Explorer*, Collected Edition (1967).

Melville, Herman, *The Complete Stories of Herman Melville*, ed. Jay Leyda (New York, 1949).

——, 'Hawthorne and his Mosses', collected in *Hawthorne: The Critical Heritage*, ed. J. Donald Crowley (1970).

——, *The Letters of Herman Melville*, ed. M. R. Davis and W. H. Gilman (New Haven, 1960).

——, *Moby-Dick*, ed. Charles Feidelson, Jr. (Indianapolis, 1964).

——, *Typee*, ed. George Woodcock (Harmondsworth, 1972).

Montaigne, Michel, *The Essayes of Montaigne*, trans. John Florio (1891).

Rousseau, Jean Jacques, *Confessions*, trans. J. M. Cohen (Harmondsworth, 1953).

Sterne, Lawrence, *A Sentimental Journey through France and Italy*, in *Works of Sterne*, 2 vols (New York, 1900).

Swift, Jonathan, *Gulliver's Travels*, ed. Peter Dixon and John Chalker (Harmondsworth, 1967).

Verne, Jules, *A Journey to the Center of the Earth* (1864).

Webster, J. Provand, *The Oracle of Baal* (1896).

Wells, H. G., *The Island of Dr Moreau* (1896).

White, Patrick, *The Eye of the Storm* (1973).

——, *Flaws in the Glass* (1981).

——, *A Fringe of Leaves* (1976).

——, *Voss* (1957, 1980).

Woolf, Virginia, *To the Lighthouse* (1927, 1977).

Wordsworth, William, *The Prelude*, ed. Ernest de Selincourt, rev. Helen Darbishire (Oxford, 1959).

Index